Nonfiction Chapter Books

D1300890

Lucy Calkins, Kristine Mraz, and Barbara Golub

Photography by Peter Cunningham

HEINEMANN ◆ PORTSMOUTH, NH

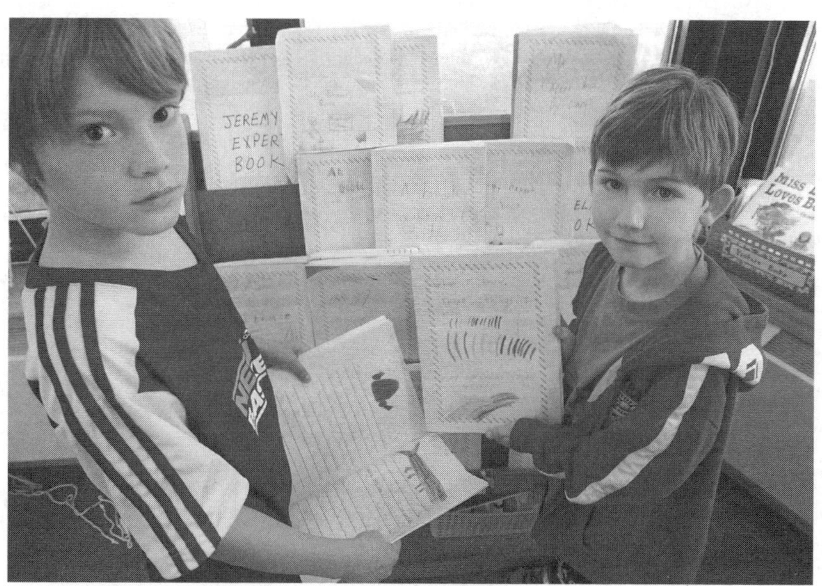

This book is dedicated to Laurie Pessah, who joins me at the helm of the Teachers College Reading and Writing Project, co-leads all the organization's primary work, and co-wrote the book upon whose shoulders this one stands. —Lucy

This book is dedicated to my grandma, who always looked out for me, and for Geoff, who looks out for me still. —Kristi

This book is dedicated to Mama and Papa, who gave me a bigger life than I could ever have imagined. —Barb

*first*hand
An imprint of Heinemann
361 Hanover Street
Portsmouth, NH 03801–3912
www.heinemann.com

Offices and agents throughout the world

© 2013 by Lucy Calkins

All rights reserved. No part of this book may be reproduced in any form or by any electronic or mechanical means, including information storage and retrieval systems, without permission in writing from the publisher, except by a reviewer, who may quote brief passages in a review, with the exception of reproducible pages, which are identified by the *Units of Study in Opinion, Information, and Narrative Writing* copyright line and can be photocopied for classroom use only.

"Dedicated to Teachers" is a trademark of Greenwood Publishing Group, Inc.

The authors and publisher wish to thank those who have generously given permission to reprint borrowed material:

Reprinted with permission from the book: *National Geographic Readers: Sharks!* by Ann Schreiber. Copyright © 2008 National Geographic Society.

Material from *Change It!: Solids, Liquids, Gases and You* written by Adrienne Mason and illustrated by Claudia Dávila used by permission of Kids Can Press Ltd., Toronto, Canada. Text © 2006 Adrienne Mason.

Cataloging-in-Publication data is on file with the Library of Congress.

ISBN-13: 978-0-325-04725-6
ISBN-10: 0-325-04725-1

Production: Elizabeth Valway, David Stirling, and Abigail Heim
Cover and interior designs: Jenny Jensen Greenleaf
Series includes photographs by Peter Cunningham, Nadine Baldasare, and Elizabeth Dunford
Composition: Publishers' Design and Production Services, Inc.
Manufacturing: Steve Bernier

Printed in the United States of America on acid-free paper
17 16 15 14 13 ML 3 4 5

Acknowledgments

PRIMARY TEACHERS know that sometimes young kids write a text through a process that is often referred to as Share the Pen, and portions of this book were written that way as well. We're grateful to all the extra hands with whom our pen was shared. In addition to the three of us, Anna Gratz worked tirelessly on this book. Anna is coauthor of the fourth-grade information writing unit and has taught and led curriculum development across the elementary grades, so she brought a very deep knowledge of nonfiction writing to the book. Kim Thompson helped to reveal a clear message that lay under sometimes wordy, excessive prose, as did Julia Mooney, and we thank them both. And the book itself stands on the shoulders of the all-about book that Laurie Pessah coauthored, almost fifteen years ago, blazing the trail for the learning the TCRWP has done since then.

Of course, a whole cast of characters helped with the knowledge base upon which this draws. We are grateful to those in the Project community who have especially contributed to the organization's knowledge base on Common Core State Standards and to Webb's Depths of Knowledge—a special nod to Mary Ehrenworth and Janet Steinberg. We are grateful to those who have helped with our knowledge of phonics—Donald Bear, author of *Words Their Way*, as well as Enid Martinez, Rachel Rothman, and Christine Cook Robson. We are grateful to the people who have especially extended the organization's knowledge of information writing—a special nod to Colleen Cruz for that. We are grateful to the people who have been the great thinkers about K–2 instruction within our organization—especially Amanda Hartman.

We've had our own supporters who've kept us going, with cheerleading and celebrations. That list is different for the three of us, but together, it includes Kathleen Tolan, Ali Marron, Celena Larkey, Jennifer Serravallo, and Maggie and Kate Roberts.

We are grateful to a host of teachers who have nurtured our learning and provided student work. We are grateful also to Emily Jones, who worked with us in classrooms, helping to maximize all that we learned from children. And we thank all the classroom teachers and all the schools with whom the three of us have worked, especially the teachers and children at Taipei American School in Taipei, Taiwan, particularly Molly Hobbs and Laura Walter, the teachers and students at PS 277, Rosie Young from PS 1, and to Rochelle Rosenblatt and Christina Ragusano at PS 78.

At Heinemann, Felicia O'Brien and lead editor Teva Blair went far beyond their expected roles. We are grateful to Felicia and Teva for making the manuscript as coherent, complete, and seamless as it is now. Finally, the book is beautiful, and that is due to the craftsmanship and high standards of the production team. We thank Jenny Jenson Greenleaf for her stunning design of all the interiors, covers, and brochures connected to this project. We thank Peter Cunningham for dazzling photographs and David Stirling, project manager, for tagging and sorting, cropping and placing thousands of photos into this series. We thank Abby Heim for overseeing that effort and everything else related to production, and doing so in a way that has created a breathtakingly beautiful and complex mosaic. We thank Elizabeth Valway for impeccable standards and tireless efforts to decipher every revision, to enter changes on every page, to make every word as perfect as possible. We thank Roberta Lew for multiple, year-long negotiations with publishers, agents, and authors to secure permissions to use excerpts and images throughout these books. All of these people and scores of others have been able to devote themselves to this project because Lesa Scott believes in it, and we thank her for that confidence.

The class described in this unit is a composite class. We wrote the units this way to bring you both a wide array of wonderful, quirky, various children and also to illustrate for you the situations and responses this unit has created in classrooms across the nation and world.

—Lucy, Kristi, and Barb

Contents

Welcome to the Unit

THERE IS PERHAPS no more transformational year for your children than first grade. This is the year when they learn to deepen the meaning behind their reading work, to strengthen the conversations of their partner work, and to dive deep into the expression of their writing work. Your children will come to you at the beginning of the year, insisting that they are "big kids," bursting at the seams to share all that they know about the world. You'll hear this in their joyful chatter as they work, the conversations they have on the playground, and the accounts they eagerly recount on Monday mornings.

This unit prepares children to write information texts of all sorts across this year's curriculum. Because the unit is foundational, undergirding children's reading of information texts and enabling their cross-curricular writing, it is well positioned early on in first grade. You may wonder if your little ones are actually ready to wrestle with expository structure at such a young age. They are! After all, many six-year-olds believe they are experts. Watch them title their books: "The World's Greatest Book on Cats!" "All You Need to Know about Bikes," "Everything You Need to Know to Feed a Chicken." These titles alone exude youthful confidence.

There's truth behind that confidence. Every first-grade classroom is teeming with youngsters full of areas of expertise. There's the child who knows everything about dolphins, the child who can tell you countless facts about cooking, the snake enthusiast—the list goes on and on. One of the wonderful things about working with first-graders is the delight they take in their own knowledge. This unit channels that energy into writing. First-graders will love the chance to teach you and the world. Go ahead and announce to your kids, then, that their beloved bicycle, their fairy tale collection, and their favorite topics—horses, insects, dinosaurs—are book-worthy!

Then, too, this may not be your children's first time trying out this kind of writing. Many, if not all, of your kids spent time in kindergarten writing teaching books. Last year, for example, your children may have written teaching books with titles like "All About Families" or "All About Soccer." This year you will show them how to teach even more by writing about a focused topic. This year, those books may sound more like "Sisters" or "Scoring Goals."

There's another good reason to teach this unit at this stage in the year. Students who were reluctant story writers often come alive when given a chance to teach what they know. The lengthy discussions you field on the value of Xbox vs. Wii will now have an outlet on paper—as will any other topic that children are eager to share with others.

Finally, although this is a writing unit of study, it is also designed to grow young students' reading abilities. Children will become much more skilled at reading information books once they have an insider's perspective on how to structure this kind of writing themselves.

During this unit of study, each child will write lots of information books about lots of different topics and will revisit his or her writing to self-assess and revise, as expected by the Common Core State Standards (CCSS W1.5). This unit is designed to give children the support and practice they will need to organize their information; again and again over the course of the unit, children will name a topic, give facts, and provide a sense of closure (CCSS W1.1). In addition, this is one of the first times children will delve into research to add to their knowledge of a topic (CCSS W1.7).

This unit also addresses other important standards for first-graders. For example, you will continue to build on your students' understanding of language by introducing additional spelling strategies (CCSS L 1.2E), working on ending punctuation (CCSS L1.2B), and teaching children that writers use commas when writing a list (CCSS L1.2C). This unit also offers many opportunities to work with partners, especially around asking and answering questions to clarify what someone is saying (CCSS SL1.3). Partners will have chances to talk about their topics, reflect on what they are learning, and ask questions to help each other teach even more information.

Expect that your children will learn information writing in leaps and bounds over the course of this unit. The Common Core State Standards are a call for preparing even our youngest students to get ready for the lives ahead of them. Standard 1.W.2, which expects first-grade children to "write informative/explanatory texts in which they name a topic, supply some facts about the topic, and provide some sense of closure," builds upon what children do naturally: study and become experts about the world in which they live. This unit, then, helps you and your children meet this standard while supporting the independence upon which your writing workshop is founded.

In fact, the expectations that the CCSS lay out are not as ambitious as this unit; it is our belief at the Teachers College Reading and Writing Project that children can do far more than these minimal standards. We believe it is wise to launch youngsters into writing well-developed information books because writing expectations rise quickly, starting in third grade, and because the opportunity to write information books will help students become more active and insightful readers of nonfiction texts. Therefore, we recommend you teach not only toward the standards that the Common Core sets for *first*-graders, but toward the work that students will do as lifelong writers and readers of informational texts. Lay the groundwork now, and then watch as your children rise to the occasion again and again.

OVERVIEW OF THE UNIT

This unit takes children on a writing journey that builds in sophistication. It begins with instruction in how to make a basic type of information book—a picture book—and ends with children creating multiple information chapter books, filled with elaboration, interesting text elements, and pictures that supplement the teaching of the words. If your students come from a history of writing information texts, you may find you move through the first bend quickly. On the other hand, if this work is new to your kids, you may opt to linger a little longer as children become accustomed to this new style of writing. Likewise, the middle bend, which teaches the nuts and bolts of writing a teaching book, may require a little more time in some classrooms and may be a quick few days in others. As with all the units, the path you take is meant to be tailored to your students and their experiences—more on that in the assessment section below.

In the first bend, "Writing Teaching Books with Independence," youngsters will write a giant folder full of information texts, revisit many of those texts repeatedly, and revise them independently. These first books will resemble nonfiction picture books. Don't worry just yet about introducing traditional nonfiction features, such as tables of contents. What matters most is that children are immersed in this new kind of writing. From Day One, this bend will spotlight using a teaching voice and writing a lot, so that each page teaches new and interesting information. Writers will also learn how to answer readers' questions and to use those questions to add and subtract information. Over the course of this first bend, children will revisit some of the skills they learned in *Small Moments:* planning, tackling brave and fancy words, and drawing—in the context of this new genre.

Throughout this bend, children will self-assess against the informational writing checklist. Introducing this tool on the first day and revisiting it continually will help children build the habit of reflection and goal-setting. The first version of the checklist that children look at will contain only a few basic skills. As the bend (and children) progress, the checklist will become longer and more elaborate. During this bend, you will also be producing the first of several class books, which will serve as a touchstone throughout the bend. Additionally, you will introduce a close study of the pictures in the mentor text *Sharks* by Anne Schrieber. It is likely that first-graders will produce a book every day or two at this time in the year. Before the end of the first bend, then, they will have a chance to choose one for further revision and editing prior to a mini-celebration.

During the second bend of the unit, "Nonfiction Writers Can Write Chapter Books!," children will progress toward writing chapter books, which of course gives them opportunities to work on structuring their texts. It is likely that the pace of your children's writing will slow down during this bend because the books they will be producing will become longer and more ambitious. Where children were once writing a book every day or two, it may take three or four (or more!) days for them to complete these longer books. During this bend, you will revisit the mentor text *Sharks* once again to investigate how chapter books are written. The first lesson in this bend involves a close study of a few tables of contents. You will write another class book at this time, which will serve as a model to demonstrate, as well as a place for children to practice the new skills they are learning in the minilessons.

The books children write in this second bend of the unit should, from the start, include elements that might have been revisions to other, earlier books—for example, teaching pictures, brave and fancy words, as well as answers to readers' questions. This second bend will introduce many of the more common elements found in information books: how-to pages, stories, introductions, and conclusions. You will teach this new information in a more step-by-step fashion to support the complexity of the work. This bend will also spotlight new ways to elaborate: comparisons, examples, and elements of persuasion. This means that children may need paper with more lines and access to plenty of strips and extra sheets to attach. As children write, they will also continue to self-assess to make their books stronger. Partner work will be important again in this bend, as a way to check for clarity, generate more ideas, and cheer each other on. Once again, you'll celebrate the work in this bend on the last day, giving children one more chance to practice revision and editing before showing off what they have learned.

In the third, and final, bend, "Writing Chapter Books with Greater Independence," children will write chapter books, this time with increasing speed and independence. Whereas in the previous bend children learned how to structure a chapter book, in this bend children will take all they have learned and set goals to write new (and better!) chapter books. In addition, there will be opportunities here to teach six-year-olds simple ways to research their topics by studying photographs and asking questions. As in any bend, there will be plenty of opportunities to push writers who are excelling in the genre and to support writers who struggled with moving into chapter books. Finally, lessons around craft and thoughtful punctuation will add a flourish to the powerful writing first-graders are now doing in their information books. All of this work will lead to one last celebration, during which children will choose their favorite book of all the ones they've written and share with an audience what they know and have written.

ASSESSMENT

Just as you began *Small Moments* with an on-demand assessment, we suggest you do the same here. We have certainly found no better way to ensure that you tailor your path through the book for the students in front of you.

As in *Small Moments,* you will want to give children five-page booklets. This work will be assessed as part of a K–5 learning progression, so we hope you are willing to give children some information so that every child receives the same prompts and opportunities. The prompt we suggest is in the *Writing Pathways: Performance Assessments and Learning Progressions, K–5* book and below:

> "Think of a topic that you've studied or that you know a lot about. Tomorrow, you will have forty-five minutes to write an informational (or all-about) text that teaches others interesting and important information and ideas about that topic. If you want to find and use information from a book or another outside source to help you with this writing, you may bring that with you tomorrow. Please keep in mind that you'll have only forty-five minutes to complete this. You will only have this one period, so you'll need to plan, draft, revise, and edit in one sitting. Write in a way that shows all that you know about information writing.
>
> "In your writing, make sure you:
>
> - Introduce the topic you will teach about
> - Include lots of information
> - Organize your writing
> - Use transition words
> - Write an ending"

As children set off and begin these books, we recommend that you stand back and watch them during the workshop. Loris Malaguzzi, in *The Hundred Languages of Children,* advises teachers to "stand aside for awhile and leave room for learning, observe carefully what children do, and then, if you have understood well, perhaps teaching will be different from before." Check to see who is off and writing right away, who begins a story, who sketches first and then dives into writing, and who chews on their pen while staring dreamily into space. All of this will become grist for the teaching mill as the unit begins to unfold.

One more suggestion for the on-demand: although your students' writing will have progressed since the first unit, you may find that you still need to walk around and get the dictation for any student whose writing is difficult to read. This will provide an invaluable tool in determining what such children will need in the upcoming unit.

When you step back and collect this work, you will want to assess where each writer falls on the Information Writing Learning Progression and where the majority of your class falls. This information, added to the data gathered during the actual on-demand, will inform your unit. Explore what this new group of students knows about genre and organization: does it sound like the writer is giving facts, or does it run into the realm of story? Does each page have new information, or does it seem like the writer just put down each thought as it came, without a sense of what should go together? What about elaboration? How much can the writer say about one idea before veering off to the next one? Do you see words like *because* and *when,* for example? What about the pictures? Are those trying to teach as well? Last but not least, study spelling and conventions. What does this writer know about letter and sound relationships? Is there a sense of sentence? These questions (and the answers!) can guide you in tailoring the unit ahead and forming small groups as you see fit.

We suggest you also read each student's work, comparing it to the benchmark texts within the Information Writing Learning Progression first. Then read the specific descriptors to identify next steps for each child. This work is sometimes best done in the company of colleagues, allowing you to calibrate your responses with each other's. Rest assured, there will be variation between a text and the benchmark pieces, with many children's pieces falling in between two levels. This is where the descriptors will become particularly helpful in naming next steps. These pieces of writing should stay someplace accessible to you and students as a baseline from which to measure growth throughout the unit.

After your students publish their final pieces of writing for this unit, you will once again ask them to compose an on-demand piece of writing. The second on-demand will measure growth across the unit. You will once again want to study the behaviors of the students during the workshop and look closely at the pieces. Did the children grow in the areas you targeted? Where else do you see gains? Where will children need support in the next unit?

On-demands will not be your only source of data for this unit. You will also want to study a high-frequency words assessment as well as a spelling assessment to determine which language standards you need to focus on. Within the unit, you should also rely on your formative assessments, such as your conferences and small-group work, to guide your teaching. Use this information to assess that students are on track and to teach into the things they are not yet grasping to support their progress. It can be helpful to keep a copy of the Learning Progression, or an abbreviated version of it, with you as you confer so you can check back in on the goals of the unit as you teach.

GETTING READY

You will want to prepare for the unit by acquiring (or making) paper that can support the variety of writing your students will do. Analyzing your students' on-demand assessments can help you make decisions about the kind of work you can expect your children to do in the unit, and those decisions will have implications related to paper choice.

You may decide to have five-page booklets available, which resemble (or actually are!) the paper choice your writers used for narrative writing, with a box for a quick sketch and plenty of lines for filling with information. You may want to have booklets available but also plenty of stacked loose paper so that, from the start, your writers know that they will be adding pages and parts because of all they know and need to teach.

You will also want to select grade level complex texts that can be the center of close reading and study. In this book, we recommend the mentor text *Sharks!* by Anne Schreiber, part of the National Geographic series. There are others from the National Geographic series that would work well for this unit, such as *Trucks* and *Trains*, both level 1, but of course, you can select whichever texts you think will be worthwhile for your students to study. We do encourage you to keep an eye on text complexity and on the quality of the writing in the text you select. Make sure that studying this text will ignite students' interest in learning about the world as well as teaching them about the genre. It will be helpful to select a mentor text that will enable you to do the teaching you have in mind to do. For example, you will want to rally students to study mentor texts that contain tables of contents, chapter titles, and diagrams. Consider, too, whether the text uses the elaboration strategies that you want your children to strive for. Will the text structure teach children about ways to organize their writing? Some children may benefit from a list-like structure (similar to the books that they are reading), while other children would benefit from mentors with sophisticated text structures and elaboration strategies. You may turn to the nonfiction books in the Rigby PM Pets series, such as *Goldfish*, *Mice*, or *Cats*, because these are good examples of all-about texts, and they will be accessible for your first-graders to read. You may also want to refer back to the texts that the students likely looked to in kindergarten when writing all-about books.

Writing Teaching Books with Independence

BEND I

Session 1

Writers Get Ready to Write by Teaching All About a Topic

IN THIS SESSION, you'll teach children that writers teach all about their topic by organizing their information and using a teaching voice.

GETTING READY

- ✔ You may decide to have five-page booklets available—the same paper you used during the *Small Moments* unit. Keep the paper in your writing center, clearly labeled and easily accessible to children.
- ✔ Single sheets of paper for children who want to add on an extra page in the beginning, middle, or end of their books
- ✔ Half sheets of paper, so that children can make flaps for additional information they may want to add into the middle of specific pages
- ✔ The same two-pocket folder that each child had from the last unit of study
- ✔ Baskets of pens, tape, and date stamp on each table
- ✔ A basket of mentor texts, perhaps labeled "Our Writing Teachers," available in the writing center for children to have access to. Titles include: *Bugs, Bugs, Bugs* by Jennifer Dussling, *My Football Book* by Gail Gibbons, *Star Wars: R2-D2 and Friends* by Simon Beecroft, *The Story of Chocolate* by Caryn Jenner, *Invaders from Outer Space* by Phillip Brooks.
- ✔ Mentor texts for the minilesson: *Sharks!* by Anne Schreiber, *Animal Families* by DK Publishing, *Star Wars: Spaceships* by Scholastic, *Trucks* by Wil Mara (See Connection)
- ✔ Information Writing Checklist, Grade K (see Share)

Common Core State Standards: W.1.2, W.1.5, W.1.7, RI.1.1, RFS.1.1, SL.1.1, SL.1.4, SL.1.5, SL.1.6, L.1.1, L.1.2

THE FIELD OF WRITING instruction owes its existence to a teacher of writing named Donald Murray. Murray died a few years ago. His funeral was held in a field house at the University of New Hampshire—a gigantic venue that would more traditionally house major sporting events, rock concerts, or perhaps funerals for movie stars. The hundreds upon hundreds of people who traveled across the nation to honor this teacher of writing came, saying, "Before I studied with Murray, I had no idea that anyone would want to hear the things I have to say." They said, "He made me realize that I know things, and that by writing, I can teach others."

Pulitzer-Prize-winning author of a score of books on teaching writing, writing coach to journalists from across the nation, and columnist for the *Boston Globe*, Murray's wisdom has shaped the way nonfiction writing is taught in K–12 schools and colleges. This unit of study, and especially this lesson, is informed by one of the most famous passages in all of Murray's writing. In *Learning by Teaching,* he reflects:

> I am tired, but it is a good tired, for my students have generated energy as well as absorbed it. I've learned something of what it is to be a childhood diabetic, to raise oxen . . . to build a bluebird trail . . . to bring your father home to die of cancer. I have been instructed in other lives, heard the voices of my students they had not heard before, shared their satisfaction in solving the problems of writing with clarity and grace . . . I hear voices from my students they have never heard from themselves. I find they are authorities on subjects they think ordinary . . . It is a matter of faith, faith that my students have something to say and a language in which to say it. (1982, 157, 160)

Writers of information books are teachers, teaching others about the subjects they know well. Before introducing this session, think for a moment about the youngsters in your class. Can you think of a few topics that each one knows well? Don Graves, another influential figure in the field of teaching writing, once suggested that a competency test for teachers of writing might involve asking teachers to list the names of their students, and alongside each name, to list four or five topics that each student knows well. One of your youngsters is a dinosaur buff. Another is a horse enthusiast, a bicycling pro, a Lego maniac, a fashion stylist, a musician. This unit channels children's enthusiasm for these and other topics into writing.

First-graders will love being asked to teach what they know. They will be thrilled to learn that their beloved bicycle and their collection of action figures are book-worthy! During this unit of study, each child will write lots of informational books about lots of different topics. Instead of immediately pushing children into researching and drafting formal reports on distant subjects, you will help them to recognize their own funds of knowledge and empower them to write with authority about those topics. Of course, you will also help children know that research is part of being an expert.

"First-graders will love being asked to teach what they know."

Today's session aims to launch kids in writing up a storm, so that they produce something like a book a day, each on a different topic of personal expertise. As the week unfolds and you teach students more skills and more concepts about informational writing, they'll be able to use what you teach on both the new book that they will be writing and on the folder full of books they wrote earlier.

You will have noticed that the structure of this unit involves children writing books that don't contain tables of contents, chapter headings, or subheadings during this first bend in the road of the unit, allowing you to spotlight these structures later in the unit when you teach organization skills. For this week, then, provide children with booklets that do not contain pages for tables of contents. If there are kids who make tables of contents and the like, don't spotlight what they have done so that others emulate it just yet. Hold that exciting and challenging work at bay until the second bend of your unit.

Once you *do* teach children to organize books into chapters, then your children can, with your support, reread and rethink some of their books written during Bend I, perhaps, at that point, scissoring them apart to categorize some of the information into chapters. For now, expect that the books your children write at the start of the unit will probably contain a hodgepodge of facts, in no particular order. Ideally, however, the information is somewhat parsed out by pages, so one page addresses one subtopic.

You'll notice that in the share section of the session, we suggest you bring the Information Writing Checklist from kindergarten into your first-grade classroom, using the checklist to remind children of all they learned earlier about information writing. If you are following the trajectory of units in this grade, your students will recognize this checklist as being similar to the Narrative Writing Checklist that they encountered in the *Small Moments* unit. Of course, many of you will teach students who did not encounter such a checklist during kindergarten. The items on it are very easy and accessible. You can reword the share so that instead of reminding them of what they learned the preceding year, you note that you already notice many of them doing these things. Then say, "I'll read this checklist over, and you can think about whether you are already doing some of the items on it."

MINILESSON

Writers Get Ready to Write by Teaching All About a Topic

CONNECTION

Drumroll the start of a new unit. Read a few pages of an information book, contrasting with a storybook, to help writers talk about and grasp a few essential differences.

"Writers, this is a really exciting day because we start a whole new unit of study. You used to be storytellers, writing true stories of your lives. But now you will be experts, writing to teach others what you know. You used to write stories like these." I held up some story books. "But now you will be writing teaching books like these: *Sharks!*, *Animal Families*, *Star Wars: Spaceships*, and *Trucks*.

"Let's start with an investigation and try to figure out the differences between the storybooks you used to write and the teaching, or informational, books you will be writing now. I'll read just a bit of our storybook," I gestured to show this was one option, "and then read just a bit of our informational book." I gestured to show this was another option. "Will you and your partner listen, and try to list across your fingers all the ways that teaching books are different than storybooks?"

I read just two pages of each book and then said, "So how are the teaching books that you'll be writing for the next month different from storybooks? Turn and talk."

Listen as children talk about the differences between narrative and information texts, not letting this get too detailed. Then recap, stressing that writers of information books use a teaching voice, not a storyteller voice.

The room erupted in conversation. I listened as Tamara told Karl, "A teaching book doesn't really sound like a story."

Karl responded, "Yeah, it's just like lots of facts."

Tamara thought for a moment, her eyes raised as if trying to pull a thought from the sky. "A storybook is just like, like, like . . . like what happened *one* time. A teaching book is all the stuff you want to *learn*."

Karl perked up. "I already know what I'm going to write about—Just Dance 3." And he made some moves to accompany his topic.

◆ COACHING

Notice the repeated use of the refrain: "You used to be . . . but now you are. . . ."

My goal is to give writers a big sense of the genre they'll be writing and to elevate their work by linking it to the work of professional writers.

Notice that this unit starts with a small investigation. I could have told children the main differences between story writing and informational writing, but I'm quite sure they can deduce these themselves, and I want them to have the experience that every writer has of looking at a text that resembles the sort of text one plans to write, and thinking, "What's particular about this genre? What is the work I need to do to write like this?" I'm also mindful that by embedding a tiny bit of inquiry into the start of this unit, I raise what Norman Webb would call the Depth of Knowledge (DOK) level of this minilesson.

After a minute, I spoke over the hubbub. "Writers, I heard some of you say that the authors of information books use a teaching voice, not a storyteller voice, and write with facts and information. Let's think now about what authors do to get ready to write teaching books so you can write one today."

Channel writers to quickly locate a topic they can teach today by showing them the way you inventory your knowledge base to generate topics you could teach others.

"I'll show you some questions I ask myself when I want to come up with a topic to teach others. Will you give me a thumbs up when you have thought of a topic for the book you'll write today? I ask myself," and I switched into the role of a writer, musing, "what do I do a lot that I know and can teach others? Is there a sport or a game or a show or a kind of animal that I know a lot about?" I mused, looking in the air, letting my own potential topics surface. Then I muttered a parenthetical comment: "If you think of something you know a lot about that you could teach others, thumbs up." I saw thumbs rising across the room. With urgency, I said, "Fast, tell your partner what you are thinking you could write about!"

Name the teaching point.

"Writers, today I want to teach you that to get started writing a teaching book, a writer often becomes a teacher and teaches people all about the topic. When doing that teaching, many writers find it helps to use a teaching voice and to use fingers to organize information. That way the writer teaches one thing and then another and another about the topic."

TEACHING

Recruit children to notice the way you use a teaching voice and fingers (as graphic organizers) to teach about a topic in preparation for writing an informational book.

"Writers, watch me as I get ready to write my teaching book by using a teaching voice and fingers to teach you one thing and then another about my topic. Let's have you guys pretend to be students in a class I'm going to teach about yoga. This is a fancy class, so sit up nice and straight, with your whole body facing me. Take out your imaginary notepad so you can pretend to take imaginary notes on what I am teaching you. Yes! You look like official students!

"Are you ready to watch how I teach, because then you will have time to teach each other your topics?"

Role-play being a professor, teaching all about the topic on which you'll eventually write a demonstration text. Use your fingers to differentiate one subtopic, another, and another.

Shifting into the role of a professor of yoga, I adjusted myself on my chair and cleared my throat, as if getting myself ready for the teaching I was about to do. "Welcome, students. Today I am going to teach you about yoga. I am going to tell you some really important things that I know about yoga. First," I said, holding up one finger, "in yoga, you do lots of stretches." I held up another finger. "Also, to do yoga, you need a mat." I held up a third finger. "Another thing, in yoga you have to work very hard on breathing right." I paused, thinking aloud to myself, "Hmm, let's see, what else

I aim to be brief and not to repeat everything I heard. This is not a time for children to report back. Often the decisions one makes in a minilesson are guided by a fierce commitment to protecting time for writing.

It isn't usual to channel writers to decide on a topic during the connection of a minilesson, but the truth is that it is no big deal for first-graders to come up with one topic that they know a lot about. They'll end up generating close to a topic a day throughout this unit, and the children will listen differently to the rest of this minilesson if they do so with their topics in mind. Of course, I do not worry if some children don't have a topic in mind just yet, but I know the vast majority will. In the conferring section, you'll find ways to help children who end the minilesson still uncertain about their topics.

Gestures matter. When I have tried to illustrate the use of fingers to organize information, I hold up one finger, then another, as I say, 'That way, the writer teaches one thing, then another. . . ."

Again, it helps to gesture and to act. Whenever I talk about organizing information, I hold up one finger and then another. Fingers are the best graphic organizer in the world—and always on hand! When I talk about the students sitting up straight, ready for their first class, I'm definitely going to sit straight and tall myself. You can't do this acting if you are gripping this book. Set it aside and ad lib the lesson, doing so with a twinkle in your eye. This should be light, quick, and fun.

do I know. If I only know three things, I'm not sure I'm going to be able to write a whole book about yoga. Oh yes!" I held up a fourth finger. "Also, yoga comes from India. And one more thing." I held up a fifth finger. "Yoga helps people to feel better. I hope you enjoyed what I taught you about yoga."

Name what you have done in a way that is transferable to another day and another topic.

"Did you see how I got ready to write my book by teaching you all about my topic, yoga? I thought of as many things as I could about yoga, and I held up my fingers to show each time I shifted to a new subtopic—a new thing about yoga. Now I can start filling up pages in my very first teaching book."

ACTIVE ENGAGEMENT

Channel children to think of a topic they could teach others, and then ask one partner to teach the other, using a teaching voice and also using fingers to distinguish one point or part from another.

"I'm going to call you 'Teachers' now, because that's what you are going to be doing—teaching! Teachers, now it's your turn to give this a try. Thumbs up if you have a topic in mind that you think you could teach others."

After a moment, I said, "I see that not all of your thumbs are up. I'll wait just another moment for you to think of a topic that you could teach."

When most students' thumbs were up, I continued. "Teachers, it's your turn to give this a try. You are going to take turns teaching each other all about your expert topics. Partner 1, you are going to begin. Partner 2, you are the student, so adjust yourself so you are ready to learn. Partner 1, the teacher, when you are in position, you can start."

The room erupted into a chorus of voices, and I moved from partnership to partnership, listening in. I coached into their conversations, voicing over compliments. "Joey, I love how you are touching a finger each time you teach something new." "Alfred, that is amazing. You have already taught your partner *four* things! Keep going." "Hattie, I can see that you are very enthusiastic about your topic, and you are telling your partner lots of interesting stuff. That's lovely."

After a few minutes, I channeled the partnerships to switch so that Partner 2 could have a turn.

When you shift from the demonstration to debriefing, students should feel the different moves you are making just by the way your intonation and posture changes. After most demonstrations, there will be a time for you to debrief, and that's a time when you are no longer acting like a writer. You are the teacher who has been watching the demonstration and now turns to talk, eye to eye with kids, asking if they noticed this or that during the previous portion of the minilesson.

Throughout this book, you will see that we try to signal instances when you give the children a bit of silence. Notice that after telling the children they will now teach each other, I let a moment go by. It is absolutely critical to leave white space in a minilesson. Pay attention to the times when we nudge you to give kids a bit of time to think, to react, to do something, before you move on, and don't bypass those times.

If you worry that you are asking students to do something that is hard for them, keep in mind that they will find it easier if you leave open which partner goes first. If you channel Partner 1 to assume a particular role, and Partner 2 to assume a different role, then you aren't allowing the writer who feels more able to do this to step forward.

It is important for you to realize that usually partners do not switch roles. That is, usually if one teaches and the other learns, that provides sufficient support for both. Don't buy into the idea that each child needs to have a turn doing each thing during every turn and talk! This time, however, I did think it was advisable to let each child have some time to teach the other.

LINK

Restate the teaching point, making it applicable to not only today but every day.

"Teachers, let's come back together. Wow! I am so amazed at all of the things that you know. It's like I've become smarter just by listening in to what you had to say. I learned about skateboards and dinosaurs and the Buffalo Bills and Dominican food. You guys know so much! Now it's your chance to write a teaching book on the same topic that you just taught to your partner.

"And after this, for the rest of your life, always remember that one way that writers of informational books can get ready to write is to teach someone all about a topic. It can help to use a teaching voice and fingers or pages to organize information so the writer teaches one thing, and then another, about their topic. Put your thumb up if you feel ready to write. When I see you are ready, I'll send you off so that you can get started."

Remind Children that They Are Experts Who Have Many Lessons to Share

WHILE IT MAY BE TRUE that if *you'd* been asked to write an information book, you might panic over topic choice and worry that you have no area of expertise, the truth is that most first-graders have no trouble reeling off areas of expertise, especially once you've given them an idea of the sort of ordinary and accessible topics you are imagining. So today, be wary of the tendency to project your own writers' block onto six-year-olds. Guard against the assumption that they will all need help choosing topics for today's writing. Instead, convey to kids an absolute rock-solid conviction that it will be easy as pie for them to think of a ton of things that they could teach others about—dogs, ballet, Joy Cowley's books, wearing tights to school, doing tricks on the monkey bars, and so on. Channel children toward topics of personal expertise and toward topics that others would like to learn about. That is, a book on laundry may not give the young writer any social cachet, but a book on magic tricks or slugs or skateboard wheelies might—which will tend to make the young writer all the more willing to invest in writing in the future.

On the other hand, you may have a few children who *do* need helping arriving at topics to teach. For these youngsters, keep in mind that your goal will not be to help them come up with topics, so much as to teach them a few strategies they can use often so that they are able to generate ideas on their own. One of the most straightforward strategies you could teach involves the writer brainstorming things throughout their day that they know well (morning TV shows, the school bus, outside line-up at school, the class pet . . .).

A second strategy is that kids can turn to someone who knows them well and ask that person, "What topics do I know about?" The kids, then, will say things like, "Tonia should write about Littlest Pets toys. She has so many," or "Henry should write, 'All About SpongeBob SquarePants.' He always talks about SpongeBob."

But don't go overboard teaching strategies for generating topics, because most children will have no trouble generating ideas for things they could teach. First-graders will be more apt to have trouble using partners well as a support for rehearsal. You

MID-WORKSHOP TEACHING **Writers Aim to Write Something Interesting on Every Page**

"Writers, can I stop you?" I waited until all eyes were on me. "Earlier, we talked about how you are writing to teach people about something you know about. I'm doing that with my yoga book. There's one thing I have been working on in my book that I am pretty sure you're going to work on as well, and it is this: I'm trying to make my book interesting. So sometimes I reread what I have written and give it a 'Will this be interesting?' test. Are you willing to help me test out my yoga book? And then you could help each other test your books as well.

"So what I do is I read over my book, and at the end of every page, I ask, 'Is there something at least sort of interesting on that page?' And if there isn't, I try to squeeze my mind and come up with something interesting to write. So do you want to try it? Here is page 1 of my yoga book:

Yoga is a way to move your body. It is not hard.

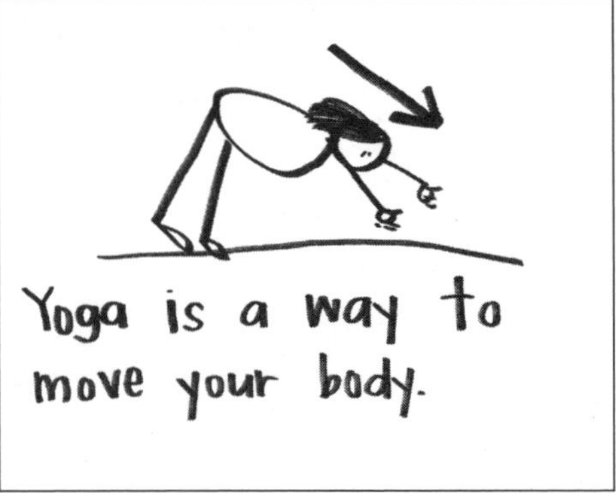

FIG. 1–1

"What do you think?" I feigned shock and horror. "*What?* You think my first page was a little bit *boring?* Oh, no. I'm going to have to think about what I can say that would make it more interesting! And here is one tip that will help me: details almost always make something more interesting. So let me think if I could add a detail to that page. Hmm, I know." I quickly added:

Yoga is a way to move your body. You can bend from side-to-side and you can even go upside down! You can even touch your toes.

"So, writers, will you try this with each other? For now, just read pages 1 and 2 of your book to your partner, and partners, see if you can point to a part on every page that is at least sort of interesting. If there isn't an interesting part on the page yet, that's okay, because what do you think you could do today?" The children grasped my point, with a few suggesting they could add interesting stuff. The youngsters then worked with partners, helping each other add interesting parts to every page.

may want to teach the listening partner to listen with eyes, ears, and whole bodies. Help the listener to know the difference between the unengaged listener (who is fun to act out!) and the engaged listener and to realize that a good listener's presence makes writers say so, so much more.

Good listeners also ask questions that elicit information, and your listeners could develop little crib sheets containing the kinds of questions writers ask one another as they move through the writing process. You can certainly give kids "starter questions," such as "What else can you teach your reader?" and "What will your next part be about?" Then, as children become more adept at having conversations about their writing, encourage them to add onto their crib sheets independently, pointing out the smart ways their writerly conversations are evolving.

Meanwhile, be prepared to be a partner to all the writers in the class, listening with responsiveness to all that they have to teach. There is nothing like a rapt listener to help any one of us realize that in fact we *do* have lessons to teach and information to share. Remember that this entire field of work relies on the wisdom of Donald Murray, who described his role by saying that he helps writers realize they are experts on topics they think are ordinary. If one child's mother just had a baby, that child may need you to help him or her realize that the rest of us would love to know what it's been like to have a baby in the family.

This is important work indeed!

SHARE

Looking Back and Looking Forward

Tell children that you collected a checklist showing all they learned about information writing in kindergarten. Read the checklist aloud while kids note if today's work reflects each item.

"Let's gather for a share session," I said. Once children had settled in the meeting area, I began. "This is the very first day of our unit, but many of you are already writing books that show that you know a lot about this kind of writing. Watching you work, I remembered that last year, when you were in kindergarten, some of you wrote teaching books. So I sent a messenger to one of your kindergarten classrooms and borrowed one of the checklists you made last year. I'm going to read this over while you and your partner look at the writing you each did today."

To help children get ready to listen, I said, "Lay the writing you did today on the carpet in front of you." Once they'd done this, I said, "As I read off each item, will you evaluate your writing? When you hear an item from last year's checklist, give yourself a thumbs up if your writing shows you have mastered that skill and a thumbs down if that item is not yet in your writing." I read one item at a time, leaving tiny intervals for children to scan their work, looking for evidence. Occasionally I said, "Point to where you did that." The Information Writing Checklist, Grade K can be found on the CD-ROM.

Information Writing Checklist

	Kindergarten	NOT YET	STARTING TO	YES!
	Structure			
Overall	I told, drew, and wrote about a topic.	☐	☐	☐
Lead	I told what my topic was.	☐	☐	☐
Transitions	I put different things I knew about the topic on my pages.	☐	☐	☐
Ending	I had a last part or page.	☐	☐	☐
Organization	I told, drew, and wrote information across pages.	☐	☐	☐
	Development			
Elaboration	I drew and wrote important things about the topic.	☐	☐	☐
Craft	I told, drew, and wrote some details about the topic.	☐	☐	☐
	Language Conventions			
Spelling	I could read my writing.	☐	☐	☐
	I wrote a letter for the sounds I heard.	☐	☐	☐
	I used the word wall to help me spell.	☐	☐	☐
Punctuation	I put spaces between words.	☐	☐	☐
	I used lowercase letters unless capitals were needed.	☐	☐	☐
	I wrote capital letters to start every sentence.	☐	☐	☐

End with a note of celebration and resolve, by reminding children that tomorrow they'll have more time to write in ways that reflect all they already know about this genre.

"How many of you found that you remembered to do many of the things you learned in kindergarten?" I looked around. "Great. And did some of you learn about things you can work on tomorrow?" I scanned the room, nodding as if there's nothing better than learning about some work one can do. "Lea noticed she wants to label her illustrations tomorrow. She'll always remember she can teach even more by doing that (see Figure 1–2). Isn't it the best to have some goals!"

Then I added, "I'll leave this checklist at the front of our meeting area, and tomorrow, before you start a second book, will you check the things you will want to remember to do? Soon we're going to learn even *more* things that make teaching books really terrific. For now, give yourself a pat on the back." They did. "And stand and take a bow." They did.

Dogs play and they look like wolves. And eat dog food.

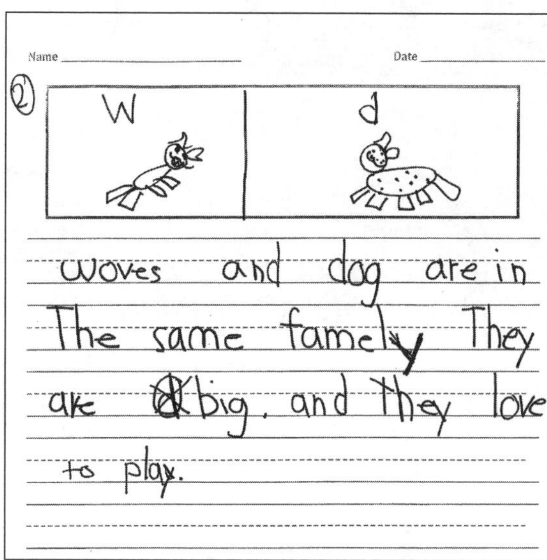

Wolves and dogs are in the same family. They are big. And they love to play.

Dogs can be good friends. I got a dog and her name is Nala. I love her so. That is how it was.

Dogs like balls like we do. We like balls. They like balls too.

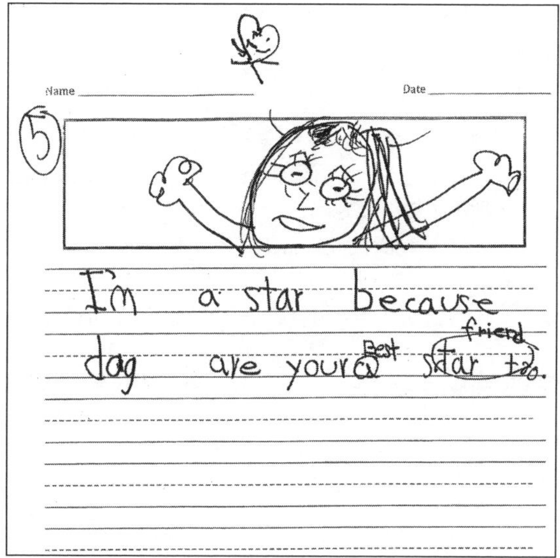

I'm a star because dogs are your best friend. You're a star too.

FIG. 1–2 Lea's first draft

Session 2

Writers Tell Information across Their Fingers, Sketch, then Write

IN THIS SESSION, you'll teach children that writers plan what they are going to say before they write. They do this by telling information across their fingers, sketching, and then writing.

GETTING READY

- ✔ An example of a keepsake: a decorated folder, backpack, or key chain (see Connection)
- ✔ Information Writing Checklist, Grade K, on a large chart (see Connection and Share)
- ✔ Anchor chart titled "How to Write a Teaching Book" (see Connection)
- ✔ Small copies of the "How to Write a Teaching Book" chart, one for each partnership
- ✔ A giant-sized book of your own demonstration writing made out of chart paper, which you will use to demonstrate today's strategy (see Teaching)
- ✔ Student writing to assess against the Information Writing Checklist (see Share)

Common Core State Standards: W.1.2, W.1.5, RI.1.6, RI.1.7, RFS.1.1, SL.1.1, SL.1.4, SL.1.5, SL.1.6, L.1.1, L.1.2

I REMEMBER LEARNING TO PLAY TENNIS. My mother would holler at me, day after day, calling, "Keep your eye on the ball." I would think, "What do you think I am looking at? Birds? Of course I'm keeping my eye on the ball." Then one day I saw the ball as it hung, suspended at the top of a bounce, and saw my racket hit the ball, too, and I realized that prior to that day, I had never actually kept my eye on the ball.

I say this because when teaching writing, we, like my mother, will need to call out a handful of instructions, over and over. Kids will think they are doing exactly as we say, until one day, they actually *do* what we've supported all along, and it will come to them that, Holy moly, it really makes a difference when I do that.

Today's session contains very little new content. Instead, you return to work that you taught earlier this year and to content you touched on lightly yesterday. Today you essentially say to kids, "The work that you did yesterday, and also earlier this year, is still important today." You'll recall that you ended yesterday by reading through the Information Writing Checklist that you hope your children encountered during kindergarten. You begin today by returning to that checklist and to the important idea that even though this is children's very first unit this year in which they are writing informational books, they bring prior knowledge to this unit and need to use all they know, right from the start.

Then, you'll remind children that yesterday's lesson emphasized that writers of information books are teachers and often prepare for writing by teaching others. More specifically, you channeled students to use a teaching voice and to use their fingers as graphic organizers, helping them divide their content into different pages of information (each represented by a finger). Today you remind students to prepare for their writing by thinking and saying what they might write, and more specifically, you spotlight the notion, mentioned in passing yesterday, that writers can use their fingers as tools to support organization. This is a slightly different planning technique than what children learned for writing small moments. Rather than touch the exact page they will write on, children use their fingers to represent each page. This will become important later on as children construct booklets with different kinds of paper. Rather than touching a preconstructed booklet, children will plan their teaching book on their fingers and select the type of paper (out of several choices) that will best teach that information.

> *"Transference is something we can never take for granted. Experienced teachers know that instead, it is wise to explicitly teach for transference."*

The simplest version of this is for children to say one thing they know about a topic while touching one finger and another thing they know about that topic while touching another finger. This might sound something like, "One thing that I know about recess is that kids get exercise during it." Then, next finger, "Another thing that I know is that a lot of kids play games like tag during recess." After you remind children that it helps to tap fingers as they ramble off information about their topics, you can build on this by teaching children that, actually, they can say a few sentences about each fact before moving to the next fact. This rehearsal doesn't take more than a few minutes, so children can engage in rehearsal and still have time to write a second book during today's workshop.

To help aid with transference from the *Small Moments* unit, you will want to create a new version of the "How to Write a Story" chart, altering the wording slightly to match this new type of writing students will be doing. You will title this chart "How to Write a Teaching Book." And under "Plan," rather than "Touch and tell," you will write, "Say it across your fingers."

This session, then, revisits the planning session from the *Small Moments* unit and teaches the broader concept that much of what children learned to do during their previous unit of study will apply now to this new unit. Transference is something we never can take for granted. Experienced teachers know that instead, it is wise to explicitly teach for transference.

There are about a score of other things that you taught children to do during the previous unit that you'll want them to transfer into this unit. Make this explicit. For example, come right out and say something to the effect of, "I am so proud of you all because last month, you learned to. . . . So, did you forget all about that now that you are writing informational books? No way! That is totally cool. Let me list other things that you learned to do during our first unit, and for each of these things, will you and your partner give yourself a thumbs up or a thumbs down, depending on if you are still doing it?"

MINILESSON

Writers Tell Information across Their Fingers, Sketch, then Write

CONNECTION

Share an example of a keepsake—perhaps a sticker on a notebook or a key chain on a jacket zipper—that jogs memories, just as anchor charts do.

"Writers, I was looking at Charlie's backpack this morning. Look at it!" I held it up. "You see how it has badges that remind him of things he's done? Charlie, this badge says, 'Red Jacket Ski Hill.' When you look at that badge, what do you remember?"

Charlie stopped bobbing back and forth long enough to say, "Skiing." I nodded, accepting that underdeveloped answer with enthusiasm. "And I bet that just looking at the badge helps you remember all about the Red Jacket Ski Hill, right?"

Then I spoke to the whole class. "It is important that people have ways to remind them of things they never want to forget. Some people use their backpacks to remind them of stuff. In our classroom, we use teaching charts to remind us of stuff, don't we? And yesterday we studied a chart—a checklist, really—that shows stuff many of you learned in kindergarten. We want to make sure that we are doing *all* these things so that we can learn new and harder things about writing teaching books."

Read aloud the checklist on information writing from kindergarten, asking writers to consider, then talk about, how many of the things on the checklist they have already done in their writing.

"So before you start writing today, I'm going to read this kindergarten checklist that we looked at yesterday one more time. Will you and your partner talk about things on this checklist that you aren't yet doing—things you want to try hard to do today? You ready?" I read aloud from the checklist we'd studied yesterday. The Information Writing Checklist, Grade K is available on the CD-ROM.

"Writers, turn and tell your partner the items on our checklist that you are going to work hard to do today. Go!"

I listened as Alfred told his partner he was going to add labels on his pictures. Annie said she would check that her book had a good ending. Then I reconvened the class. "Writers, your goal is not just to write teaching books, like we discussed yesterday. Your goal is to write books that are better and better every day. Will you look at yesterday's book and think

◆ COACHING

In an instance like this, you will want to be mindful that Charlie's badges are not the point. Don't let the discussion of the backpack and skiing become more than a passing reference. You don't want the kids to be confused over whether you are teaching about backpacks and skiing or about anchor charts and the writing process. Always remember that you need to be clear about what you are emphasizing. Streamline things, make your point, and then let kids write!

Teachers, you may decide that instead of reading the whole checklist and then popping this all-important question, you may read just three items, then ask this question, then read another few items, and again ask children to weigh whether one of the items might become a personal goal.

not just about the things you are going to fix up in that book, but also about what you will do to make the new book you start today *even better*?" I left a little pool of silence for the children to do this thinking.

Name the teaching point.

"Today I want to remind you that before you write a teaching book, you plan how your book will go. And guess what? You *already know* how to plan your teaching books! You plan your teaching books by saying your information across your fingers and then quickly sketching something you'll write on each of the pages."

TEACHING

Point out that just as teachers plan for our teaching, writers, too, must plan. Illustrate this by suggesting your minilesson would be chaotic had you not planned.

"Writers, last night, I was sitting at home, *planning* what I would teach in today's minilesson, when all of a sudden I realized, 'Wow. I know what I better tell the kids. I better tell them that teachers *plan*!' Remember, nonfiction writers are a kind of teacher. That means that you are teachers, too. Wouldn't it be *crazy* if I can up here to do a minilesson and it went like this?"

> *Hi, mathematicians. No, uh, wait, Hi, um, whoever you are. Ah! Yes! Hi, writers. Today we're gonna, um, well, we'll learn about* something. *(I'm not sure what.) One thing is that writers use colons before a list. But no, colons aren't that important. We should talk about About the Author sections. No, wait.*

Make sure you play up the confused nature of your teaching so it sounds completely and totally chaotic. I've tried to write it so that the kids will be laughing at how silly this kind of teaching (or writing) would be. This lesson actually revisits the topic from yesterday, emphasizing that writers structure their writing and address one thing at a time, but the minilesson gets at the same content from a different avenue.

Point out that some writers of teaching books neglect to plan, resulting in chaotic books. Stress that planning for teaching books resembles planning for narratives. Model planning.

"It would be really crazy if my minilessons went like that, wouldn't it be? I'm telling you this because some people actually *forget* to plan their teaching books, so their writing just jumps from one topic to the next to the next, like I just did: 'I'm going to teach about . . . no wait . . . no, not that, but. . . .'"

Notice that I am teaching what to do by accentuating what not to do. I want writers to be able to monitor their own work and realize when they are doing something that is not working. I want them to realize that teaching, or writing, in a fashion that lurches from one subtopic to another is far from ideal, and I'm hoping to accentuate the problems of doing that.

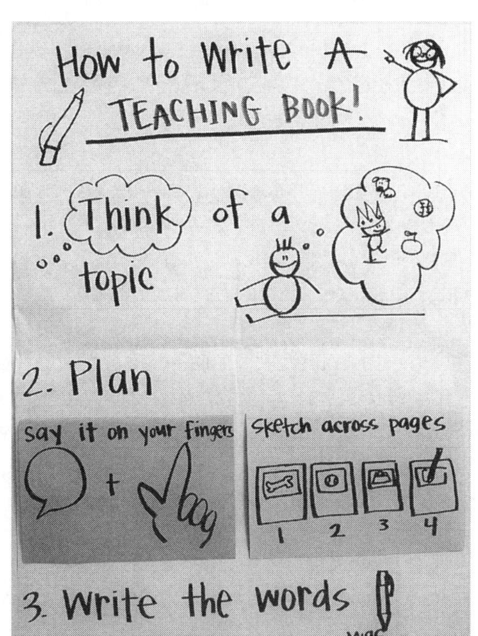

"I've given you and your partner a small copy of a chart that is similar to the one we made together during our *Small Moments* unit. The "How to Write a Teaching Book" chart can be found on the CD-ROM.] Do you remember how we learned that when writers are writing Small Moment stories, it helps to think of an idea, then plan, then write? Well, now that you are writing teaching books, I made a few little changes to match this new type of writing you are doing. Writers of teaching books think of a topic they want to teach others about, plan their information across their fingers, sketch, then write.

"Try to notice whether I do each of those things as I plan my teaching book, okay?" I shifted into the role of writer, holding a giant chart-sized book. "Let's see, first I need to think of a topic. Well, I can use places I go. I go to yoga every day, so I will write about that." I looked up and thought.

"Now let me plan." I held one finger up and dictated. "I'm going to tell you all about yoga. In yoga, you do lots of stretches. Also," I held up my next finger, "to do yoga, you need a mat." I held up one last finger, smiling. "Yoga helps people to feel better." In an aside to the children, I said, "Are you noticing what I have done so far to plan?" and I gestured toward the bullet for saying the text across your fingers.

Pointing to the phrase "Sketch across pages," I sketched. Pantomiming, I stuck my tongue out and quickly sketched a page and then in a stage-whispered aside told the children that I would do that on every page. "Let's read the list together to make sure I am ready to write the words." The class read together as if this was a shared reading.

It is not common to demonstrate so many steps or to rehearse the entire process of choosing a topic and planning a book during a teaching component of a minilesson. This is more steps and more content than you will usually demonstrate. But today, you want to give kids a sense of the flow of the whole process, so isolating just a part of it wouldn't work. The essential thing is that you need to be quick, confident, and economical in all you say or do. Don't get feeling so comfortable that you become chatty and start embellishing things!

Debrief by stressing the way this lesson is transferable to other days and other topics.

"That was easy. I'm ready to write my teaching book! Remember, writers, whenever you want to plan your teaching book, you do this in almost the exact same way that you planned your Small Moments books: think of an idea, say your information across your fingers, sketch, then write."

ACTIVE ENGAGEMENT

Channel children to locate topics for today's informational writing, then to plan with partners.

"Will you do the same kind of planning for the book you'll write today? I know a few of you will first finish up yesterday's book. Before you can plan today's writing, each of you needs to come up with a topic, so I'll give you a minute to think."

During those thirty seconds of silence, if you actually sit in the chair and think of a topic you could write—even though, yes, you already have a book started—the fact that you are mentally doing what you want the kids to do has a magical power, and kids are far more apt to do what you want them to do. Try this. You'll be amazed at the power.

After a minute, I said, "How many of you have a topic in mind for your next book? Thumbs up." When many children signaled, I said, "Turn to your partners now, and will one of you, whoever has a topic and is ready, plan the book you are going to write today? Say your information across your fingers, remembering to teach your partner something interesting on each page, on each finger. If there is time, partners can switch roles and hear a second book."

The room erupted with talk. The children couldn't wait to teach their new topics. I circulated among them, noticing their work. After a minute, I stopped them. "Hattie," I started, "you were saying your information across your fingers and adding details when something wasn't clear. Wow! And Anessa, you were saying your information across your fingers using a teaching voice. Most of you have a topic, and said what you will write, using the same teaching voice that Anessa used. That means that when you go back to sketch and then write, you will be thinking about your readers the whole, entire time. Well done!"

Teachers, it is okay that children get started and do not completely finish this, and certainly it is okay that there often is not time for the partners to exchange roles. Your point is to teach writers that this sort of planning helps, not necessarily to make sure that every writer has completed his or her planning during the minilesson.

LINK

Coach writers to use their best teaching voice when they touch and tell and then to quickly bring their voice to print.

"Writers, you are using beautiful teaching voices when you touch your fingers and say what you will write, but sometimes when you turn to write those great words and sentences in your books, that beautiful teaching voice disappears. Hold onto it!

"You are doing some good work when you take the time to get ready to write your teaching book. Will you look at our Information Writing Checklist and remind yourself that you will also want to remember all those items on that list?"

Channel writers to get started saying information across their fingers, sketching, and writing—and then send them off to continue writing.

"Can we try something together, writers? I want you to turn to your first page and make a quick sketch. As you sketch, *say in your mind* the words you are going to be writing on that page." After a minute, I said, "In a second I am going to suggest you get started writing the words you are saying on that page. But before you write, say the words you are going to write aloud to yourself one more time. Then start to write."

As I saw writers working with absorption, I signaled for one, then another and another, to move to his or her writing place and continue working.

CONFERRING AND SMALL-GROUP WORK

Rally Kids to Get Started on the Big Work of the Unit—and Don't Sweat the Small Stuff

AT THE START OF ANY UNIT OF STUDY, you will want to use small groups and, to a lesser extent, conferring to issue a generous invitation into the unit, helping all your children feel at home doing the new work. For today, then, it will be important for you to keep your priorities straight and to use your time in ways that generate enthusiastic participation in the new work of the unit.

You'll want to lead lots of informal small groups during conferring time, so it helps to think in advance about some of the teaching methods you'll use and about some of the content you'll teach.

If you could watch teachers doing small-group instruction in a writing workshop, you'd notice right away that youngsters don't start and finish a piece of writing within a small group. Instead, the small groups give a teacher a chance to "teach into" kids' ongoing work. There are two main kinds of groups. Sometimes, the teacher arrives at a table full of writers, watches long enough to sense what many of the kids need, and then teaches that group, perhaps by using one child as an example. Other times, the teacher gestures for a few youngsters who need similar help to pull together and then teaches a common topic to those children.

Let's for today imagine that you arrive at one table, then another, and then another, watch for a bit, and then teach into the work the children are doing. Start by planning your time frame. You'll be at a table no more than, say, four minutes and sometimes, half that time. During that time, you watch what kids are doing, and this clues you in to what you will teach. Then you ask for and get everyone's attention. You teach kids what to do, perhaps helping them get started doing that. Then—and this is the hardest part—you leave. You don't stay to watch them work, to perfect what they are doing, or to prop up the level of their work. Instead, you circle to a new table, knowing that in so doing you are giving the original group time to approximate. After working with two or three more groups, you circle back to the first group and ramp up the instruction you gave earlier.

MID-WORKSHOP TEACHING **Remind Writers that Once They're Done, They've Just Begun**

"Writers, today I reminded you that when writing teaching books, you can touch and tell, sketch, then write, just as you did when writing Small Moment stories. There are *lots* of things you already know, as writers, that you need to remember to do still. Watch me get stuck and see if you can draw on things you already know to help me."

I shifted into role-playing a six-year-old writer. Holding up a booklet, I said, "I'm all done. I finished my teaching book. All done!" Then I put my feet up on the table and leaned back in an exaggerated "I'm done" pose.

Children clamored to talk. Hattie said, in her best teacher-imitation voice, "When you're done, you've just begun. Do another book!" Others added. "Put it in the Done folder." "First add on." "You gotta put more details in."

Nodding, I said, "I'm totally impressed. You know that when writers are done, they've just begun. Today I'm going to watch all the totally cool things you can do once you're done. Because Hattie is right. Once you're done, you've just begun. You can make your book even better."

All of this will require thinking on your feet and making snap decisions, and frankly, the only way to do that is by being prepared. If you come to a group of kids and you already anticipate that you'll teach one of four possible things, it is not hard to decide which of those four possible topics will be most useful to that group. Don't allow yourself to become deeply invested in helping any one child write a terrific text or even do well whatever it is that you teach. Deep work with one child will be at the expense of bringing half a dozen other youngsters into the gist of this unit.

So what are some of the things you can anticipate teaching? For one thing, writers tend to tackle gigantic topics: a five-page booklet is titled "The Whole Wide World of Dogs." You will want to coach writers to focus their topics somewhat so that, for example, the writer tackles one breed of dog or one dog show rather than writing all about every kind of dog. Then, too, young writers tend to put one or two pieces of information related to a subtopic on a page and then they jump to another subtopic. More development will help. For youngsters, this means literally writing more about each subtopic before moving to the next. Since young writers tend to add in everything but the kitchen sink, rereading to take out stuff that "doesn't go" can be important. Also, writers don't always realize that the drawing stage of writing can be generative. They draw and then write and then turn the page. If the writer began to habitually return to the picture, adding more to it, this could fuel a second round of writing work on that page.

SHARE

Writers Learn to Assess Their Own Writing by Assessing Shared Texts

Set one writer up to read his information book aloud while the class evaluates that text to see ways he does (and does not yet) show that he is meeting the criteria for good informational writing.

"Marco has finished his teaching book, and he wondered if I could help him check that he has done everything on the Information Writing Checklist that we brought up from your kindergarten classrooms. I thought maybe we could *all* help Marco check that he has done all those things that he knows how to do. Marco, in a minute I am going to ask you to read your book aloud to us and we'll talk about places where we saw you doing all the things you guys already learned." (This checklist can be found on the CD-ROM.)

"Let's all take jobs. Who wants to see if Marco seems interested in his topic?" Some children volunteered. "And who will listen to see if he teaches the reader about his topic? Who can check for that?" Soon we had listeners checking that the pictures teach, that the writer ended his book with a final thought, that he put spaces between words *and* did his best to spell each word, and so forth.

Marco read his piece aloud (see Figure 2–1).

The class agreed Marco had done some of the items on the checklist and still needed to add a final thought about his topic.

Channel all members of the class to transfer this work to their own books, rereading their own writing to self-evaluate it against the same criteria that the class used to assess Marco's writing.

"Now, writers, here is the big job. Can you apply what you just did to your own book? Read your own book and self-evaluate it, then decide what to do—and do it!" The children began doing this work. "And remember, anytime you are writing a teaching book, you can refer to our Information Writing Checklist to see if you can add anything to your book."

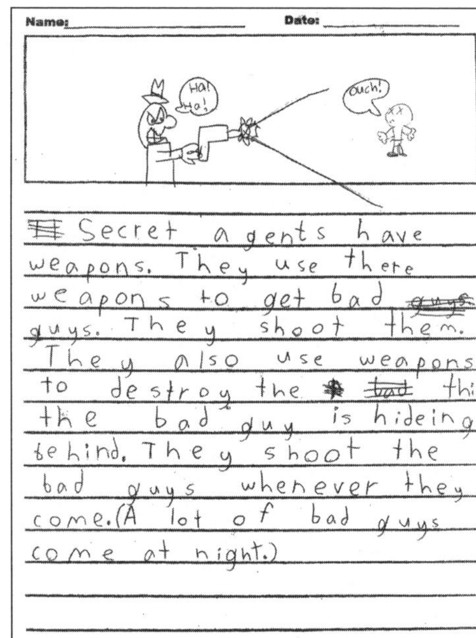

FIG. 2–1 The class used Marco's draft with the checklist.

Session 3

Writers Keep Readers in Mind, Writing to Answer Their Questions

EVERY GENRE OF WRITING has predictable challenges, and when writing information books, one of the most important challenges is including lots of information! In this session you will help your students elaborate, or say more. To support this, be sure that your own exemplar piece of writing is the length that hope your students will produce so that you are modeling the same volume you expect from your writers.

The Common Core State Standards (CCSS) highlight the importance of this goal. When writing informative/explanatory texts, first-graders are expected to "name a topic, supply some facts about the topic, and provide some sense of closure" (1.W.2). That, in and of itself, doesn't sound like a demanding goal, but the student samples included in Appendix B of the Common Core raise the expectations. The grade 1 information writing sample is a long report on Spain, brimming with information.

This session will help children tackle the work of supplying lots of facts from the get-go, which will build volume in their writing. You may see that as children write informational books, they often write just one sentence, almost a topic sentence, on each page before heading to the next page. Writing several sentences on a page before starting the next page is important work for your first-graders at this point in the year.

It is good to begin to stress the value of elaboration and evidence early on in a student's writing career because expectations in this dimension of writing increase rapidly over the upcoming years. In the CCSS, few things matter more than the fact that students are expected to provide increasing amounts of elaboration and evidence. And elaboration is equally important in opinion and narrative writing, so the work you do helping students to elaborate when writing information texts will carry over when they are working within other genres.

There are lots of ways to teach children to say more. At its simplest level, this session teaches them that they can think about the questions readers will ask (for your students, this means the questions that other kids will ask) and then put answers to those questions into their books. More specifically, you can teach them that people want details. They want

IN THIS SESSION, you'll teach children that writers try to picture who their readers will be. Then, to reach their readers, they imagine and answer the questions their readers might ask.

GETTING READY

- ✓ Anchor chart titled "How Can I Teach My Readers?" to start during the minilesson and add onto during mid-workshop teaching
- ✓ Your own demonstration writing from the previous session—giant-sized—on which you will demonstrate today's strategy (see Teaching)
- ✓ Students need to bring the teaching books they wrote yesterday to the meeting area (see Active Engagement).
- ✓ Post-its® to add examples (see Conferring and Small-Group Work)
- ✓ Scissors, revision strips, and tape (see Share)

COMMON CORE STATE STANDARDS: W.1.2, W.2.2, RI.1.1, RI.1.4, SL.1.1, SL.1.2, SL.1.3, L.1.1, L.1.2, L.1.4, L.1.6

to know what things look like, for example, and that means they'll ask about numbers, sizes, shapes, and colors. They want to know how things work, and they'll ask about what happens first, next, and next.

"This session will help children tackle the work of supplying lots of facts from the get-go, which will build volume in their writing."

To teach this session successfully, it is important that your expectations for the volume of writing that your students can produce and for their fluency and stamina are properly high. If a child can write one sentence on a page, that same child can write three sentences on that page, and if a child can write three sentences on a page, that same child can write six sentences. And frankly, you want to aim toward helping all your children write five or six sentences on a page, on four or five pages, and to do that in a day. If you are startled by these expectations and find yourself protesting them, think again. After all, these books have grown out of three decades of work in thousands of schools, including many schools throughout many major cities. If the expectations feel too high to you, perhaps you are underestimating your students' abilities.

Of course, motivation matters. To motivate children to write more, you might want to tell them that now that they are writing books like real authors, they'll want to study what real writers do and think about doing likewise. One thing writers do, of course, is write a lot more than a sentence on a page. That is, they "say more." Be stubborn in your expectations, and you will find that students surprise you with how much they can do.

The work of this session, considering questions a reader might have, can be supported in partnerships. You can set partners up to take turns telling each other what information they are planning to teach next, listening carefully to questions the other has, and then composing in ways that answer those questions. If a child has said, "There are a lot of bad guys in Star Wars," then another child might ask, "What are their names? Who are the bad guys?" The author, then, can add this information. To support this kind of elaboration, you can scaffold writers by prompting them to ask *what*, *when*, *why*, and *how* questions of their partners' pieces as well as their own. By the end of the session, children will have new tools for saying more in their informational books and will have begun the challenging work of anticipating and answering readers' questions, an important skill that will become even more crucial as students write increasingly sophisticated information, opinion, and argument texts in the months and years to come.

MINILESSON

Writers Keep Readers in Mind, Writing to Answer Their Questions

CONNECTION

Recall that like teachers, writers plan. Like teachers, writers also think about their "students," their readers. Writers answer readers' questions.

"Writers, you have learned that when you write teaching books, you become teachers for your readers. And so one way to get better at writing these books is to remember that as authors, you are acting as teachers and you need to do the things teachers do. For example, you already learned that teachers plan—and I know you all are planning your books, by teaching your content to your friends and by touching and telling, sketching then writing."

Name the teaching point.

"Today I want to teach you that teachers do more than plan. They also think about their students. Teachers think, 'Who am I teaching?' And then, when they have their students in mind, they try to teach in ways that will reach those students. As writers of information books, you are the teacher, and your readers are your students. You need to ask, 'Who am I teaching?' To reach your readers, imagine and answer their questions."

TEACHING

Set children up to think about readers' questions by helping them generate topics for writing.

"Let's try this. Before we start, tell your partner what you might write about. (I should say, 'What you might *teach about*.') That way you will have your topic in mind as we work." I gave them a minute, coaching, "Don't forget that you can write about things you do, places you've been." I left a little pool of silence in which they could think.

"Although most of you had time to finish your books yesterday, I am still writing my yoga book. A few of you will still be working on yesterday's book, too, and that's okay. Does each of you have a topic in mind you will write about—teach about—today?" I checked that most of the children were ready to listen to today's minilesson with topics on hand.

◆ COACHING

One of the marks of effective teaching is that it harkens back to prior instruction, keeping that instruction alive for students and showing them how the new instruction builds on and fits alongside the prior instruction. This is often the goal of the connection.

Notice the way this teaching point—and almost all teaching points—is carefully sequenced. It has a lot of words in it, and I certainly tried to tighten it. But I am careful to make the sequence feel precisely accurate.

You will see that in this unit and in many units. you persist with your one or two texts while children crank out a lot more books. The reason you return to the same text is that this way you can demonstrate just the new aspect of writing, in an intact book. So while you do want the children to have repeated practice writing whole books, your minilessons essentially allow you to spotlight one aspect or another of writing, and it is easiest to do this by zooming in on just one aspect of a text that is familiar to all the children.

Demonstrate asking "Who will my readers be?" "What will they ask?" Write (or rewrite) to answer their questions.

"Watch what I do to think about my readers and about the questions they'll ask, because then you can do this too."

Shifting into the role of writer, I mused. "Hmm, I need to think, 'Who will my readers be?' Am I writing for the other people in my yoga class, people who do yoga with me every week?" I thought about that and shook my head. "I don't think so, because they already know the steps we're taught and all. So who am I writing for?"

Answering my own question, I said, "I guess this is a book for people who *wish* they were in my yoga class but aren't. So I picture my readers will pick up the book, hoping it will teach them what to do. They're probably ready to follow the directions in the book and do the yoga moves. I want to be able to imagine my readers. Let's see, maybe my dad will be one of my readers."

I got up, away from my usual seat, put on a baseball hat, and then walked in my best father imitation, approaching my seat. As this imaginary reader, I shook the now nonexistent teacher's hand and said, "I hear you are writing a book for me about yoga. I hope your book answers my questions. I want to know, Do people have to wear tights and a tutu to do yoga? Also, do I have to go to a special place to do it? Is it for a special day like my birthday or just for any day?"

I took off the hat and resumed my seat, making a big show of becoming myself again. "Whoa, writers, did you hear the questions my dad had about yoga? My book better answer some of his questions." In my book, I wrote:

> People do yoga in a studio. A studio is a special room with a lot of space and mirrors. It usually has a nice smell.

"Next, I can add more to my book by answering the questions about wearing a tutu."

Debrief, reminding writers of the steps you took to add to your book.

"Did you see, writers, how I imagined my reader and, specifically, my reader's questions, and then I made sure I answered the questions? Let's start a chart that captures this skill so we don't forget this important way to teach our readers more about our topic." I revealed a chart on which I'd written, "Think about questions my reader might have" under the title "How Can I Teach My Readers?" "This way, writers, you'll remember how to teach your readers more about your topics. We'll add to this chart as we learn more ways to teach our readers.

Pay attention to methods we use for demonstration teaching. I am thinking aloud so that children can see the decisions I make as I plan ways to answer questions I anticipate readers will ask. But I am not sitting with my hand poised before the page, rambling along about all sorts of thoughts. Instead, I ask a question, then generate an answer I reject and then an answer I accept. Then, I do the next step of writing work, which involves imagining a reader's point of view, but to make this more concrete, I act out what I am imagining. After imagining a reader, I shift back to the role of writer and shift into naming what I'll write next. This is a far cry from rambling on and on and on about all my thoughts.

FIG. 3–1

ACTIVE ENGAGEMENT

Set authors up to work with partners who role-play being real-world readers and who ask questions.

"Partners, can you look at the book you are working on and think about one of the pages you are going to write today? Partner 2, tell Partner 1 what that one page might be about." I gave the partners a minute to name the information they'd write on one page.

"Now both of you pretend to be someone outside of school, who is reading this page. Pretend you found the book in the library. You will have to change from kid to actor and act the part of a busy reader, just like I pretended to be my dad, who is learning this information for the first time. First decide who you'll be." I gave them a few seconds to do this. "Now take a minute and just think about some of the questions this person might have about the information. Just like I did with my yoga book." I gave the partners a minute, and as they thought I quietly said, "The person might ask *How*?" I left silence. "Or When? Where?" to support children as they thought of questions.

Teachers, you'll notice that most minilessons contain what I call "tucked tips." These are added bits of information that are tucked into the teaching or active engagement sections of a minilesson and are not highlighted in the teaching points. They presumably go over the head of some students and extend what others have learned. In this session, the suggested questions that one can ask of writing were the tucked tips: "How?" "When?" "Where?" Of course, the biggest question is the unspoken one: "Why?"

"Turn and talk." The room erupted into chatter and giggles as people assumed the roles of strangers. I listened in as Anessa shared, "I am gonna write about the monkey bars at the park. Probably people don't know how to go on the monkey bars, but I do because I do it all the time." She nodded smugly. I whispered in her partner Jacob's ear, who was staring at Anessa stone-faced, "Hmm, can you ask her a question, like when or why?" Jacob thought for a moment and asked, "Why do you go on the monkey bars?" As Anessa burst forth with an answer, I returned to the front of the rug.

Debrief, reminding readers that they can read by pretending to be a stranger, generating questions they then answer.

"Okay, now that you guys have learned how to think of questions readers might have, you should have a technique that can help you say lots more in your writing. You'll probably add on so much that you write to the bottoms of your pages!

"In real life, it is actually the *author* (not the partner) who needs to pretend to be a stranger to the book, who needs to act as if he or she sees the book on the shelf in the library and thinks, 'Hmm, I want to read this book about (whatever) because I have lots of questions.' You can plan your upcoming book and revise your old book by imagining the questions readers will have."

LINK

Remind writers that they can plan for a new book or first add new pages to a recent book, doing both by generating and answering questions.

"I can tell you are all just dying to get back to your writing. Some of you will be finishing up revising yesterday's book and all of you will start new books—either right away, or after a few minutes. Either way, I know you will read your writing like you are a stranger and answer questions you think strangers are apt to have. Use those questions to make sure your book will teach readers what they want to know. Okay, writers, teachers, actors, off you go!"

CONFERRING AND SMALL-GROUP WORK

Challenge Kids to Increase Their Productivity and to Elaborate More, Writing Longer

THERE ARE LOTS OF WAYS to teach students to elaborate. You might start by pointing out that now that your youngsters are writing books like real authors, they'll want to study what real writers do. For starters, writers write a lot more than a sentence on a page. That is, they say more. Try challenging your kids. "Can I give you a challenge?" you can say to three kids. "I read that kids your age can actually write a whole book—like five or six pages long—in *one day*. And this person said those books can have a whole lot of lines on each page, too." You might, in a tongue-in-cheek way, add, "At first I thought that *would* be too hard for seven-year-olds. But then I got this thought that maybe, just maybe, you actually *could* write a six-page book, with a bunch of lines on each page, in a day. Would you be willing to try? Just to see?" The kids will be bursting with excitement to show you and will rise to the occasion. And from that point on, your expectations for the whole class can leap ahead.

MID-WORKSHOP TEACHING **Elaborating by Writing in Twin Sentences**

"Writers, can I stop you? Like many of you, Becky has been writing a page in her book, then asking herself questions that readers might ask. After writing a page about cats eating food in the morning and at night, she asked herself, 'What kind of food do cats eat?' But this is the cool thing that she has done. She has answered her question by writing in *twin sentences*, as she calls them.

"Let me show you what this means. Remember, Becky had written this."

Cats eat in the morning and at night.

"Then she asked, 'What kind of food do they eat?'

"So she went to add, 'They eat wet and dry food.' But she stopped. She thought, 'Can I answer not just in one sentence but in *twin* sentences?' And then she wrote, 'Cats eat wet and dry food. *They like the wet food the best.*' Do you see that she didn't just write one sentence about what kind of food cats eat? She wrote in twin sentences—in two sentences!

"Right now, Partner 1, go back to the last page that you were writing in your book and would you read that page to Partner 2 and talk about whether you can find a way to revise it so that you are doing what Becky did and writing in twin sentences? Then Partner 1, you can start revising that page to add a twin sentence. And after this, it would be totally amazing if some of you decided to push yourself to write from the start in twin sentences, without anyone reminding you!

"Since we just learned a new way to teach our readers more—writing in twin sentences—let's add this to our chart. Anytime you're not sure what to write or how to teach your reader more, you can look at this chart for ideas."

How Can I Teach My Readers?

- ✓ Think about questions my readers might have
- ✓ Write in twin sentences

One strategy that helps children make leaps in volume is thinking of the specific audience that is apt to read their book and to think, too, about what that audience needs to know. For example, José insisted, "I want to write all about basketball for the people in the after-school program because I think they want to know how to play better." Becky said, "I want to write all about cats for my friend Nora because she doesn't got a cat yet but she is telling her mom she needs one. Her mom thinks they are hard, but they are not." When children know their audience and know why this audience needs their information, they will have an easier time thinking of information to put in their books.

You can also lure kids to write more by teaching them that writers reread a page and think, "Can I add an example?" and then add onto the page. Some teachers suggest children use giant colorful Post-its to add an example. The Post-it alone lures the writer to want to elaborate. Of course, the child's elaboration could almost certainly fit beneath the text just fine without the Post-it but if the process of adding more to a text feels like carpentry, writers are keen to roll up their sleeves. Flaps hanging off the sides of a book work equally well. After Becky wrote, "Cats are easy pets," she returned to that page, reread, and then asked herself, "What else can I teach Nora's mom about this part?" Then she added, "Cats can stay alone all day. They do not have to go to the bathroom outside because they poop in a litter box. And they like to relax so you don't need to take them for walks or anything."

Although nudging your children to reread and add on is important, you will also want children to know that what they do early on through revision can be done in a first draft in future books. In the end, you will want your writers to produce longer chapters right from the start. If a child has written a chapter titled "The Parts of a Bicycle," and has written only, "Bicycles have handlebars," you hope the child will say, "Oops! I gotta say more about the parts of the bicycle," before progressing to the next chapter.

SHARE

In Order to Add Information, Regard Your Pages as Malleable

Emphasize that writers use tape and arrows to add information into their books.

After convening the children, I said, "Writers, to ask and answer questions, you have added more and more pages into your books, and you have used arrows to tuck more information into extra spaces on your pages. You are finding that writers are like carpenters. Sometimes you practically need a hammer and nails to work on your writing! I'm joking, really. You wouldn't put nails in your beautiful books.

"Gabriel, for example, ran out of space on one page. But did he just sit there like this?" I folded my arms and leaned back in my chair, signaling I was on a break. "No way! Instead, he went to the writing center, and he got some extra paper. Then he taped that paper on to the part of the page where he needed more lines."

I held his booklet up for everyone to see. "He figured out a solution, didn't he? That's good work, Gabriel. Writers, I'm telling you this because I know many of you want to add answers to readers' questions into your teaching books, and sometimes you aren't sure how to squeeze the information into the right place on a page."

Point out that sometimes information gets put on the wrong page, and writers reread and fix that.

"Also, you need to reread your writing to make sure some of your information isn't in the wrong place, so your writing doesn't hop from one topic to the next and then back to the first in a crazy fashion.

"You can do like Gabriel did and like many of you are doing and be a carpenter. Tape pieces of paper onto your page so you can put the information where it goes. Use tools to add your information at just the place where the reader wants more information. That means that when you pretend to be a stranger, reading your writing, notice not only the questions you ask, but also where, in the book, you ask those questions. It is usually *right there* where you stick the answer!"

Restate the fact that writers reread, noticing not only the questions readers will ask but also the place in the text where those questions arise, and they add strategically.

"After this, when you reread your piece and see that you need to add information, think carefully about *where* the information should go, just as I did with my yoga book. If you need to, scissor your piece apart and insert strips at just the right place."

Notice that the act of revision is physical: cutting apart the paper, physically moving parts of the writing around, and taping the work in place makes the abstract work of revision concrete. Keep these tools well labeled in the writing center so children will use them again and again.

Session 4

Nonfiction Writers Teach with Pictures as Well as Words

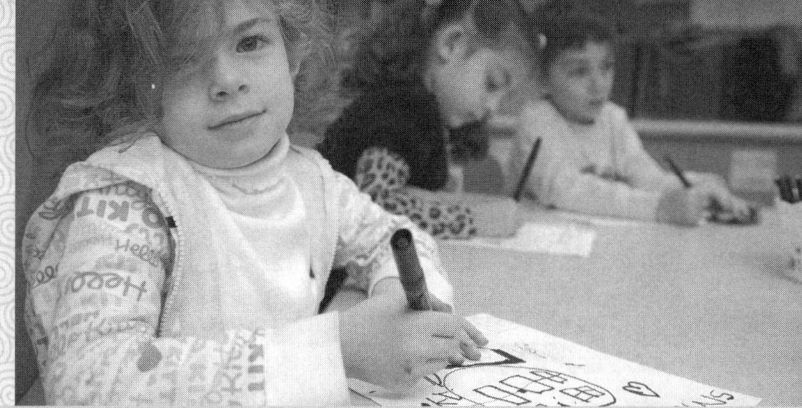

IN THIS SESSION, you will invite your writers to teach their readers through pictures as well as words. Information books for children rely heavily on illustrations. In *In Pictures and in Words*, Katie Wood Ray reminds us that when drawing, children bring the same exploratory spirit they bring to all sorts of other play: "Because it takes some time for children to become fluent and proficient with transcription (getting words down on paper), being able to represent meaning in illustrations makes so much more possible for beginning writers" (2010, 10).

The challenge is to teach children to take their illustrations seriously. They can learn to bring the entire writing process to their illustrations—thinking about what to include, omit, emphasize, show in detail, and overview. They can also assess and revise their illustrations.

Some children may feel more confident with words than with images, but they can still work zealously on their illustrations. They may decide to add details through captions and labels rather than drawings. Either way, illustrations can help your writers consider their audience, to think about particular parts of their writing/drawing in relationship to the larger whole, and to analyze the effect of their work. These skills, easily practiced when drawing, are transferable to writing.

As for your modeling, relax. Remember, you are drawing for children. And there are many styles of drawing. Show some mentor texts, pick something you feel like you can demonstrate, and go to it. (You can shamelessly cheat by lightly penciling your drawing and then producing it in pen in front of the children). If you want to become a better illustrator overnight, Ed Emberly provides simple illustration instruction in his book, *Make a World* (2006), and samples at edemberly.com. He'll teach you about perspective and thinking in parts that will be useful for both you and your children.

This is an inquiry minilesson. It will follow a different template than most minilessons. This session invites children to inquire into ways that illustrations are different in a teaching book than in a story, concluding that drawing is one more way to teach readers. And, ultimately, the strategies your writers are learning and employing as they work on their drawings can be applied to their writing.

IN THIS SESSION, you'll teach children that writers teach with pictures and words. They include illustrations in their teaching books to help teach their readers even more.

GETTING READY

- ✔ Students' writing folders, with Post-its inside, to be brought to the meeting area at the start of the minilesson
- ✔ Anchor chart titled "How Can I Teach My Readers?" (see Guided Inquiry)
- ✔ Exemplar page with teaching pictures from a mentor text, such as *Sharks!* (see Guided Inquiry)
- ✔ A way to display illustrations from a mentor text. This could mean relying on a document camera or a big book (see Guided Inquiry).
- ✔ Transparency paper to place over the mentor text and marker (see Teaching and Active Engagement)
- ✔ A class book, started in small groups (see Share)
- ✔ White boards and markers (see Share)

Common Core State Standards: W.1.2, W.1.5, W.1.7, RI.1.1, RI.1.5, RI.1.6, RI.1.7, SL.1.1, SL.1.5, SL.1.6, L.1.1, L.1.2, L.1.5.a

MINILESSON

Nonfiction Writers Teach with Pictures as Well as Words

CONNECTION

Celebrate the way writers asked and answered readers' questions yesterday, and channel them to compare their first and most recent teaching books, looking for growth.

"Writers, yesterday you pushed yourselves to think about questions your readers might ask, and you worked hard to answer those questions. Some of you said your hands hurt by the end of writing workshop, because you wrote so much. Right now, get out the first teaching book you wrote on the very first day of this unit, and get out the book you were working on yesterday, and look to see if your writing is growing longer. Evaluate your progress—and show your partner what you notice."

"Thumbs up if your most recent writing is a lot longer than the first book you wrote in this unit." Many children put their thumbs up. "Great. Give yourself a pat on the back if your writing has gotten longer, because longer is one big part of better. And if your books haven't yet begun to get longer, the book you start today could be the longest book you've ever written, which would be really exciting.

"Writers, I know that every day, you have been going back to the books that are already done, in your folders, and you have been working on those books, *and* you have been writing new books. And I know that when you revise the books that are already done, you have been adding more *to your words*, answering questions readers might have. Then when you write new books, you have been thinking about readers' questions and answering them as you write the new book.

"Well, today I want to remind you that whether you are looking back on old writing or working on a new book, it is important to realize that writers often look back on a picture they have made and add more *to the picture*. And, on top of that, writers of teaching books have some special ways to give their pictures teaching power.

"I'm not an expert on this. I do not really know what authors do to make their illustrations instructive, but I figured maybe we could research that together."

◆ COACHING

Teachers, these sessions are meant to help you write your own minilessons for all the units that we never have a chance to plan with you. Notice the sorts of things one does in a connection—you can do those same sorts of things in any unit on any topic. On previous days you have asked students to reflect and assess by channeling them to use lists of goals to guide self-assessments. Now you support the same sort of reflection and assessment by asking students to look back to their earlier work and contrast it with their most recent work.

Throughout these minilessons, you will see tons of instances when we talk about the volume of writing that kids are expected to be doing. We harp on that for their sake and yours. One of the most serious problems we have seen in primary classrooms is that sometimes teachers teach a tiny part of the writing process in a day's minilesson, and then kids go off and only do that one tiny part of writing. Adding detail and labels to illustrations is not a day's work. Kids also need to be writing new books.

TEACHING AND ACTIVE ENGAGEMENT

Name a question that will guide the inquiry.

"Writers, today we are going to do an inquiry. We are going to explore the questions, 'How are the illustrations in an information book different than illustrations in most picture books?' and 'What are some of the special techniques that information book authors use to give their illustrations teaching power?' And then you will be able to try out some of these techniques in your own teaching books."

This minilesson is an inquiry lesson, so the format of it is different. By now you will have encountered several of these. Note that there is no teaching point.

GUIDED INQUIRY

Set writers up to investigate the photographs in *Sharks!* by guiding them through a series of steps that help them. Then listen in and coach, eliciting and collecting their comments.

"Okay, writers, I'll display a couple pages from *Sharks!*, written by Anne Schreiber and let's study the pictures together." I picked up a pointer. "And then I'm going to ask you, 'What is this writer doing in the pictures? Why is she doing it? And how is she doing it?'" I jotted "What?" "Why?" and "How?" on the easel next to me.

If you don't have a way to enlarge pictures or don't have these books, remember that these minilessons are not a script for you to follow. This is how we taught the unit—and the assumption is that you will adapt this to fit your tools, your resources, your students.

I showed the spread on pages 6 and 7 and said, "Wow, there is *so much* happening in this picture. Let's quickly scan the picture and start to name the things we see. Turn and tell your neighbor what you see in the picture."

The children talked, and after a minute I intervened and said, "Let's take a moment to look closely at one thing we notice and really think, 'What is this writer doing in the picture? Why?'" I gestured to where I'd written these questions.

Orchestrate the class to have a whole-class conversation about one part of the picture, coaching in ways that support them to notice *what* the author did and to think about *why* she did it that way.

"All eyes up here," I said. "So let's get into a circle for this discussion. You know the drill. Everyone to the edge and stay next to your partner." I gave the students a few moments to squirm into place and then gathered their attention once again.

You may decide that in whole-class conversations, children do not need to raise hands and get permission to speak, but that instead they should learn that one voice speaks at a time, and then they can monitor their own conversation. Or you can gesture to the next speaker. We suggest you encourage children to use a thumbs up rather than hands to indicate they want to talk, if they do need to be recognized before they can speak, and that by all means you avoid making a big deal about deciding who to call on next. This needs to move at a brisk pace and to be as close to conversation as possible.

"I heard Amanda and Julie say they noticed the tail." I gestured to show the tail. "Let's try on our questions. *What* is the author doing in this part of the picture?" I tapped the word *what* on the chart paper.

Liam said, "She showed the tail." I nodded and waited.

After a minute Kyla spoke up, "She showed the tail big."

Annie jumped in and said, "And she said it is big on top." I nodded again. "And she made an arrow."

I laid a clear transparency over the picture and traced the edge of the tail as I said, "So, she showed the part she was teaching about." I circled the annotation and said, "Then she labeled what she was showing." I drew over the arrow. "And she made an arrow." I paused, tapped the word *why* on the chart paper, and asked, "Why do you think she did all that? Turn and talk with your partner for a second."

After signaling for the kids' attention, I gestured for Anessa to talk. "She did all that to teach us, the arrow it um, it um, it shows the part so you know." When the children acted confused, Anessa got up to point to the page. "The arrow, it shows that this," pointing to the annotation, "goes with this," pointing to the tail.

I jumped in. "Ahh, so the arrow makes it clear what the writing is teaching about. And the words next to the arrow tell us more about one part of the picture. This reminds me of something most of you learned last year, when you were writing your how-to books. You used *labels* next to your pictures to help teach your readers more and sometimes you drew an arrow to the specific part you were teaching. This is just what Anne is doing, isn't it? She's just using even *more* words to teach." I gestured to the whole page and said, "Turn and talk to your partner if you see another part where she did the same thing." The children quickly noticed another arrow pointing to the shark's mouth and the writing that accompanied it.

Obviously, this scrutiny of the picture will be easiest if you have a way to enlarge the picture.

I pointed to the word *why*. Marco pitched in, "She did it at the important parts." Thumbs went up again. "To teach us about the tail and the mouth."

Move the conversation to another picture, and scale back your support.

I turned to the illustration of shark skin at the bottom of page 7 and said, "Okay, let's again use those questions—*What did the author do? Why* did she do it?—to think about this part." Get your minds going on this by thinking quietly.

After a minute, I asked for a child to launch the next part of the class conversation. "Who noticed something that the author did that can get us started?"

Mica said, "She made a circle and made the skin." Alyssa added, "She wrote too. She wrote what the skin is like."

I tapped the word *why*, and Liam jumped back in the conversation. "She showed us the skin in the circle so we could see it. And she wrote about it so we could learn."

I jumped in. "Isn't it interesting that she didn't show us the skin on the picture of the shark, but made a separate space for it. I am really wondering why." I tapped my head and a few children mimicked the pose.

Some children made a few guesses. Kim jumped in. "No, no because it's close!" She jumped up excitedly to the page. "See its *bumpy* here," pointing in the circle, "but not *here*," pointing to the shark. It's a close-up!"

Bring this conversation to a close and begin to name what the students noticed in a way that is transferable to other texts. Coach into children's work.

"So, researchers, get together with your partner, and two partnerships get together—or three; don't leave a partnership out. Put your minds together and see if you can come up with some ideas from all that you are learning. As you are working, I'm going to add to our 'How Can I Teach My Readers?' chart because I can tell already that you are learning so much about including pictures in your books, and I want to capture this thinking." As children worked, I added "teaching words," "lines and arrows," and "zooming in" under the bullet "pictures."

LINK

Channel students to reread and evaluate their folder-full of teaching books, deciding which of the things they have learned during the unit they will draw on as they set out to improve those books.

"Writers, if you get out your writing folders, you will see that inside your folder, I've put a collection of Post-its. You can use these to flag things in your writing. Spend a bit of time looking over the illustrations in all the teaching books you have made so far this year, and will you flag places where you think you can revise your illustration to add more detail to it or to increase its teaching power?

"You will need to reexamine each of the books, evaluating what is working and what isn't. Think especially about the teaching power in your illustrations, but you will want to reread the words, too, and think about whether you do have something interesting on every page. Once you have evaluated your books, left flags where you want to do some work, and made some decisions about the work you will do today, signal to me that you are ready to start. But for now, we need absolute quiet because this is *hard work*!"

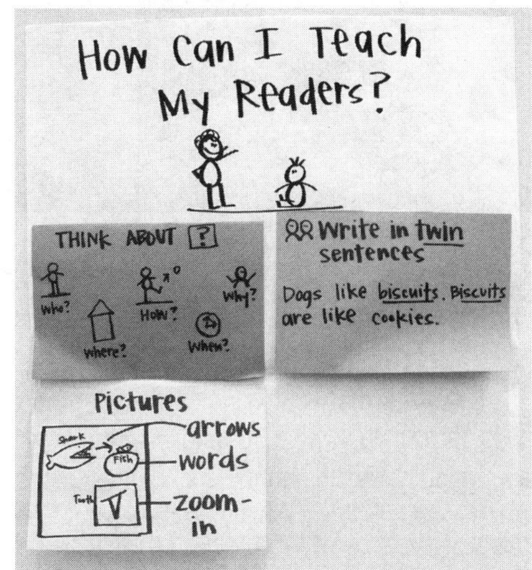

FIG. 4–1

Children will be eager to assess and add to their illustrations, so you are using a focus on illustrations to slyly coach them into revision.

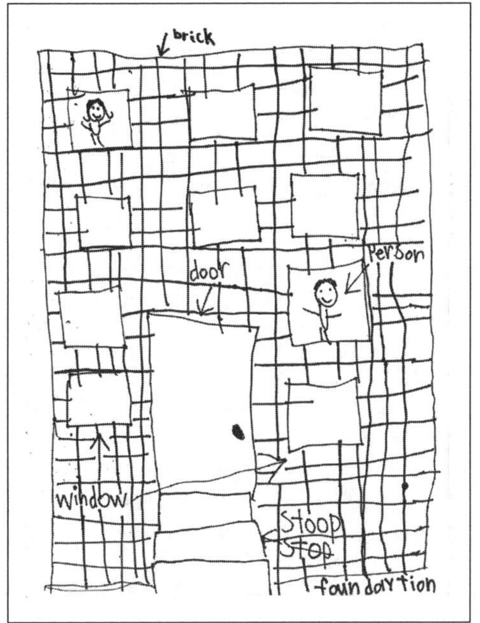

FIG. 4–2 This student used labels and arrows to teach about buildings

CONFERRING AND SMALL-GROUP WORK

Making Today's Focus on Illustrations Bigger and More Ambitious

BE AWARE that conferring and small-group time is meant as an opportunity for you to help writers accumulate all they have learned across the year, recalling and standing on the shoulders of prior instruction. It is a problem if your conferences regularly focus mostly on the content of the day's minilesson, because this is meant to be a time when writers draw on their full repertoire of strategies and make strategic decisions. One of the ways to be sure your teaching doesn't wear blinders, focusing only on the specific topic of the day is for you to always think, "How does today's topic relate to work youngsters have done earlier in the year?" and then to

MID-WORKSHOP TEACHING **Emphasizing the Importance of Specific Information about Number, Size, Color, and Shape**

"Writers, put down your pencils for a moment. Writers, earlier we studied the pictures in Anne Schreiber's book *Sharks!* I want to remind you that we can also learn by studying *each other's* illustrations. Right now, will you each choose one of your *own* pages of illustrations? Choose a page on which you have done something another writer could learn from." I was quiet while students evaluated their work. "Look up when you have selected a page." When many children had looked up, I continued. "Let's try studying each other's illustrations and coming up with ideas for what we could do in our own books. For example, let's look at this page from Alfred's 'All About Super Mario Brothers' book." I displayed it. "Tell your partner what you see Alfred doing that you could try."

The room buzzed, and then I said, "Eyes up here. What are you saying that Alfred did that you might try as well?"

Peter's hand shot up. "Colored pants?"

I looked at Alfred's page, noted the varied colors of overalls, and nodded. "So I'm hearing that you noticed that Alfred gave each person in his illustration different color overalls. And one has a hat." I tapped the word *why* on the chart paper and waited for children to generate the next question themselves. Then I nodded and voiced what they were thinking. "Alfred, can you explain *why* you did that?"

Alfred said, 'So you can tell the Mario Brothers apart. 'Cause Mario wears a red hat and overalls and Luigi wears a green hat and overalls, and Luigi is bigger than Mario."

"Class, the goal is to let Alfred's illustration help *us* learn something that we can use in our illustrations. And I do not think the lesson is that all our characters need to wear different color overalls. No way! But we can learn things from him, and one of them is that he added details about color. And it is true that details about color, number, and size all matter.

"Alfred's details about the different colors of overalls made each of his people different from the others. He found ways to make his characters look different from each other. I am going to go back and look at my yoga book to see if I made me and the teacher in different sizes. Will you look at your book and see if you, like Alfred, added details about the color or sizes?" While the children looked at their writing, I leafed back to a page in my book where the yoga teacher was much taller than me.

"So, writers, pictures have more teaching power when they show and tell specific shapes, colors, numbers, and sizes. Some time today, take a second to find at least one page in your writing where you can add specific information about the shape, color, size, or number of your subject. Here is one last tip. You can add that information to the drawing *or* the words. We have twenty more minutes for writing." As students got back to work, I added "Use color, shape, and size words" to our class chart, "How Can I Teach My Readers?"

help children see those connections, so that your teaching is braided, a goal that is important to many who help teachers implement the CCSS.

Today, for example, you may want to approach some small groups and conferences, planning to remind children that all year long, it helps to study the work of mentor authors. "Writers," you might say to a small group, "earlier this year you studied *Night of the Veggie Monster* (2008)." Holding the book up you could add, "And you researched the neat things George McClements did that you could try. Remember how you noticed George used uppercase bold letters that *popped* out! He used that bold font not just once, but in a few places, didn't he? I remember how you all got going on the question of 'Why?' Why might he have wanted those particular words to pop off the page?

"And today you studied the illustrations, the pictures, that are included in an informational book by Anne Schreiber and asked, 'What neat things did Anne do that I could try?' I hope that from this day forward, you always notice what authors do, and think, 'Could I try some of that?' Will some of you probably be thinking this way during reading time? When you are reading from your book baggies, will you be noticing what those authors did and thinking whether you can remember to do that in your writing? Fabulous!" Then, of course, you could support children in doing any of this work—including studying illustrations.

It can sometimes feel risky to emphasize illustrations in a writing workshop lesson, because some children then devote an entire workshop to drawing each little scale on the dragon in their teaching book about dragons. If you find that some children are so intent on using pretty, nice-smelling markers to decorate their pages that they are forgetting to convey information, you might gather a small group and teach them that illustrators, like writers, always ask themselves, "Does this help teach my reader?" You might teach these students that they can run a finger around the parts of their drawing, asking themselves at each touch, "Does this help teach my reader?" If the answer is no, then perhaps that doesn't need to be in the illustration. If it does, it may need a label or an arrow to become more powerful.

You might also teach students that it is helpful to ask whether the content that is contained in the pictures is also contained in the print (although in real life, this actually does not always need to be the case.) Again, you may teach these children to touch each thing in the picture, only this time, asking themselves, "Did I write about this yet?" If the answer is no, the writer can then add more to the print. You may even let writers know, "When I see a lot of teaching details in your pictures, I know you must be planning to write *a lot!*"

Last, but not least, you may find that you have a group of children who do not want to draw. A few children are probably trying to recruit others (including you) to draw for them. These children may feel intimidated because their drawing skills are not advanced, in which case you may want to teach a few simple drawing techniques using shapes and sticks. To do this, you could grab an overhead transparency and lay it over the cover of a book, say, the book, *Sharks!*, as in the teaching demonstration. You can then point out to children that what seems at first to be an ornate drawing is actually comprised of several simple shapes. Trace over the cover (on the transparency with a dry erase marker) to show the underlying structure of the picture: an oval for the shark's head, triangles for the teeth, and two small circles for the eyes.

Of course, identifying the shapes in an object—say, a coat—is not always easy for a child whose knowledge of geometric shapes is still emerging, so you may want to provide a shape chart for reference. Once the underlying shape structure is in place, children can add more detail.

Drawing will decrease in importance as the year unfolds, but in these beginning months, thoughtful drawing instruction can help beginning writers develop important habits of mind.

SHARE

Using Diagrams and Labels to Teach

Bring a text that several children started together about a topic the class knows well, suggesting it become a class book, and show an instance where the children used diagrams and labels to teach.

"Writers, Anessa, Kevin, and Alex started a book today in their small group called 'All about School,' and they said that we can all help with this book—making it sort of belong to us all. The good news is that they already began to make teaching pictures."

I revealed a page full of diagram-like sketches. "Do you see how this page has lots of little pictures about lunch? You might see they used a zoom-in, arrows, and labels." I sat quietly as the students peered at the pictures. I flipped the book to the next page. "And on this page they showed how you watch movies in the auditorium." I paused as the students studied the pictures of a large screen and the backs of heads looking at the screen.

Point out that the children ran into trouble depicting a sequence of activities, leading to the suggestion that they write in three pictures boxes.

"But then they ran into trouble!" I said leaning in close. "They came to the page where they wanted to teach about getting ready to go home, and they couldn't figure out how to draw that in just one picture since there are three steps." I ticked the steps off on my fingers as the students listened, "First, you put your homework folder and books in your backpack. Then you put on your coat. Then you put your chair up on your desk." I held up three fingers and the children mirrored me. "Maybe you can help. Turn and talk with your partner about how they might be able to show all three steps in one box.

"Writers, to help these writers out, please use your white boards and draw what a 'going home' page could look like. Remember some of the teaching pictures you have seen in *Sharks!*" I propped the mentor text open on the easel. As students worked, I whispered tips like, "Try to draw each step," and "Think about the order."

Carrying one student's white board with me, I reconvened the class. "I see many of you drawing detailed pictures of going home. Great job. I notice a bunch of you have drawn these steps like Marco, dividing the picture box with lines so you made three smaller picture boxes, and then drawing one step in each box. Marco even numbered his boxes 1, 2, 3." I pointed to the corner of each box. "Others of you, like Kim, drew three pictures and then put an arrow in between each picture to show the order. When you want to show steps or to show a certain order, you can divide your picture box into smaller boxes or you can use arrows to show the order of the steps."

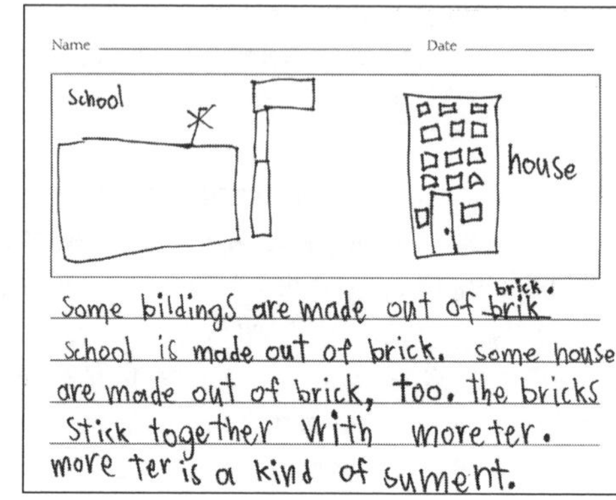
Name Date
School
house
Some bildingS are made out of brik brick.
School is made out of brick. Some houses are made out of brick, too. the bricks Stick together With moreter. moreter is a kind of sument.

FIG. 4–3

Session 5

Being Brave Enough to Spell Domain-Specific Words (Spelling Fancy Words)

IN THIS SESSION, you'll teach children that writers bravely spell the challenging, expert words that help teach about their topic.

GETTING READY

- ✓ Your own teacher demonstration text (e.g., "All about Yoga")
- ✓ "Ways to Spell Words" chart from the *Small Moments* unit, to add to during the teaching
- ✓ Shared class book: "All about School" (see Active Engagement)
- ✓ "How Can I Teach My Readers" anchor chart and Information Writing Checklist, Grade K, to refer to (see Link) 
- ✓ White boards and dry erase markers (ideally one per student and teacher), alphabet charts, and class book (see Conferring and Small-Group Work)

FOR A WHILE NOW, you have taught children to spell by listening for sounds at the beginning, middle, and end of words. By now, children spell many simple one-syllable words with the correct consonants in the correct places, or they at least make reasonable approximations. You may not see the same success with vowels just yet. Vowels often present a particular challenge to children in the beginning of first grade because at this age many children still rely to some extent on the *names* (not the sounds) of the letters of the alphabet to help them as they spell, and that system doesn't always work out too well when writing vowels. For example, a child reaching to spell the word *bedtime* may find himself stuck on the vowels because in *bed* the *e* sounds much more like the letter name *a* then the letter name *e*. (Try saying the short *e* sound and then the letter name *a* to hear the similarity.) This, then, might lead to a spelling such as *badtim*. However, children's ambitions to use more sophisticated words should not be tethered by developing spelling knowledge. (If I waited until I could run three miles to start running, it's fair to say I wouldn't get off the couch anytime soon!) Therefore, you will want to teach children strategies to take on the big words they want to write. Although your children may not yet have a full command of letters and sounds, their effort to approximate challenging words is a step forward in their development as writers.

This session, then, aims to take what students are doing well—writing simple words with correct consonants and some vowels or logical vowel substitutions—and transfer this knowledge to the work of tackling more complex multisyllabic words. And it also aims to rally youngsters to use the correct, domain-specific vocabulary words when writing about a topic. The value of this writing work is also supported by the Common Core State Language Standards, in which using domain-specific vocabulary is an expectation across the grades. This session lays the groundwork for this important skill.

Before teaching this lesson, you will want to drumroll the importance of vocabulary to your nonfiction writers, which is easy to do because when a nonfiction writer teaches

COMMON CORE STATE STANDARDS: W.1.2, W.1.5, RI.1.6, RFS.1.1, RFS.1.2.b,c,d; SL.1.1, L.1.1.a, L.1.2, L.1.6

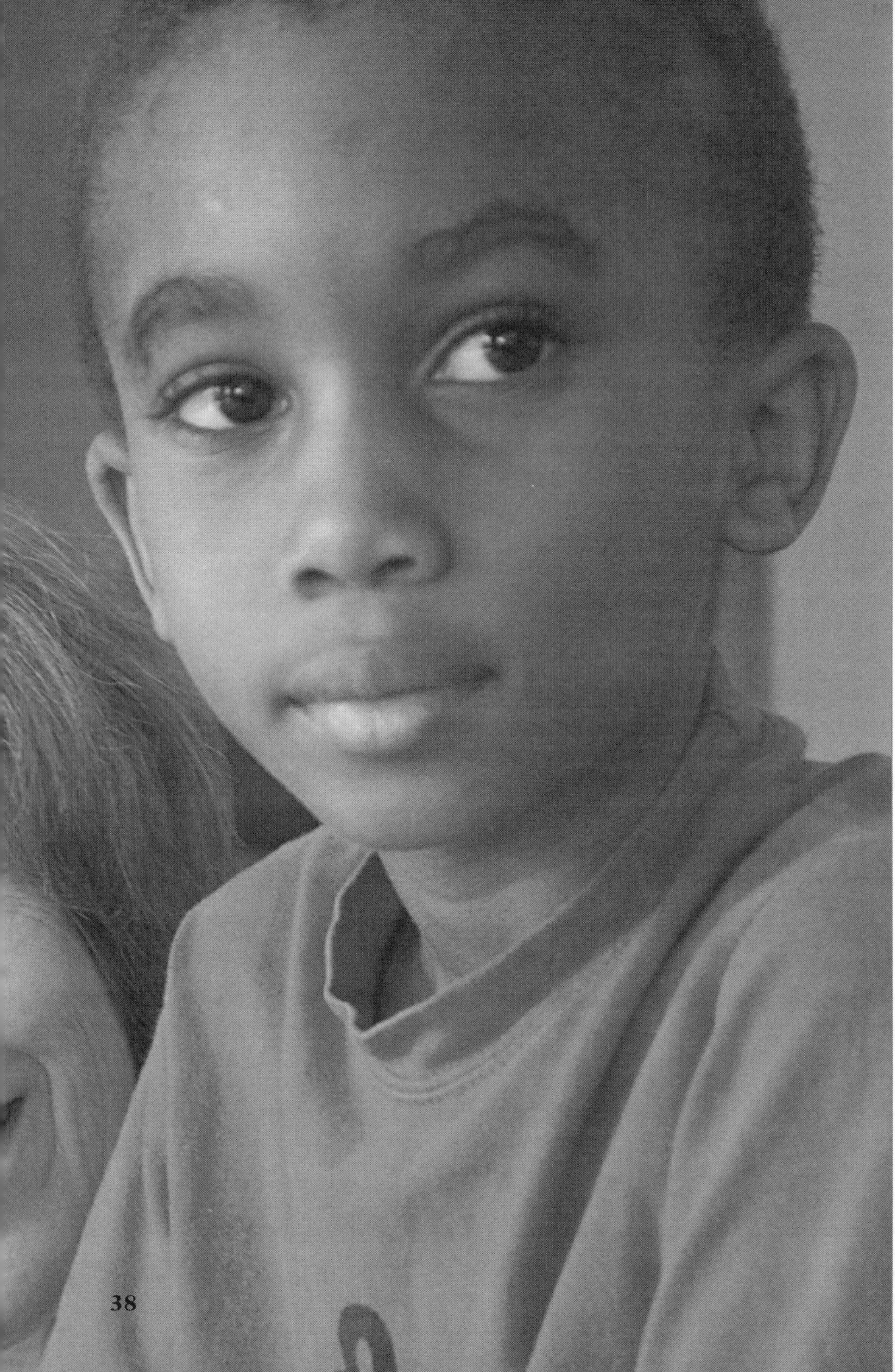

readers about a topic, a big part of that instruction involves teaching the words and concepts of the topic. It is important for your writers to realize that it is important for them to have the chutzpah to tackle challenging vocabulary words.

"This session aims to take what students are doing well—writing simple words with correct consonants and some vowels or logical vowel substitutions—and transfer this knowledge to the work of tackling more complex multisyllabic words."

By the end of the year, first-graders will be expected to use conventional spelling for words with common spelling patterns (i.e., digraphs, short vowels, simple long vowel patterns) and for frequently occurring irregular words (word wall words). They should also be able to spell more complex words phonetically, drawing on phonemic awareness and their knowledge of spelling conventions. Additionally, children will begin to use syllables as a way to help them encode (write) and decode (read) longer, trickier words. By foregrounding the importance of spelling, this session will help your young writers meet and exceed these goals.

MINILESSON

Being Brave Enough to Spell Domain-Specific Words (Spelling Fancy Words)

CONNECTION

Tell a story about a time when you wrote an information text and avoided the domain-specific vocabulary because of a fear of misspelling.

"Writers, today I want to share with you a problem I had with my writing. As you know, I am writing a book about yoga. Well, yesterday after school I was working very hard at making sure my book had something interesting on each page." I pointed to the chart that reminded me to do this. "I was writing about stretches, and I remembered that there is one stretch that is very, very challenging. I've sketched it here." I flashed the sketch at the class and then set it down. "You see, in this stretch what you do is," I bent at the waist and stretched my arms in front of me, letting my hair hang down. "You stretch out on the floor on your stomach, but I'm just going to demonstrate it standing up, and then," I lifted my calf slightly, "you take this one leg and you stretch it out," I wobbled on one foot, "until it goes all the way in front of your head. I'm not kidding! It's really hard! Phew!" I stood up. "Now, I really wanted to write about that in my book. I thought it would be so exciting. So here is what I wrote (see Figure 5–1)."

> In yoga you do lots of stretches. The hardest stretch in the world is called the thingy.
> To do the thingy you have to put your foot over your head!

"I was so proud of what I wrote that I read it to my friend Hannah, and do you know what she said? She said that my book sounded like I didn't know what I was talking about! 'There's no yoga move called the thingy,' she said."

Tell about your realization that you needed to use precise words, becoming a brave speller.

"That's when I realized that to make my book really interesting for my readers, I have to use precise words. When I write in a teaching voice, I have to use the fancy words an expert uses. That way I show my reader I really know what I'm talking about. If I am writing about a horse, I can't call the girth of the saddle," I motioned to show where it goes, "a belt. It is a girth. Even if I'm not sure how to spell *girth*, I need to be brave enough to try. And if I am writing about the Yankees, I can't be so worried about spelling things right that I chicken out and call the place where they play their games a *hall*, just because that word is easy to spell, because the precise, fancy word for where the Yankees play is *stadium*."

◆ COACHING

The opinion units of study teach youngsters that when they want to persuade someone to do something, it can help to mention the "or else" consequences. That is, you can persuade by saying, "You better do this, or else. . . ." That is exactly what this connection does. The message is that writers better use precise, domain-specific vocabulary words "or else. . . ."

I hope the kids find it silly that you write with a word like thingy. *Use* what-you-call it *if that will create an impression. Humor is one of the best ways to get through to kids (or to any of us!).*

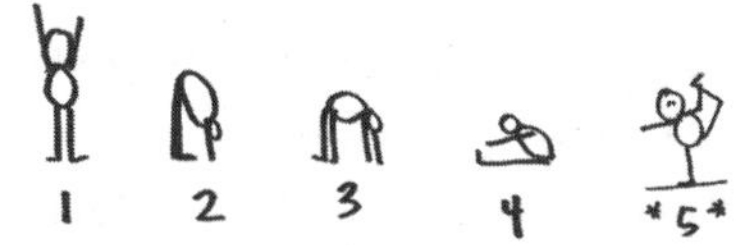

In yoga you do lots of stretches. The hardest stretch in the world is called the thingy. To do the thingy you have to put your foot over your head!

FIG. 5–1

"The problem is that sometimes fancy words are hard to spell. That really hard stretch in yoga is called the crocodile. When I got to the word *crocodile* in my book, I was so afraid I couldn't spell it, I just wanted to leave it out. But what Hannah helped me realize is that nonfiction writers don't just chicken out from using big words. To make my book really sound like a teaching book, I will have to use all of the strategies I know for spelling tricky words. If I am brave, I can even write *crocodile*."

The minilesson is, of course, teaching the importance of domain-specific vocabulary while also highlighting brave spelling.

Name the teaching point.

"Today I want to teach you that nonfiction writers use fancy words to teach others about a topic, and if they aren't sure how to spell the word, they are still brave enough to try using those fancy words, saying, 'Oh well, I'll try my best.' Writers sound out fancy words by listening to each syllable, sliding their finger across the page, and writing the sounds they hear."

TEACHING

Demonstrate spelling a "fancy word," syllable by syllable.

Taking out the oversized page of my book, I began, "So today, writers, I am ready to be brave. I am going to make my 'All about Yoga' teaching book sound just like an expert book by using a precise word and by trying my best to sound out each syllable of the word as I write it. I want you to watch me as I work hard to spell this word *crocodile*. I'm going to listen for the sounds in each syllable of the word, slide my finger across the page, and write the sounds I hear.

The challenge when teaching writers a strategy such as this one is to really spell the strategy out, bit by bit, in such a way that children can actually use it to good effect.

"/croc/" I said loudly, and slid my finger along the page, then wrote "croc" quickly.

"/o/" I continued in the same strong voice, sliding my finger on the page and writing an *o*.

"/dile/" I finished in the same way, and then I reread the whole word, "Crocodile."

"Writers, did you notice what I did to spell my fancy word? I said each syllable, listening for the sounds, I slid my finger along the page, and I quickly wrote the sounds I heard. When you wrote your Small Moment books, you sounded out words part by part. Now you know how to listen for syllables to help you write tricky words!

"Wow, writers, now that you know so many ways to spell tricky words, let's review the chart we started when you were writing Small Moments. And remember, you can draw on any of these strategies when spelling the fancy, expert words in your teaching books."

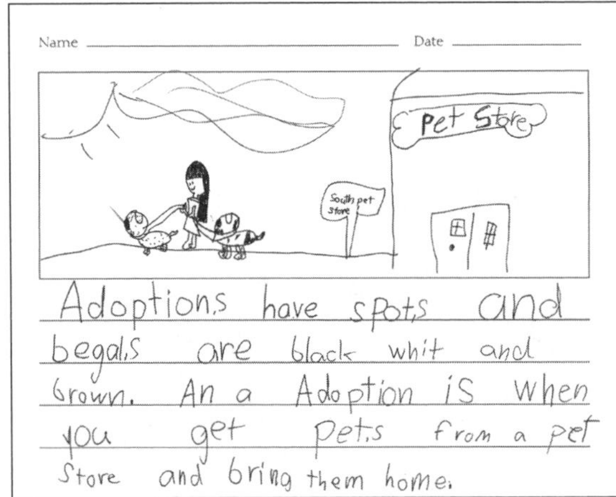

FIG. 5–2 This student used a precise word—*adoption*—to teach about her topic.

FIG. 5–3

ACTIVE ENGAGEMENT

Invite the children to help you use a brave and fancy word in the class story. Ask pairs to work through the spelling.

"Writers, can we try to use brave and fancy words in our class story, 'All about School'? Yesterday we helped Anessa, Kevin, and Alex make their drawings better. Remember the first drawing of everyone lining up for lunch?" I held up the drawing from yesterday's lesson. "Today we should help them write about the lunch place.

"Writers, will you turn to your partners and talk for a moment about the fancy words you might use to write about the place where we all have lunch?"

Pairs of children chatted, reaching a consensus almost instantly. "Okay, writers, I heard most of you saying we should use the word *cafeteria* in our book. *Cafeteria* is a precise word that an expert would use. Do you think that working with your partners, you could spell *cafeteria*? Use your white boards and slowly say the word *ca-fe-ter-i-a*, listening for each syllable. Remember that each part of the word, each syllable, includes a vowel. As you slowly say the syllable, slide your finger across the white board, and then write each sound you hear."

Notice that the active engagement sections of minilessons are designed to take just a very few minutes of time, and note that you tuck new tips into this teaching. Here, the tip about each syllable containing a vowel is tucked in. That will go over the heads of some children but that's okay.

If you think this word is way out of reach for many of your students, you will want a more accessible one. But if you are not aiming for perfection, this word does contain a lot of clear sounds. Just don't correct children if they record a k *instead of a* c*. The point now is not for perfection!*

Remind children of all the strategies they know to spell words, including rereading what they have written to see if it sounds right.

I circulated among the students as pairs worked. "Don't forget to slide your finger along the page as you say the sounds," I reminded them. "After you work through the whole word, read what you have written again to see if it sounds right."

After pairs worked on the task for a minute, I asked them to hold up their white boards to share with the class. "Writers, you have been very brave. I see lots of you doing your best to write a fancy word by listening for each syllable and writing what you hear."

LINK

Channel students to return to their writing, reminding them that many will be starting new books. Reread charts of goals and ask them to choose goals, in addition to the goal from today's minilesson.

"As you go off to write now—some of you starting a new book, some of you finishing the book you worked on yesterday—I want you to remember today and every day that nonfiction writers use precise words to teach about their topic. When they get to a word that experts use to teach about their topic, they bravely try to spell the word, even if they aren't sure. They just do their best, and they use strategies like spelling syllable by syllable.

Notice even the different ways to send kids off to get started on their work. If one of these ways works especially well for your class, then use it often, even if the minilesson write-up suggests a different send-off.

"Of course, nonfiction writers have *lots* of goals. Let's look back at some of our charts and remember all the other goals that will be important as well." I brought the "How Can I Teach My Readers?" chart (see Figure 4–1) and the Information Writing Checklist (page 10) front and center in the meeting area and used a pointer to support the class in rereading the charts as a shared reading activity.

"Will you tell your partner what you will be doing today—finishing a book, starting a book, or both—*and* tell your partner two goals that are going to be important to you, drawing on everything you see on our charts? Maybe one of your goals will be to use the fancy words that go with whatever you are talking about, but what else will you try to do, whether you are starting a new book or finishing yesterday's? Turn and talk."

As partners talked, I listened in. "Once you know what your goals are for today's writing, you can get started."

It is important to weave references to anchor charts throughout a unit, because you want kids to become accustomed to using charts as references to guide their work even when you do not remind them to do this.

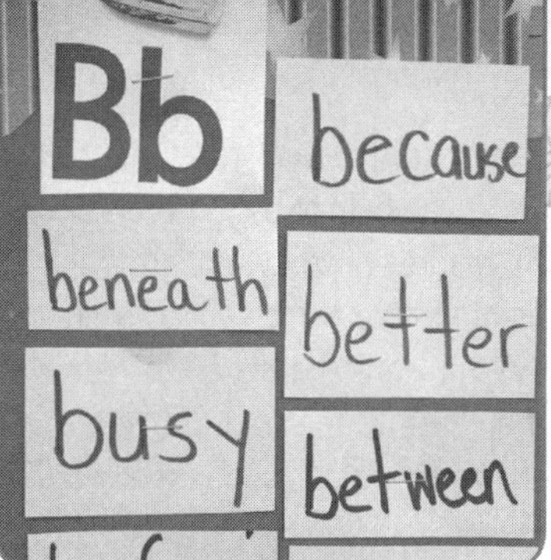

Small-Group Work to Support Vowels and Other Challenges

THE WRITING WORKSHOP is a time to help your children see that one of the big reasons to learn about letters and sounds is that this helps a person communicate effectively. Oftentimes children will excel in phonics knowledge when working on repetitive ditto drills, but when they need to orchestrate phonics within all the other concerns that are paramount to writing a book, this becomes more challenging. We encourage you to use Donald Bear's assessment from *Words Their Way* (2007) or another system to identify each child's stage of spelling development. Some are ready to work on short vowels and others will also need support on consonants.

For about ten minutes of the workshop, you may want to work with a small group of children to bring their phonics knowledge into the writing workshop. Equip the children with alphabet charts, blend and digraph charts, white boards, and markers. This particular work could aim to help children draw on what they know when they write, which means the group could be multilevel, including children who need help with short vowels, blends, long vowels, and so on all mixed together. Once you convene the group, you could begin work on the next page of the class informational book. As you work to stretch out words, prompt children to use not just the strategies on the "Ways

MID-WORKSHOP TEACHING **Getting Ideas Down First, Then Going Back to Tricky Words**

"Writers, I have to stop you and celebrate for just a minute. Earlier we talked about tackling some brave and fancy words using syllables to help you. Can you find one place where you did that—chose a fancy word and bravely solved it—and show your partner?" I waited while students flipped through their books and pointed out a word in their writing.

As the chatter died down, I gathered their attention again. "When I was working with David earlier, he was stuck at his fancy word. When I asked what was going on, he said he had been thinking so hard about the word, he forgot what he was going to write!" I put David's paper on the document camera with only the first word showing: "Knights."

"David has a lot more to say, but he wasn't sure how to spell his next word, so he has been thinking and thinking—and waiting. That simply cannot happen! We can't let our brilliant ideas get lost. David decided that what he is going to do from now on is to write the word the best he can, to circle it, finish his sentence and *then* go back and try to fix the word." I uncovered the rest of the page. It read, "Knights prout (circled) the casl." So now that David has his whole idea down, he can go back and work on that word a little bit more. Let's help him out. His word is *protect.*" I gestured for David to come to the document camera with his pen.

"Tell your partner the first syllable. *Pro-*. Write the letters for the sounds you hear in *pro-* in the air as David writes it up here." I leaned in and nodded encouragement as David wrote *pro* above the circled part. "Next syllable?" The class chimed, "-tect." "Say it and write the letters for the sounds you hear. *T-e*. It next sounds like a *k*, but it is *c-t.*" David finished the word on his paper and headed back to his seat.

"So, writers, you can use David's plan if you are worried you will forget the words you want to write. Write the best you can, circle the word you want to come back to, and when you get all the words down in that sentence or on that page, go back and fix it up. You have about fifteen minutes left before our share, so make sure you get a book written today!"

to Spell Words" chart, but also what they know about letters and sounds from word study. You can prompt certain children to tackle certain words or parts of words so that each youngster is channeled to tackle work that is within his or her reach, but all children can see the way writers set about using what they know to spell as best they can.

For example, you may want to write a word like *folder*, so you might remind youngsters that each word—and actually each syllable—has at least one vowel. Remind them of their vowels by singing the version of "Old MacDonald" that they sang in kindergarten, where Old MacDonald's chorus was not E-I-E-I-O but was, instead, A-E-I-O-U. "Remember to say the vowel slowly, stretching it out, and to use the vowel chart," you can coach children, encouraging them to try spelling the word on their white boards. Then you can call on one child, record the word on the small-group's shared version of the text, and keep the pace moving quickly.

After working with the small group on a shared writing of the class information book, you will want to ask children to take out their own writing and move forward in that piece, working with an eye and an ear on using what they know from word study to help them spell the words they want to write. Again, encourage children who are at the spelling stage of development where they are using and confusing short vowels to work on those, and meanwhile support children who are still learning ending sounds to focus on that. That is, your emphasis will vary based on your knowledge of what is within range for a particular writer. Before you send them off to keep working on their own, you will want to reinforce that as writers, their job is to use the knowledge they have about words to help them spell as best they can.

Of course, after working with that group, you will need to put your roller skates on, checking in with lots of the children in the classroom. It can help to assign yourself one lens and move quickly about the room, looking at children's work through that one lens. You could, if you want, look through the lens of vowels. Which children do you see that regularly spell words with consonants only? You could gather those individuals and tell them what you notice and ask them to go back to the start of one of their books, any book, and reread it, asking themselves, "Do I have a vowel in this word?" and then work to hear and record vowels in every word.

Then again, you could look through the lens of elaboration, noticing whether children are writing several sentences on a page, which may not necessarily mean they are elaborating, but certainly if they are writing just one sentence on a page, they won't be! Again, you could convene that group, tell them they need to set a goal for themselves, and show them how to reread, adding a thought about each thing they have said. In the same way, you could look for whether children seem to be trying to write something interesting on every page, for the use of detail, for labels in the illustrations, for some attention to sorting information so that unrelated information is not included in a book. Because your first small group was an extended one, whatever teaching you do will probably be decisive and quick. Work on being especially powerful, launching a whole group of writers to work with tremendous energy based on a quick, clear challenge you give to them. It's a trick to rally a group of writers to do some work when you aren't going to hover to make sure it happens, but if you teach with power, you can pull this off.

SHARE

Checking the Spelling of Fancy Words

Remind the class that spelling is something to check for when they think they are done.

"Today you used fancy words to teach in your topics. I saw words like *shin guards* in a soccer book, and *pedal* in a bike book. Writers, many of you had two or even three finished books before you learned about the fact that writers of teaching books try to use the fancy words that experts use when talking about their topic. Before today is over, you may want to reread one of the books you wrote at the start of this unit to see if there are more fancy words you could add to those books. You could add fancy words to your sentences or to your labels.

"And, writers, if you are not sure how to spell the fancy word, I'm pretty sure you and your partner can be brave, hard-working writers who work together to figure those spellings out as best you can. When you do this, remember that it helps to break the word into parts—into syllables. And remember, there will be one vowel in each of those syllables. So writers, go to it! I'm going to admire the work you are doing with each other."

I listened in and heard Takuma begin to share his teaching book, "Coloring," with his partner, Karl. He continued, telling his partner, "I want to add that drawing is a fun activity. But I don't know how to spell *activity*." Karl told him, "Say the parts. /Ac/." Takuma picked up from there. "/Ac/," he began, and quickly wrote *ax*. Then he continued, "/Ti/ /vi/," writing the sounds he heard for the last two syllables, ending with /ty/ spelled *dy* (see Figure 5–4).

If you are bored, drawing is a fun activity to do. Even if you are on a long car trip.

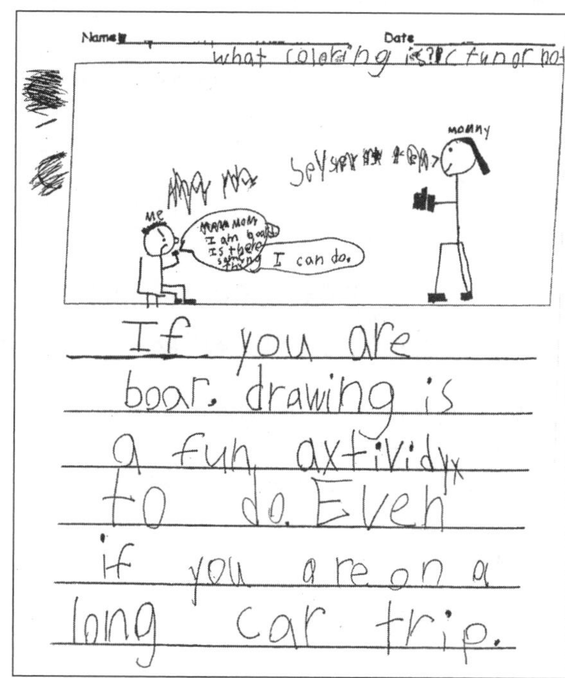

FIG. 5–4 Takuma adds a fancy word—*activity*—to his writing.

Session 6

Nonfiction Writers Use Readers to Help Them Add and Subtract

IN THIS SESSION, you'll teach children that writers need readers to help them revise. Readers help writers know where to add more details and where to subtract details.

GETTING READY

- ✔ Your own demonstration text (e.g., "All about Dogs"), with missing words or information (see Connection)
- ✔ Class story ("All about School"), with a new page added that has confusing, irrelevant information (see Teaching)
- ✔ Blank writing booklets (see Conferring and Small-Group Work)
- ✔ Students need to bring one teaching book from their writing folder to the meeting area (see Share)

Common Core State Standards: W.1.2, W.1.5, RI.1.1, RI.1.4, RI.1.6, RFS.1.2, RFS.1.3, SL.1.1, SL.1.2, L.1.1, L.1.2.e, L.1.6

AT THIS POINT IN YOUR UNIT, your writers' folders will be starting to fill. Most of your children will have written a small pile of informational books. You may think, as you stand back and look at the bulging folders, that work is going well. A visitor could come to the classroom, and you could give that person a tour, strategically going from one carefully chosen child to another, one folder to another, and everything could look very impressive.

But meanwhile, you may also carry a niggling awareness that if you are being really honest with yourself, the truth is that you do not really want that visitor to just roam the room as he or she pleases, checking in with every writer, because you are also thinking, "Yes, most children have written a lot of books, but some of them are, well, confusing. And some are only half done."

There. You've said it. You've let the cat out of the bag. Jim Collins, in his book, *From Good to Great*, suggests that the way to excellence involves "confront[ing] the brutal facts of reality, while retaining resolute faith" (2001, 126). I love the combination of terms—the brutal facts, the resolute faith. So you can feel good about the fact that you aren't just sweeping the loose ends, the tangles and problems, under the carpet and pretending all is well with all of your writers. And it is a good thing to help your writers, too, face the brutal facts. Everything is not perfect. There are some messes to clean up, some unfinished pieces to work on, and in some instances, there is a frightening lack of general productivity.

So take a deep breath and know that up until this point, the emphasis has been on diving in and approximating the work of informational writing, so it makes sense that the work is filled with whatever approximations children have produced. Some of their writing *will* be chaotic or messy or incomplete. And the truth is that is one reason why you build in revision sessions like this one, and like the one after this as well, when you will ask students to assess their writing against an updated informational writing checklist, with new expectations for your first-grade writers. It is important for writers to learn to take a step back, to look at their writing, and to think, "How will readers receive this? What should I add? What should I subtract?"

MINILESSON

Nonfiction Writers Use Readers to Help Them Add and Subtract

CONNECTION

Tell a story about a time when a reader questioned your informational writing, leading you to revise for more clarity. Tell this in a way that supports the need for readers.

"Yesterday I dropped my dog off at Ms. Young's house, and I gave her an 'All about Dogs' teaching book that I had written earlier this week." I held up the book.

"When I went to pick my dog up, Ms. Young said, 'I looked everywhere but I couldn't find the balls sticks.' I looked at her like she was crazy, and I said, 'What's a ball stick?' Then she showed me a page that I had written in 'All about Dogs' that talked about dogs liking to play." I flipped open to that page. "And it said, 'Dogs like balls sticks.'"

I slapped my hand to my forehead, almost falling over backward. "That's not what I meant! I meant balls *and* sticks! Do you know something? I had already reread my own book, but I had never noticed that confusing part of my book. It wasn't until someone else read my book that I learned my book was still confusing. So I'm thinking we can maybe institute a ritual that allows us to check whether our books make sense to readers—and if not, to fix them up."

Name the teaching point.

"Today I want to teach you that writers of teaching books especially need readers who point out places that don't make sense. Those parts might not make sense because of missing words or information, and they might not make sense because things have been added that don't belong."

TEACHING AND ACTIVE ENGAGEMENT

Recruit the class to be readers for a new (and confusing) page that has been added to a class book.

"Writers, some little writing elves helped add pages to our book about school. I would love to have you be the readers for it, deciding if there is a part of it that doesn't make sense either because information has been left out that readers need or because things have been stuffed in that don't really go. So listen up, will you?"

◆ COACHING

One of the goals of a connection is to do just that: to connect! A personal anecdote like this connects. Just be sure to keep it brief because sometimes children get so enthralled by the personal stories that they lose any sense of how the stories build toward a point related to writing.

When you write your own minilessons, one of the tricks to remember is that they are written to be said aloud so you need to write them by speaking aloud, then recording what you say. This connection is a perfect example of a text that I first said aloud, complete with gestures, and only later recorded.

You can use the book you started with your small group in Session 4. Add a page with the error you need to make the teaching and active engagement easier.

I read a new class-book page. (See Figure 6–1.) Don't be subtle. When you read your writing aloud, you can read in ways that make the mess-ups you hope children detect even more blatant.

"What do you think? Are there parts that are confusing, where you need more information? Are there parts that don't go? Turn and talk." After children talked for a tiny bit of time, I called on a few.

Debrief in a way that teaches children that readers can spot places where more information is needed or where irrelevant information has been included where it does not belong.

"It is important to do what you just did when you said that the hot dog doesn't go in this book. I know how you have been adding more and more information to your books. Well, have you ever added colors together? You start with yellow, and you add blue. You get a nice shade of green. Then you think, 'Hey, this adding thing is fun,' so you add red and purple and orange—and all of a sudden you realize, 'I've got the weirdest color on earth. I've got a color that is mud.'

"Sometimes, your revisions make your pieces great, and sometimes they make mud. So absolutely, after you hear from readers, sometimes you need to add more, and sometimes you need to subtract."

Notice that I've moved along to debrief after hearing only two children. If you think that was a mistake, that I should have heard from more, you are wrong. I'm always watching time. The real participation that matters is the participation that occurs during writing time.

At the start of every day in first grade, first graders take out their homework folders, hang up their coats, do do-nows and read the morning message. It tells what will happen in the day. That takes five minutes. ~~It tells that lunch is hot dogs. I love hot dogs. One time I dropped mine and it looked like blood on the floor with the ketchup.~~ Then first graders look at the flow of the day and learn what the first part of the day is. Usually reading is first.

FIG. 6–1

LINK

Send students off in groups of four or six to have new readers read their stories.

"Your first step today will involve getting yourself a reader. Will two partnerships get together into a foursome, without leaving anyone out? There can be a six-person group if necessary." They did this. "For today, I think you need a reader who has not read your work, so within the groups you just formed, switch partners, just for today. That way someone who has never read your writing will join you in reading your pieces." As I saw new alliances formed, I gestured for them to head off to work. Once I'd dispersed half the group, I suggested the others work on the rug.

"I think you will want to start by each rereading one book, with the readers spotting places where writers can add to make things clear or take away to keep pages from containing stuff that doesn't 'go.' Then switch places." After a few minutes, I asked partners to switch and look at the other partner's book, and before five minutes were over, I channeled everyone to go from talking to writing.

CONFERRING AND SMALL-GROUP WORK

Giving Students Strong Direction in Writing Whole New Drafts

In today's minilesson and others, you will have encouraged students to initiate revision based only on responses from a peer. Some will do this, and you can celebrate that. But you also need to be prepared to use your conferences to support the revision that you have in mind for children to do.

The revision that will be easiest to support is that which involves marking up or even taping onto an existing draft. But the revision that will probably help the most will require writers to start a whole new draft, writing the whole piece over again from scratch. You may find yourself worried about this, projecting the resistance you would feel if you were nudged to start your writing all over again. Keep in mind that for youngsters, writing time will be for writing. The choice is either to work on the existing piece—finishing it, revising it, or rewriting a new draft of it—or to work on another piece altogether. It is not necessarily a lot harder to rewrite a piece altogether than to start a new one. So go ahead and nudge writers to do this.

When I sat down next to Gabriel, I had no particular plan. He had clearly finished talking to a reader and was working on a still-unfinished teaching book. He looked up and said, "I am working on the words. I did all my sketches already." Gabriel then went right back to writing.

"Can we talk about your writing?" I asked, signaling for him to pause and pay attention to the conversation. "What topic are you teaching in your book?"

"I am teaching how I went to Playland. I played all the games and I played smack the mole." I read the piece quickly, to myself, and saw that Gabriel was indeed writing about Playland. Gabriel's piece started:

> Pg. 1: I went to play land and had so so so so much fun. I played smack the mole and put the tail on the monkey and put the nose on the clown.

The one thing that had struck me the most was that the piece had the tone of a story more than of an information book. My instinct was to say this to him, but I have learned to locate something the writer has done well and to start with that. And indeed, when I tried to see strengths, they weren't hard to find. "Gabriel, one thing that really works in your writing is that you decided to write about a topic you care about, one you have expertise in, and that makes this writing feel alive. Your voice is strong in the writing. It doesn't sound like a robot wrote it, but like you wrote it. And you are able to include particular details, even the fancy names for specific games, because this is a topic you know well.

"I also noticed that you have been writing quickly, and I bet that when you know the topic well and write almost as if you are talking, that helps you write quickly. So all of those good things go together. Whenever you write teaching books, you can remember that it works for you to write about a topic you know well, to write quickly, and to make your writing feel almost as if you are talking."

(continues)

MID-WORKSHOP TEACHING **As Deadlines Approach, Writers Work with New Urgency**

I stood in the middle of the room and said in a voiceover, "Within a few minutes, both writers should be revising up a storm. Tomorrow you are going to evaluate all the work you have done so far in this unit, so work like crazy today to finish every book, to make sure everything makes sense, and if you haven't written *at least* two books that are at least five pages each, with a bunch of sentences on a page, then you *really* need to write fast and furiously. I'm not going to interrupt you because you have so much to do. Just work, work, work."

Gabriel nodded in agreement, explaining, "I went to Playland on my birthday, and I think I will get to go on my next birthday, so I know all about it."

I then said, "I do have one suggestion for what you could do to become an even stronger writer of teaching books if you are willing for me to give you a pointer." Gabriel was more than willing so I continued. " Although you have a strong voice in this writing, it is sort of the voice of a storyteller, telling the story of your trip, and you are going to want to use that strong voice of yours to be a teacher, teaching a class all about Playland. Gabriel, will you pretend to be my teacher, and I am your student?" I had him sit on the edge of a desk, and I sat on a chair, like a student, with a few other chairs holding imaginary students to my right and left. "Pretend all these chairs are filled with your students, and we have come for a class on Playland. Teach us about it."

Gabriel took a big breath and started in. "On my birthday we went to Playland and first we–"

I intervened. "Gabriel, you are telling a great story about one time when you went to Playland. You are telling what you did first and next and next. That's a great way to tell the story of your trip. But what I am hoping you will do instead now is to teach us a class. Remember how you learned that you think about the parts of your topic—the parts of Playland—and you use your fingers to help you teach all about one part, then all about the next?"

Gabriel nodded. "At Playland, people can play smack the mole. They have a big hammer and . . . " I smiled and gave him a thumbs up. He continued telling about that game and then moved to a second finger and a second subtopic. "At Playland, people also go fishing. But you can't eat the fish because it's not real."

I nodded and said, "Gabriel, I love the way you are still using that strong voice of yours and still working with a topic you know well, and this time, instead of telling a story you are teaching a class. That's what writers of teaching books do. Do you see that in your first draft, you were writing a story more than a teaching book. It was a long and detailed story—you are great at writing stories—but you also want to learn that there are different ways of writing, and informational books, or teaching books, sound different than stories."

Before I left, I provisioned Gabriel with a new blank book and with assurances that I'd be back to admire his efforts soon.

SHARE

When Writers Teach about Their Topic, This Helps Them Add More

Remind students that information books are teaching books, and sometimes it helps to stop writing and to teach. Orchestrate the formation of several topic-related groups, with one writer in each group teaching about the subject he or she has been writing about.

"Writers, lots of people who write teaching books about a topic end up teaching classes about that topic or giving speeches about that topic. In a few minutes, I'm going to orchestrate things so that you can teach other people about one of the subjects you have been writing about. You won't be reading your book. You'll put the book down and look at your class—that will be other kids—and you'll try to teach as much as you can about your subject, remembering to plan out your teaching across your fingers so that you say a lot about one thing, then go to the next thing, and say a lot about that. So right now, will each of you get ready to teach about your topic? Plan across your fingers."

If your classroom topics are too diverse to make groups, you can still gather them into "classes." Even though children may not have written about the same topic, they often know about the topics of their classmates. Instead of calling out the different topics, you can just pull children into groups that you know will work well together.

I gave the children a minute or two to plan, and as they planned, I did so as well. Then I intervened. "So I'm going to divide you into classes. In a minute, when I tell you it is time, will all of you who have written anything that has anything to do with a sport go to this corner of the classroom and sit in a circle? And will any of you who have written about an animal go to this corner? And will all of you who are not in one of those groups but who wrote about something you do outside school go to this corner? Go!" Once the children got to their corners, I asked them to sit in small circles.

Channel one child from each group to teach about his or her subject, and then get the other students to compare how their subjects are the same or different.

I quickly surveyed each group, selecting an able presenter from each, and said, "I'm going to ask one person from your group to teach you all about his or her topic. I want the rest of you to listen and get ready to talk about ways your topic is similar and ways it is different."

In each group, a writer talked about his or her subject, and then as one group and another finished talking, I channeled them to talk in partners about ways their subjects were similar and different.

"The reason to teach about your subject is that this gives a person more ideas of what to write. And the reason to listen to someone else's teaching, is that this, also, gives a writer more ideas. Right now, will each of you go back and add something to your writing that you just realized you could add?"

Session 7

Taking Stock

Self-Assessing and Setting Goals

IN THIS SESSION, you'll teach children that writers assess how well they are doing and set goals to become even better writers.

GETTING READY

- ✔ Information Writing Checklists, Grade 1 and Grade 2, enlarged on chart paper (see Guided Inquiry)
- ✔ Copies of the Information Writing Checklists, Grade 1 and Grade 2 for each child see Guided Inquiry)
- ✔ Red and green Post-its (see Guided Inquiry)
- ✔ Index card to record personal goal (see Guided Inquiry)
- ✔ Mentor texts to hand out during the mid-workshop teaching, at least one text for each small group or table (see Mid-Workshop Teaching)
- ✔ Student writing folders and Post-its (see Share)

Common Core State Standards: W.1.2, W.1.5, W.1.7, W.2.2, RI.1.1, RI.1.2, RI.1.5, SL.1.1, SL.1.2, L1.1, L.1.2

TODAY YOU'LL AGAIN ASK CHILDREN to use checklists to evaluate their writing and set goals. The power of setting goals cannot be understated—knowing what you are reaching for, and having clear and concrete steps to get there, is one of the best ways to improve measurably and quickly. We know from John Hattie's review of thousands of studies of achievement that learners of all kinds are most apt to accelerate development if they are working toward crystal clear, ambitious goals.

Sessions like this one are critical for students to identify the things they are doing well and set goals for how they will improve.

Today you'll show children a far more ambitious checklist than the one you used at the start of this unit. This checklist features two columns—one with the CCSS goals for first grade and the other for second grade. We have found that most first-graders can meet most of the second-grade goals by the end of first grade, so we include that checklist now. You may choose, however, not to teach into it yet. You'll want to return to this checklist throughout the unit, reminding students to keep working toward the more ambitious goals. You will find the checklist on the CD-ROM.

This session is an inquiry lesson and therefore will not follow the regular structure of a minilesson, as you'll recall from Session 4. This session is particularly well suited to be taught as a guided inquiry, because the work of assessing one's writing and setting goals should be work that students can eventually do on their own, without your prompting, anytime they sit down to write. Having students take the lead on this work today will mean they have more practice learning how to set crystal-clear, ambitious goals and then work like the dickens to reach those goals.

MINILESSON

Taking Stock

Self-Assessing and Setting Goals

CONNECTION

Tell writers that instead of a regular minilesson, they'll be inquiring into ways they can and cannot yet do all of the end-of-year expectations for first-grade writers of informational texts.

"Writers, tomorrow is going to be the end of the first part of our unit, and then next week we are going to begin something new and really challenging. Starting next week, you won't just be writing teaching books. You'll be writing *chapter books* that teach! That's going to be really hard work, but I get the feeling that this is a whole team of hard workers, right?

"Before you can start on that new challenge, you need to make sure you have *mastered* writing information picture books. I am pretty sure that all of you have learned to do a lot of things, but I am also pretty sure that each of you has more work to do before you are an expert at writing information picture books.

"So today, I was thinking that instead of a regular minilesson, I could help you evaluate the book you think is your best so far. That way, you can figure out the things that you do well and compliment yourself on those things, and figure out the things you need to work on, so you can give yourself some goals. And maybe, with help from other kids, you could work on one of your goals today.

"This means that today will be a different kind of day. It will start with a minilesson where *you teach yourselves.* Are you up for doing that?"

◆ COACHING

Throughout these books, you will see that we have been influenced by research that suggests that kids profit from realizing that doing well is a result of hard work, not of luck or brains. We make every effort to glory in opportunities to work hard, to help kids identify themselves as hard workers. We're apt to ask, "Has one of you done some hard work today that you feel really good about?" "I want to tell you about a writer who worked really, really hard to figure something out." The larger point is that language matters. It is a conscious choice to revel in the class being a team of hard workers.

TEACHING AND ACTIVE ENGAGEMENT

Name a question that will guide the inquiry.

"Writers, today each of you is going to investigate the questions, 'What have I already learned to do as a writer of teaching books? What do I still need to work on?'"

GUIDED INQUIRY

Set writers up to evaluate their writing by guiding them through a series of steps that will help them develop ways to compliment themselves and to set goals.

"So, writers, put your best teaching book in front of you. I'll give you a minute to choose that book and get it in front of you." As I saw children begin to be ready, I said, "Will you also get out the Post-its that I've put in your writing folder? Green ones (for go!) and red ones (for stop! oops!)."

Once children were ready, I began in earnest. "You'll remember that at the start of this unit, I read over the Information Writing Checklist—a list you worked toward in your kindergarten classrooms. Well, I'm going to introduce a new checklist today that has new goals now that you are first-grade writers of information books. (This  checklist can be found on the CD-ROM.)

Information Writing Checklist

	Grade 1	NOT YET	STARTING TO	YES!	Grade 2	NOT YET	STARTING TO	YES!
	Structure				**Structure**			
Overall	I taught my readers about a topic.	☐	☐	☐	I taught readers some important points about a subject.	☐	☐	☐
Lead	I named my topic in the beginning and got my readers' attention.	☐	☐	☐	I wrote a beginning in which I named a subject and tried to interest readers.	☐	☐	☐
Transitions	I told different parts about my topic on different pages.	☐	☐	☐	I used words such as *and* and *also* to show I had more to say.	☐	☐	☐
Ending	I wrote an ending.	☐	☐	☐	I wrote some sentences or a section at the end to wrap up my piece.	☐	☐	☐
Organization	I told about my topic part by part.	☐	☐	☐	My writing had different parts. Each part told different information about the topic.	☐	☐	☐
	Development				**Development**			
Elaboration	I put facts in my writing to teach about my topic.	☐	☐	☐	I used different kinds of information in my writing such as facts, definitions, details, steps, and tips	☐	☐	☐
Craft	I used labels and words to give facts.	☐	☐	☐	I tried to include the words that showed I'm an expert on the topic.	☐	☐	☐
	Language Conventions				**Language Conventions**			
Spelling	I used all I knew about words and chunks (*at, op, it,* etc.) to help me spell.	☐	☐	☐	I used what I knew about spelling patterns (*tion, er, ly,* etc.) to spell a word.	☐	☐	☐
	I spelled the word wall words right and used the word wall to help me spell other words.	☐	☐	☐	I spelled all of the word wall words correctly and used the word wall to help me figure out how to spell other words.	☐	☐	☐

"These are the things that hundreds of teachers decided first-graders should be able to do by the very end of first grade. You are not supposed to be doing *all* these things just yet! But I am pretty sure that if you listen to this list, you will find that—wow—you already do some of these things! I am also showing you the list for second grade, just in case you want to *really* reach for the stars, but, for now, we'll focus on the first-grade checklist. You ready?"

Scaffold students' self-evaluation by reading aloud the goals under the "How does my piece go?" heading of the checklist.

I started reading the list, item by item, sometimes elaborating on an item, and often giving instructions about ways to use Post-its to note examples of that item. For example, after reading the first item on the list, I said, "The trick is to check that you didn't by mistake throw in information about some completely different topic—information that should go in a different book. If you wrote on one topic that you named up front, put a green Post-it by your title, and write 'one topic' on it." I gave children time in between each item for them to scan through a page or two of their book but did not wait until every child felt he or she was done before progressing to the next item. The goal was exposure more than perfection.

You should focus first on using only the green Post-its by having children mark what they did well. When children have several tools (green Post-its, red Post-its, and index cards), working with one first before progressing to the next can reduce confusion.

Scaffold children to continue self-evaluating. Read aloud more items of the checklist, again channeling students to Post-it evidence that they'd done these things.

I read the rest of the items on the checklist. I then asked students, "Which of these things are you finding that you are already doing? What are you already *great* at? Take a moment to look at your writing and use the green Post-its to mark the best evidence of the things you are doing well."

Listen in to students' self-evaluations, accumulating your observations about what they say they do well, so that you can remark on these to the class.

"Writers, I'm noticing that a lot of you think you do a good job of including words that experts use in your writing. If you don't know how to spell one of these words, do you just give up and use an easier, nonexpert word?"

The children chanted, "Nooooo."

"*And* many of you said that you are including pictures and labeling your drawings. Right now, quick as a wink, find one page where you have a detailed drawing with labels and hold it up so everyone can admire it."

The children tore through their books and then held the chosen pages to their chests and proudly pointed so that everyone could admire their drawings and labels. I pointed out the prowess of one or two (surprising) writers, whose detailed drawings suggested they had worked hard.

Coach children to listen not only for what they already do well but also for what they do not yet do well, setting goals for themselves.

I paused from my reading at this point. "Writers, many of you are finding that you did lots of things already in your writing, and that is great. But to become a much better writer, you also need to be hard on yourself and to be able to say, 'I can do more. I'm not yet great at that.' So let me reread the first part of the list again and ask you to think, 'Which of these things am I *not* great at yet?' Then you will have time to tell a partner what your goals will be for the next part of our unit, for the next week or two. So listen up, and think, 'Which of those things should I be better at?' and then mark it with a red Post-it."

Coach children to think especially about what they do not yet do well so they can set and record goals. Listen in as they talk about these.

I handed out the index cards next. "Now comes the important part! You are going to find a handful of goals for yourself. Write a word or two for each goal on one of the goal cards I've given you and use the words on the checklist to help you." After rereading the list, I was silent while children recorded a goal or two.

The Common Core emphasizes that students need to be able to cite text evidence for any conclusion they draw. Teach writers to locate evidence that they've met the goals on the checklist. Help them read closely. Eventually, students will learn the after locating and citing evidence, it is important to "unpack"or "discuss" ways that evidence illustrate the broader concept. You might already coach into this.

Very often, a writer has a choice. One could say the beginning of the text is fine, or one could push toward a higher standard. You really want children to aspire, to go for the gold, so talk up the importance of being hard on oneself and the joy of setting some goals. Deemphasize the joy of saying "I've done that" so that youngsters embrace instead goal-driven work.

This will be complicated work. Don't expect every student to grasp every part of it before you move along to more items on the checklist. You'll provide follow-up small-group support.

"Did you all discover some really cool goals that you can set for yourselves? Things you can work toward doing in even stronger ways?" My upbeat intonation suggested it is the luckiest thing in the world to have goals for oneself. "Will you read your goals to your partner and talk about them?"

I listened in as children talked.

Crystallize a few goals that many children seem to have identified, doing this in a way that celebrates goals.

"Writers, am I right that many of you want to get even better at ending your book with a final thought about your topic? That's a goal that never stops being important for every writer—even for the grown-up prize-winning writers. Stand up and take a bow if *you* want to work hard on that goal as well.

Enjoy this! It's a really nice touch for kids to take a bow because they've chosen an important goal!

"And there is another goal that I bet a lot of you want to work on, and that is writing more and *more* and *more!* Am I right? Again, if you have writing longer, elaborating more as a goal—writing at least a sentence or two for each part of your topic—stand up and take a bow." As they did this, I starred the items I had highlighted.

LINK

Channel children to meet in goal-driven clusters to help each other do last revisions, based on these goals.

"Now, writers, we're going to do something really challenging. We're going to divide into work groups and help each other work on one goal. So for now, choose—which of you want to get started working today, with the book you are holding? Will it be on the goal of including a final thought or idea about your topic? Will it be the goal of writing more and more? Will it be the goal of adding more expert words to your writing?"

You will, of course, organize the small groups in your class based on the goals most of your students want to work toward. This is why it is important to be listening in while students talk to their partners about the goals they have set.

I'd soon sent writers who wanted to work on one goal to a back area of the classroom; those who wanted to work on another goal were asked to remain in the meeting area, and those working on the third goal were channeled to yet a third space. "You are going to be in a group with a *lot* of kids who want to work on the same goal, so get started."

CONFERRING AND SMALL-GROUP WORK

Support Students in Studying and Analyzing Their Writing

IN TODAY'S MINILESSON, you taught children to take the lead in assessing their own writing. Some children were able to accomplish this self-assessment with ease, right on the rug. Yet for others, this work may have felt elusive. As you get ready to help children accomplish the important revision work in their small groups, anticipate that you may need to aid some of them in setting goals that are both realistic and ambitious and others in working toward their goals by identifying clear steps they can take.

It will be easy for children to assess themselves on the aspects of their writing with which they have already had some practice, such as using end punctuation. At the same time, there will be goals on the checklist that will be more challenging, such as using expert words in their writing. It is also fair to expect that some children will listen to you read through the checklist and quickly Post-it parts of their writing that do not match the goal. Fear not. With some guidance, children will learn how to independently use the checklist to assess their own writing, carefully thinking through each point and comparing it to the work they have done, as well as the work that they will do. All the while, children will deepen their understanding of each item on the checklist.

For your writers who are able to do this self-assessment work with ease, the challenge may be in knowing the clear steps they need to take to reach their goal. For these writers, it will be important to celebrate the self-assessment work they have done and then support them in working toward their goals, gradually releasing your support so that they learn to do this work independently.

As I approached Hattie, I already had a sense of where on the checklist she would need support. As the last unit came to a close, Hattie had worked hard to add volume to her writing. She hadn't yet succeeded in producing a lot.

"Hi, Hattie. Looks like you are hard at work. Is there anything that I can help you with today?"

MID-WORKSHOP TEACHING **Looking to Mentor Authors for Inspiration in Making Writing Interesting**

After conferring with one student writer, I surveyed the room, noticing a few writers were looking at books. "Are you studying ways the authors of those books made something interesting on every page?" I asked, knowing that was an optimistic interpretation of what they were doing. The children, however, readily agreed that that was what they'd been doing.

Speaking to the whole class, I said, "Writers, can I stop you for a moment? There are many things on this checklist that feel easy for you, and that is a great feeling. Making our writing interesting, however, may feel like newer work. Even if you have one way to add interesting things on every page, you can always have more ways to do that.

"A group of kids from your class has already begun investigating the different ways mentor authors make their writing interesting, and I think this is something we can all try. I am going to drop some books off at each table, so that you have authors available to teach you the different ways you can make your writing interesting. You can quickly look through the book, think about what's cool or what jumps out to you as a reader, and then you can try the same thing in your book."

Hattie looked up at me, knowingly. "I know I need to add more sentences," she started. "I just don't know how to do it." I read quickly through Hattie's teaching book about headbands (see Figure 7–1).

> There are lots of kinds of headbands. They all look different.
> Headbands cost a lot of money even though they are small.

(continues)

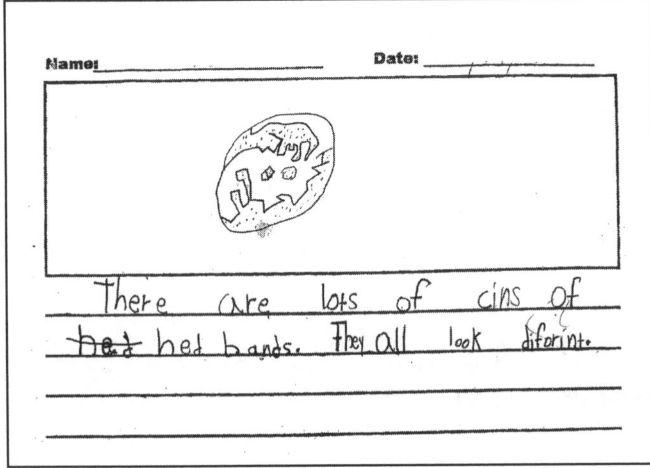

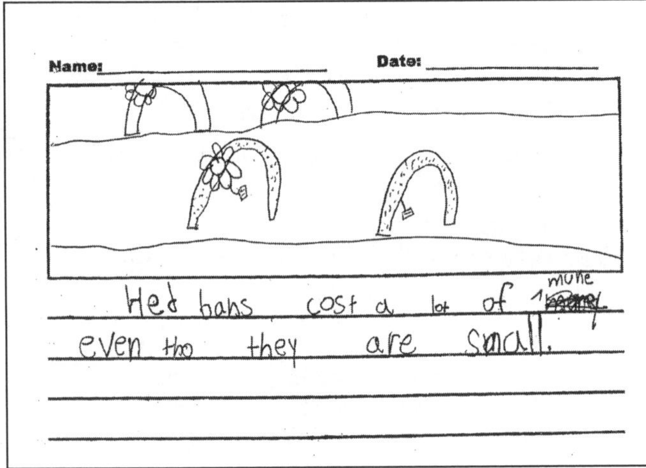

FIG. 7–1 Hattie's book on "Headbands."

"Hattie, it's true that these pages are short, but there *are* packed with information, and they each say something interesting. So you are well on your way! But now you are tackling the hard part: saying more. What strategy were you thinking of using to say more?"

At this point, I gave Hattie some wait time. This was not so easy to do, because I wanted to jump in and remind her of ways I'd taught her to add onto a text. However, the goal of this session is to help children set goals and then meet those goals with independence. So I waited.

"Well," Hattie started, "I could add more labels to my pictures."

"That's true! And then what?"

"I could . . . use those labels and pictures to help me add more?"

I confirmed Hattie's self-assessment and before I left, directed her gaze toward a chart that could help her. "Hattie, that is exactly right. One thing you can do is add more and more labels to your pictures. After you do this," I continued, getting ready to layer in some teaching, "you can add sentences to match what you've put into the pictures. That's a wise idea!" Then I added, " I also think that on many pages, if you add the phrase 'For example, . . . ', you could then begin writing about some examples. Do you know a particular headband that costs a lot?"

Hattie smiled and tapped the headband on her head. I gave her a thumbs up.

Before I left, I helped Hattie get started adding more pictures and labels to her drawing. As she did this, she began to orally rehearse the sentences she was going to add.

SHARE

Writers Learn from Each Other

Celebrate the self-assessment work students have done and ask them to share their goals and their revised teaching books with their partners.

I called the students to the rug, asking them to bring their teaching books with them and to sit with their writing partners. "Writers, there is nothing more important than being your own teacher. Of course, I love helping you all see the different ways you can make your writing stronger, but the truth is, you are your own best teacher.

"Each of you brought your teaching book to the rug. In just a moment, I am going to ask you to switch books with your partner. But before you do, turn and tell your partner what goal, or goals, you set for yourself today." After giving students a minute to share goals, I said, "Now, switch books with your partner. Take a moment to read through your partner's book, and as you do, pay attention to what your partner has done to work toward his or her goal. What do you notice in your partner's writing that shows he or she is working hard at those goals?" I gave students a few minutes to read through their partners' books, noticing the ways they were working toward their goals.

"Now, tell your partner what he or she has done to work toward his or her goal. You can say, 'I noticed that you . . . and this shows that you are working hard at your goal!' Give it a try."

As children turned and complimented one another, I went around and jotted down what they said.

"So, here are some things I heard. I heard Anessa tell her partner that she thought it was so cool how he zoomed in on one of his teaching pictures; that he didn't show *everything*, but instead drew one part really, really close up. And that shows he is working on including pictures and labels in his writing. I also heard Karl tell his partner that he thought the way he added a new sentence on two of his pages was super-duper neat and shows that he's working toward his goal of adding more to his teaching book.

"Here's the thing, writers. You can learn from yourselves, and you can learn from each other, too. If there is ever a time you are wondering how to do something, you can reread your own writing, and you can read the writing that your partner has done too. While you are all working toward individual goals, often your goals will be similar to your classmates' goals. And just like you are accountable to yourself, you can also be accountable to one another, helping each other work hard at your goals."

As you walk around the rug you can check in with students, asking, "What is your partner's goal? What do you notice?" You can help children then put what they see into words, "Oh he drew a big foot? So he really zoomed in on the important part in his picture?" Sometimes students see the strategy their partner used, but struggle with putting that into the language of writing.

Session 8

Editing

Spelling, Capitals, and Punctuation

ear Teachers,

Today we are turning over the reins to you. This letter, like others you have encountered in the *Small Moments* unit, aims to help you craft your own minilesson and plan your own conferring and small-group work, with some support from us. Your teaching today will be especially important because this session marks the end of the first bend of the unit. Much of the work today builds on the editing strategies children learned in *Small Moments*. You can lean on the editing sessions (Sessions 13 and 19) in that unit as you are crafting today's minilesson.

MINILESSON

In your connection, you'll want to harken back to the editing work students did during the last unit, reminding them of all they have learned about editing their stories, and then you will want to connect that to the day's work of editing their information books. When the children convene in the meeting area, you probably will want to display the first editing checklist from the start of the year, saying that although now they are not writing stories but teaching books, they still need to recall and use general editing strategies they learned earlier. For example, they need to check for end punctuation, capital letters, and spelling.

Your teaching point for the day might be "When a writer edits his or her piece of writing, this involves pulling in to work on things like hearing all the sounds in a word or writing with capital letters and then it involves pulling back to reread and think, 'What else?' Painters do this, too. They pull in to work, then stand back to scan their work, then pull in again. So writers, like painters, stand back to look over their work, then pull in again to fix things, then stand back again."

When planning teaching, you need to decide whether you want to work on your own writing, on a child in the class's writing, or on some perhaps fictional neighborhood child's writing. For this topic, you might choose the anonymous child, because it is not likely the

Common Core State Standards: W.1.2, W.1.5, RFS.1.2, RFS.1.3, SL.1.1, L.1.1, L.1.2

children will believe that you are really struggling to spell *leotard* or to start your sentences with capitals. Remember that in every teaching component, you essentially set children up to watch you as you either work on your own piece or show your students how another writer worked on his or her piece. So if you are telling your children about the hard work that, say, Philip, your neighbor, did to get his story ready to publish, then you step into the shoes of Philip.

You will also want to think about the specific strategies you are teaching. To highlight them, you might accentuate what Philip did *not* do. He did not just read his writing through one time and be done! He read it once, another time, and another time. You will also want to embed some tips and maybe ways to remind children of those tips. Perhaps one tip is that kids do everything many times. They stretch out a word to hear sounds, record a sound or two, then stretch out the word again, and they may repeat this four times in a given word. Some teachers literally have kids humming a little tune, a variation of "Row, Row, Row Your Boat," only this is "Stretch, stretch, stretch your word, right across the page."

The easiest way to give kids a chance to continue what you have practiced is for you to demonstrate by editing a line or two of Philip's writing, and then you can turn the job over to them and get partners to work together editing the next line or two of his writing. As partners work, you can call out voiceovers, reminding children of all you hope they have already learned. You'll want to send students off to work today with some clear goals in mind for editing the teaching books they want to publish. You may want to restate the teaching point and give children a sense of the upcoming celebration, using it to rally their energy.

CONFERRING AND SMALL-GROUP WORK

For your conferring, you might decide to divide students into groups—those who need more help with spelling, those who need more help with end punctuation and capitals—and do strategy lessons with those groups. You may be feeling the urge to spend your time in class acting as the final editor on your children's books, but it's better to use class time to help children help each other. Children can do the important work of editing together. It is true that when children read and reread their own writing, they often overlook spelling errors that you find glaring. Your work is to teach children to help one another cast a more refined lens on their writing, looking at it on a word-by-word level.

Gather two groups of partners around you and prepare to teach them to look at the *actual* words they wrote and then correct the spelling. Teach partners to hold one book in the middle and as the writer reads her book aloud, the other partner can give a gentle tap on the shoulder when a misspelled word comes up and say, "That word there. Does that look right? Try it again." Then the writer can quickly revise that word and move on through the rest of her book. When one partner finishes, children switch roles. If children are not able to go through their individual pieces by the time the small group is ready to be wrapped up, don't fret; you have taught them well, and they can go off and continue the work on their own.

For some children, using end punctuation correctly will provide a challenge. A child who has no end punctuation will want to reread thinking, "Where is the end of my idea?" When she finds it, she then needs to add a punctuation mark and a capital for the next word. Children are still approximating how they are using end punctuation, so do not expect that all sentences will be punctuated properly. As children move to write more complex sentences, they are less certain about how to mark them. If this happens, you can pull a small group to look at some pages in the mentor text, noticing how the author has punctuated longer sentences. Your goal is for children to be fascinated with and engaged by this work—it's not perfection you are after!

MID-WORKSHOP TEACHING

For your mid-workshop teaching, you might suggest that one way to be sure you are making a piece of writing easy to read is to pass the piece along to a reader who has not already read it and to ask that reader to read it aloud. Then the writer watches closely to see the places where the reader struggles, noticing if the reader raises eyebrows in a "Huh?" gesture. You could demonstrate this by returning to the story of the neighborhood boy that you wove through your minilesson, telling the kids that one of the greatest things Philip did was to learn to use readers to help him. You could recruit one child to read a chart-sized copy of Philip's writing, and the rest of the class could collect across their fingers the numbers of places in the text where Philip knows he has more work to do. Then kids could do the same work with their own and each other's writing.

SHARE

Today's share will be a mini-celebration, not the end of the unit culmination, so you will want some small way to recognize the progress that writers have made and to give children the experience of their writing reaching readers. You might, for example, decide that for a celebration, you're going to ask your first-graders to all take their books with them on a class field trip to a kindergarten room, and then in that room, they can read their teaching book to a younger child. You might suggest that children read a page, say even more about it, read the next page, and then say even more about it. That would help prepare children for the longer writing they will soon be doing.

Then again, you could with great ceremony ask each writer to put his or her book into a container that holds the class's nonfiction books. If your classroom has one bin of books on animals, writers can put their books on animals into that bin, and if there is another bin for books on sports, writers who wrote on sports could put their books there. Then there could be reading time, and you could ask writers to just read their own books, not those written by others.

Those are just two options, and you will think of better ones. Perhaps the class wants to turn the Information Writing Checklist into a display, with an item from the list written in a part of the display, with two books that illustrate that item draped nearby. The sky is the limit. Go for it!

Lucy, Kristi, and Barb

Nonfiction Writers Can Write Chapter Books! BEND II

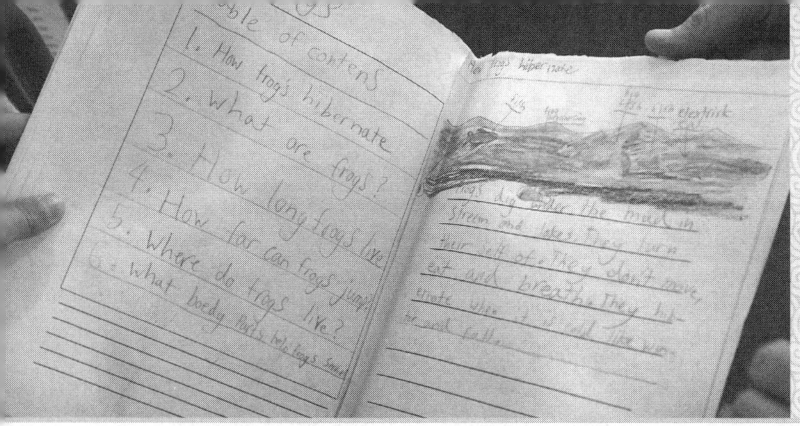

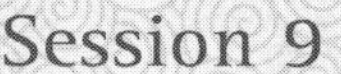

Session 9

Writing Tables of Contents

IN THIS SESSION, you'll teach children that nonfiction writers, like story writers, learn how a book might go by studying books written by other authors, including their tables of contents.

GETTING READY

- ✔ Picture of a symphony orchestra (see Connection)
- ✔ Pencil or baton to "conduct" the symphony share of topics (see Connection)
- ✔ A child's finished picture book and also a finished chapter book (see Connection)
- ✔ Mentor text, *Sharks!* (see Inquiry)
- ✔ Chart paper and markers to scaffold the questions for the inquiry
- ✔ A collection of ten or so additional informational chapter books that have tables of contents, to pass out to children during the inquiry
- ✔ Daily class schedule, to use as a metaphor for the usefulness of tables of contents for readers (see Link)
- ✔ Table of contents paper on each writing table (see Link)
- ✔ "Chapter Titles Should Usually . . . " chart, to make with students (see Mid-Workshop Teaching)

Common Core State Standards: W.1.2, W.1.5, W.1.7, RI.1.1, RI.1.5, RI.1.6, SL.1.1, L.1.1, L.1.2, L.1.5

When designing curriculum across a unit, a year, and a student's academic life, an underlying principle is to always lay out a series of challenges that build on each other, so that over time learners become ready to do progressively more complex work. Levels of text difficulty can be a metaphor for curriculum design. Readers are always reading whole texts (among other things), and as such, they are always preparing to read, reread, and rethink what they have read. Over time, the texts that students read—if they are expository—progress from being simply catalogs or lists toward being complex and structured courses of study.

So far in this unit, you have challenged students to write small books (we've variously called them teaching books or informational picture books) about topics they know well. They've experienced the full process of writing in relation to those books, planning them, drafting them, revising them, evaluating them, and doing yet more revision. And they've cycled through the process of writing at a good clip, devoting perhaps five minutes to planning a book, perhaps thirty minutes to writing the book, and so forth.

In the upcoming bend, the trajectory of students' work with informational texts rises. The challenge increases. In the upcoming bend, students will write information texts that are far longer than anything they've written before—in page numbers and in the time each part of the process requires. The chapter books they'll be writing will be more complex, too, organized into a hierarchy of information that involves topics and subtopics.

Because the work that students will be doing is challenging, you will see that their work is more scaffolded—and also, therefore, more controlled. There will be fewer times when you show them a text and simply say, "I know you can write like this. Go to it!" And students' progress from one part of the writing process to the next will be more controlled, with the whole class working in synchrony more of the time.

You should already anticipate that in the final bend of the unit, students will write information chapter books with more independence and less support from you. So if you feel uncomfortable seeing students working on a tight leash, know that this does not last too long.

MINILESSON

Writing Tables of Contents

CONNECTION

Rally students to the new challenge of spending more than a week writing one chapter book.

"Writers, I mentioned last week that today we begin a whole new part to our unit. I got the idea for this somewhere in the middle of last week when I realized that your books are so full of information that even though you are only six-years-old, I think you are ready to take on the very grown-up project of writing teaching chapter books."

Support writers in getting topics, choosing things for which they are famous.

"To do this, you need to have a topic that you will teach others about. This needs to be a topic you know really well, because you won't just write a little book," I held up one of their information picture books, "about this. You will be writing a whole chapter book on this topic." I held up a child's finished chapter book.

"It is not hard to think of the topics you know really well because those are the things you are famous for. Like you all know that I'm crazy about dogs and about teaching writing. So I could write a teaching chapter book on dogs or on teaching writing. And you all know that Matt is crazy about—what?"

The class called out, "The Yankees!"

"So let's start and get our topics figured out. Turn to the kids near you and tell them what you think they are famous for, just in case that helps. Go!"

I listened in as children talked and sometimes did voiceovers. "I'm hearing that we have experts in karate and SpongeBob and flowers, horses, and even amusement parks!"

Do a symphony share of topics, immersing children who still haven't selected one in possibilities.

After a minute I said, "Okay. I think you all have your topics in mind for your teaching chapter books. Let's do a symphony share. I'll be the conductor of you, the orchestra, at a giant symphony." I showed a picture of the people assembled on stage with their instruments. "And when I tip my baton," I held up a pencil, "toward you, "I arched it and

◆ COACHING

You'll want to drumroll the new bend in the unit.

It is not really true that you got the idea for this bend in the road because of children's prowess last week. But perhaps the children's work last week did *give you ideas. By all means, bring those into your teaching. Did it seem like kids could work better if there was music playing? Did it work best if each writing time began with ten minutes of absolute silence? Did you feel as if each child would profit from a small list of goals, propped up on a child-sized billboard at that child's writing spot? Be sure that your teaching is responsive.*

Don't get swayed by pressure to somehow channel your students to write about subjects like Rosa Parks or westward expansion. When a child knows almost nothing about a topic, the writing is bound to be problematic, and children quickly resort to copying instead of writing. You would be far better off to channel kids to write books on topics they know well, even if those topics feel entirely personal. I'd be far happier to see a book titled "My Mom" that

pointed toward one child, "then you say out your topic, loud and clear. Don't discuss it. Just say the topic, so this goes really quickly. You ready? Give a quiet thumbs up if you have your topic in mind."

I sat tall, back arched, and said in a formal presentational way, "Teaching Chapter Books, by Room 103." Then I tipped the baton, and children sang out topics: lady bugs, soccer goalie, new fashion, submarines, skateboarding. I ended this by saying, "And many more," brought my baton to rest, and leaned close to the class.

Establish the reason today's minilesson will be an inquiry lesson, and channel children to look at an example of the sort of text they will soon be writing, noticing the table of contents.

"You'll be writing teaching books that are longer than anything you have written so far. By now, you know that whenever a writer starts working on a new kind of writing—which for you will be long teaching books—it helps to study published examples of that kind of writing. I know all of you love *Sharks!*, and I do as well, so let's study that book and see if we can get some tips. Are you game for thinking, 'What did this writer do that I could do as well?'" The children nodded. "I'll be doing this study with you because I don't yet know the tips we can pull from this book."

Name a question that will guide the inquiry.

"Anne Schreiber's book *Sharks!* is longer than the books you all have been writing so far. What did Anne do that we could try as we get started writing really long chapter books?"

GUIDED INQUIRY

Set writers up to investigate the title page and table of contents page in their mentor text by guiding them through a series of steps that help them answer the underlying question and begin planning for their teaching chapter book.

"I don't have copies for all of us, so I enlarged a bit of the table of contents page so we can all be researchers together." In unison, we read the title page and the table of contents.

Chomp!

Shark Pups

Pups Grow Up

What Big Teeth You Have

Imagine This!

"Holy moly!" I said. "I thought we'd need to read about ten pages, but there is already stuff to learn, isn't there? My mind is going a million miles an hour, isn't yours? Whoa! What has she done that maybe, just maybe, someone in this

was laden with facts and specifics and elaboration, rather than the book I saw the other day that was about Rosa Parks. "Rosa Parks is a lady. She is proud. She is a lady. Rosa has parts. She has eyes and a nose and a head and legs." Just think how challenging it would be for you to write a book about your teaching. When kids write books about their pet or their sport or their hobby, that is challenging for them, too.

I try to literally wave my baton as if I am a conductor, then tip it toward one "instrument" (one child), resume waving it like a conductor, and then tip it again. I sit tall, hold my head regally, and in all ways try to bring to this an aura of pomp and circumstance. Certainly if kids chit-chat rather than saying out their topic, I suggest we try this again. I want the class to understand how to do this little ritual because it is worth returning to repeatedly.

When the method if teaching is an inquiry, you can't frame it as if you want students to inquire and see if they can come up with the answers you already know. So you need to approach this as a shared learning project and convey to them that you are learning alongside them. The pronoun of choice in this lesson will be we.

When teaching this actual lesson, we used a document camera to enlarge this page and others. If you don't have that technology or other technology that allows you to display an enlarged copy of a book, copy portions of the text onto chart paper, and duplicate other parts of the text, or simply hold it up for all to see.

classroom might be willing to try? Turn and talk. Fast. I'm dying to hear your thoughts." I jumped in on a conversation, as if I couldn't wait a second to think with them about this amazing table of contents.

After a bit, I said, "Alfred just reminded this group of those questions. Do you remember them?" I flipped the chart paper back to the page on which I had earlier written, "What? Why?" "Don't *just* talk about what you notice the author has done. Talk also about *why* she might have done it."

As children talked, I voiced over. "Your talk should sound like this: 'Maybe she did this because . . . ,' 'I think that because . . . ,' and 'Or could it have been that she did it because . . . ?'" I scrawled the first of those comments onto the chart paper.

Channel students to look between the mentor book and carefully chosen, similar information books, noticing ways all the books are similar and different in how they use tables of contents, chapter headings, and subheadings to build an infrastructure.

"I was thinking we would go on and look at other things about this *Sharks!* book, but there is so much here to learn about. Let's just think about what you have noticed so far about the title page and the table of contents. We should talk about what you notice and why you think the author has done this, but first let's look at some other books and study what those authors have done that is similar or different." I distributed about eight more informational chapter books to clusters of children and left them to buzz about those books.

After a bit I voiced over, "Are you thinking and talking about how the tables of contents in the books you are looking at is similar to the one in *Sharks!*? Different from *Sharks!*?" Then I added, "I wonder if you are asking that all-important question: '*Why* might these authors have done this?'"

Orchestrate a conversation fishbowl with a small group, surrounded by a ring containing the rest of the class. Channel first the inner, then the outer circle to compare tables of contents in several books.

After a bit, I called for children's attention. "I'm dying to learn from you about what the author is doing that you could try as well. Can you guys just talk, without me leading your discussion, while I take notes on the great ideas you have? Try to talk one at a time and to talk loudly so we can all hear your great observations." The children were game. "So let's get into a circle for the discussion. Quick as a wink, sit along the outside of the rug." As children did that, I gestured for five or six children to sit in a smaller grouping in the center of the rug. "These children will start talking about what they noticed when looking at tables of contents—what is the author doing, why, and how—and then the rest of you will chime in soon."

The inner circle children began talking. "She has chapters and she names it Chomp! and puts an excitement mark."

"It tells what it is about, like 'Shark Pups' is about pups."

"Puppies? Do they eat puppies?"

The teaching that you are doing is a bigger deal than you might realize. First, this is very grounded in the CCSS. Once children are in third grade, the Common Core reading standards ask that students be aware of the language and structure choices that authors make and be able to talk about the relationship between those decisions and the content the author is trying to focus on. That sort of talk about texts is not easy for children, so inviting them to explore this at a very early age is important. Don't expect them to produce some Right Answer. The most important thing is that children are nudged to notice the choices an author has made, reading like writers, and that they are trying to use language to talk about texts.

The books need to be simple enough that kids can read them and essentially to convey a similar message about the use of a table of contents to chunk the broad topic into smaller subtopics. Although eventually you will want children to know that books needn't have tables of contents, for now you are wise to channel the children toward this one direction, emphasizing that it can be done differently.

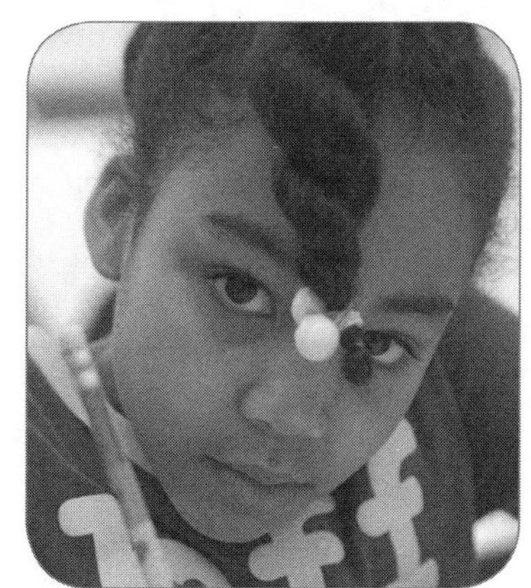

"No, the babies of sharks are puppies, like that's the name. Not dog puppies but shark puppies."

I piped in, "So you have noticed that she has different chapters, each one about a different part of her topic. Like one is about shark babies. And you noticed she tries to give names that get people wanting to read. What else did you notice?"

You'll want to be really pleased after you see youngsters talking back to whatever each other has said.

After three minutes or so, invite the rest of the class to chime in.

"Can the rest of the class now join in this conversation, and again, don't wait for me to call on you."

LINK

Debrief in ways that recap that writers of information chapter books make tables of contents that list the subtopics the book will cover, and then send writers off to do this.

"So, writers, right now, think about what *you* might do to make a table of contents for your book, and turn and talk to your partner about what ideas you have for how you can divide your whole topic into smaller parts, like you realized these books have done."

After children talked, I said, "So today you will start by working on a table of contents for your book. I've put some special paper on your tables. The table of contents is short but important. It is sort of like the schedule for the topics that readers will get to in the book. You know how when you come in the room every day, you look at our daily schedule to see what will come next and next? Well, just like the schedule lets you know the big things that will happen, a table of contents lets you know what will be coming up.

Before sending the class off to write, be sure that you have put sheets of table of contents paper on the tables. We find it helps to not staple those onto the children's books because turning back to reference the table of contents list can be difficult for very young children, so sometimes they ignore the table of contents and just generate new chapter titles. You are going to want them to essentially use the table of contents page as a check-off sheet for the writing work they will be doing.

"Once you've written your table of contents, I am pretty sure you can figure out what to do next!"

CONFERRING AND SMALL-GROUP WORK

Teaching Structure

Knowing that These Are Six-Year-Olds

YOUR CONFERRING TODAY SHOULD BE UPBEAT, because you are launching the second bend in the unit and you want children to feel up for the big work that lies ahead. The chances are good, however, that many of them will produce tables of contents that will end up needing to be revised. That is totally fine. Don't bring kids' spirits (or your own) down by feeling frantic for children to produce the tables of contents that you would produce. After all, you could cajole them into doing what you would do and bypass all the mistakes that a six-year-old is apt to make, thereby not allowing them to learn from those mistakes. So if a child has one chapter titled "Dog Eyes" and another, "Dog Noses" (I know, this is unlikely, but bear with me), then you need to say to yourself that it is not the worst thing in the world for that child to start writing those chapters. She's going to quickly realize that she does not have much information on either topic because they are too small, and with your help she'll end up revising her book to consolidate chapters. You'll be able to help her learn, then, that when a writer plans out the subsections of a book, the writer is thinking, "How much stuff will I be able to put in that subsection?" First-graders may not use that language, but they can think about pages as subsections and do that thinking. For today, you may decide to help children accelerate that process of trial and error so that their chapters are not too small, not too big, but like Goldilocks's bed, are "just right." You absolutely can lead a small group in which you help students grasp this concept. But you also can't let things go, smiling to yourself because you anticipate the fact that kids will soon find themselves discovering on their own some of the biggest principles that undergird this kind of writing.

Of course, for you to do either option—teach into the problem of too small or too large categories—it helps if you know a bit about the expectations for informational writing. You and your colleagues might look at tables of contents yourselves and try to deduce the principles that underlie these. One thing to keep in mind as you do this is this: many informational books are poorly written. The truth is, you could look at a lot of tables of contents and see fairly chaotic organizational structures. But usually, the expectation is that a book is structured a bit like an outline. If a book on the United States has four chapters, you would not expect them to be Northern US, Southern US,

MID-WORKSHOP TEACHING

Writers Draft and Revise Book and Chapter Titles

"Writers, I'm noticing some of you are making a word for each chapter title, and some of you are writing almost a whole sentence. And you are right that these are decisions authors can make. There is no one right way to do this. I do have some tips, though, about titling your chapters. The first one is that titles matter. People take time coming up with names for things, and they try one way, another way, and another way. That's true when a family is naming a new baby or a new pet, right? It is also true when naming a book or a chapter. Usually the table of contents page shows lots of cross-outs and new ideas as people work and work to get it right.

"You did such a great job of studying the tables of contents today and learning things I hadn't even realized that I am wondering if you'd like to do the same with studying a few more tables of contents. I'll put a few that have been written by kids and a few written by grown-ups on each table. Can you study them? I also have an old sheet of tips from last year, but I am thinking you guys might come up with a lot more from studying these examples. Give it a try."

Soon the class added two additional bullets to the ones I had already listed.

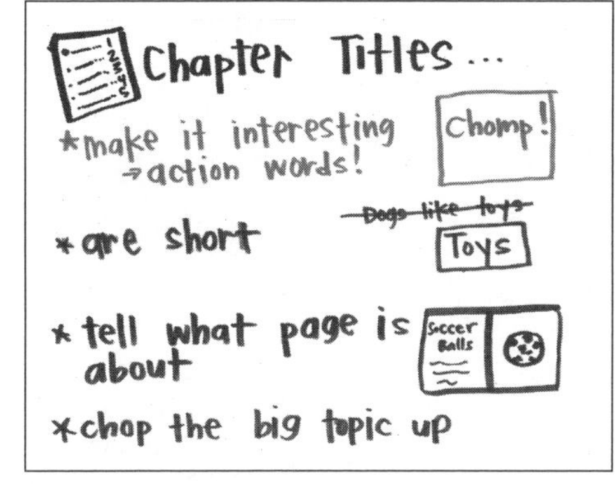

Eastern US, and North Dakota. And many topics have predictable structures. A book on animals generally includes sections of animal bodies, animal habitats, animal enemies, and so on. Books on famous people tend to have childhood, young adult years, and becoming famous. The point is not that children need to know or write within those predictable categories. They don't. But it sometimes is useful for a child writing about one sports team to look at how other books on sports team are apt to be organized. Even if the writer started a book on an entirely different sport, there will still be lessons to be learned from such a comparison.

There are lots of other ways to think about structuring informational books, and you may want to look ahead to the third-grade book on this topic if you want to develop a deeper knowledge of this. The important thing to say for now is that you are teaching organization, and it is a hefty topic. The writing demands of today are light—just lists of phrases—but the intellectual work is enormous. Don't expect to accomplish it all today or to save writers from their mess-ups. Children will be revising their tables of contents throughout the week and writing a second and better book in Bend III. For now, it is a big deal for them to plan not just across their fingers but across their table of contents and for them to begin the work of thinking about subtopics.

SHARE

Celebrating the Revision of Chapter Titles

Celebrate the work one child did in revising chapter titles and set up a museum walk for students to see all the different ways their classmates are planning their chapter books.

"Writers, I saw some of you crossing out titles and rewriting them several times to see which title would work best. I saw others of you referencing our chart for tips on what to include in chapter titles and looking at mentor texts for help. This is great work, writers, and just what professional writers of teaching books do.

"In just a moment, we are going to have a museum walk so you can see the work *all* your classmates did to plan how their chapter books will go. But first I want to share what Karl did to plan for his book. Karl had three chapter titles on his topic, amusement parks: 'Spin Rides,' 'Up and Down Rides,' and 'Circle Rides.' Karl then realized that he could add action words to his titles to make them more exciting for his reader. So, he rewrote his chapter titles to include more action. Now his chapter titles are 'Rides that Make You Dizzy,' 'Rides that Go Way Up in the Sky,' and 'Rides that Circle Around and Around.' Do you see how Karl took the same categories—the same chunks he wants to write each of his chapters about—but thought about how to make them more interesting for his reader? I bet a lot of you did the same thing.

"Writers, will you place your revised tables of contents on your desks so that they are visible for all your classmates to see? We're going to have a museum walk to look at how everyone has organized and planned for their chapter books. Okay, writers, stand up! Time for our museum walk!"

As children walked from desk to desk, these were a few of the tables of contents they saw.

What is a police officer?
Who put robbers in jail?
How do police officers get robbers?
What do police officers use?

Introduction
What's is a pet shop?
What do they sell?
Why do we go to pet stores?

How do they get the fish out of the tank?
Who works there?
Glossary
Conclusion

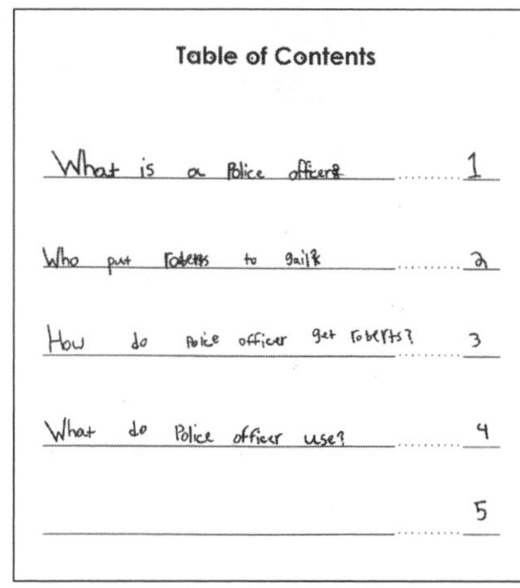

Table of Contents

What is a Police officer?	1
Who put robers to jail?	2
How do Police officer get robers?	3
What do Police officer use?	4
	5

FIG. 9–1 This entire book is focused on one particular thing, making the chapters more detailed than usual.

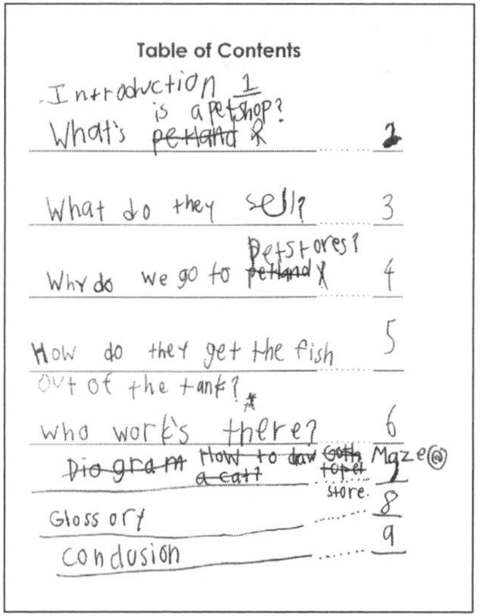

Table of Contents

Introduction	1
What's is a petshop? ~~petland~~	2
What do they sell?	3
Why do we go to Petstores? ~~petland~~	4
How do they get the fish out of the tank?	5
who work's there?	6
~~Diagram~~ ~~How to draw a cat~~ Maze	7
Glossory	8
condusion	9

FIG. 9–2 Children admired the fancy, brave words in this table of contents.

Session 10

Planning and Writing Chapters While Resolving to Get Better

IN THIS SESSION, you'll teach children that writers plan individual chapters the same way they plan their teaching books. They tell the information across—and down—their fingers before they write.

GETTING READY

- ✔ Students will need to bring their tables of contents and a writing tool to the meeting area for the minilesson (see Connection).
- ✔ Your own demonstration text for the teaching and share (we use bike riding)
- ✔ New paper choice with room for a heading on top, a picture box, and more lines on each page in bins in the middle of each table (see Link)
- ✔ Sheets of sticky mailing labels with tips for writing strong teaching books written on each label, one sheet per student (see Share)

Common Core State Standards: W.1.2, W.1.5, RI.1.5, SL.1.1, SL.1.4, SL.1.5, SL.1.6, L.1.1, L.1.2

THIS LESSON IS DECEPTIVE. It looks as if this is new and exciting and challenging work: planning and writing chapters in a nonfiction chapter book! But the truth is that you will be asking students to do pretty much the same work they have been doing across the first bend of this unit. The form into which they will write is new. Instead of writing across a sequence of pages, where each new burst of writing is supported by some time to draw, the youngsters will write on and on down a page (or so you hope).

The fact that this lesson revisits familiar work is a good thing. After all, six-year-olds are novices at all of this. Learning to write is like learning anything new: it takes practice. The fact that the work is essentially the same sometimes is not a problem because the learner is different; his or her skills are different. Then, too, when writing, the work is always fascinating because the topic is always new. One day the writer is immersed in a course on rabbits, another day on skateboarding—and always, these are topics that matter passionately to the writer. One day I write a book on informational writing, another day, on argument writing. There is something the same about that, but that doesn't stop this work from being endlessly interesting.

This session doesn't simply remind students to draw on all they know, although that would be sufficient. This session goes a step further and reminds students that when learning to do something, when working to get better at something, learners watch themselves at work and give themselves little lectures about goals and about progress. After all, the goal for your students today is not just to write a few chapters. It is also to write those chapters in ways that push their limits as writers, that take them toward whole new levels of writing skill. Developing prowess at anything requires a willingness to work toward clear goals, to watch what one does, to monitor oneself for whether something works or doesn't work, and to coach oneself. That will be the focus for today.

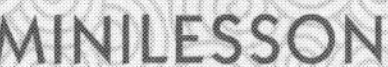

MINILESSON

Planning and Writing Chapters While Resolving to Get Better

CONNECTION

Ask students to review their tables of contents, selecting a chapter they are especially ready to write.

"Writers, bring your tables of contents and a pen or pencil, and hurry over to our meeting area. We want to make our minilesson super short so you can write a whole bunch of chapters today! When you get here, reread your tables of contents and star the chapter or two for which you are brim full of ideas. Then later today you can copy the title right from the table of contents page onto the top of a chapter page and start writing one of your chapters."

Name the teaching point.

"So, writers, today I want to teach you that when you are writing a chapter in a teaching chapter book, you can plan that chapter the very same way you planned your teaching picture book. For example, you can plan what you will say in a chapter across your fingers, saying a whole bunch about each finger, or each part of the chapter."

◆ COACHING

Although it may be hard for you to imagine that this will happen, we have seen lots of children who don't grasp that the table of contents is a plan for the chapters they'll be writing. They end up writing chapters that have nothing to do with the table of contents. So we find that it helps if we don't staple the table of contents onto the child's book until the book is completed, allowing the child to keep the table of contents as well as a chapter page both within eyesight at the same time.

TEACHING

Demonstrate how you plan a chapter by saying a bunch of things about each finger (or subtopic) that you will address on that page.

"So if we are going to write a chapter book, 'All about Bike Riding,' and our table of contents page says that one chapter will be about bike riding in the park, our job will be to plan the different things we will write in that chapter. Will you think with me about that? A chapter on bike riding in the park . . . What could the different things be that we say about bike riding in the park? Hmm.

"Oh! One thing that can go in that chapter is some information about the bike races that the grown-up bike riders have. We could tell how they all wear like stretchy outfits."

Andrew piped in, "They sometimes they wear bathing caps but I don't know why."

Notice that I am demonstrating. This is the time for the teacher to do her thing in front of the kids. But I still word this in ways that recruit kids to see this as an effort we are doing together because I know they will learn more from my demonstration if they are participants, not just observers on the sidelines. So watch the way I use the pronoun we *and get them thinking about everything that I model for them. I am convinced they learn more if they are working one step ahead of me and are able to contrast what they were thinking of writing with what I then plan to do.*

I nodded. "That will go in the chapter too. Great idea. I'm trying to think what other topics we could talk about in a chapter about bike riding in the park. Hmm. I could tell about how I got my bike on my birthday, but do you think that would go in this chapter?"

The kids all chimed, "Nooooo."

"So what other topics could go in a chapter on bike riding in the park? Oh!" I said, touching a second finger as I arrived at a second thing I could tell about in my chapter on bike riding in the park. " I could put that they have bike paths all over the place in the park, like miniature roads, only just for bikes. Then I could tell more about those paths. They go to the lake even."

Debrief and then highlight a few especially important tips that are transferable to other topics.

"Writers, did you see how we planned the chapter just like you all planned your whole books? We think of the different things that we'll say." I moved my fingers to show that fingers continue to act as graphic organizers. "We try to say a couple of sentences about each finger—a couple of things about the grown-up bike races, a couple about the kid races, a couple about the paths."

Notice that I deliberately make the mess-up I expect kids to make often and then self-correct. I do this to highlight a point I am trying to make. The chapter acts as a constraint, and the information that doesn't pertain to the topic of the chapter can't go here. I am not at all subtle in the mess-up I make because I want all the kids to grasp the point quickly.

Of course, it is not this hard for me to generate subtopics. I belabor the question to give kids time to do this work alongside me. These are strategies you will see me using repeatedly throughout all the units.

ACTIVE ENGAGEMENT

Set students up to practice planning a second chapter using the book you just started.

"So let's plan a second chapter that could go in this bike riding book, and this one won't be about bike riding in the park. I'm wondering what another chapter could be. What is a whole other thing that might go in a book about bike riding?"

Alex called out, "Cool bikes?"

I nodded. "What an idea. Okay, professors of bike riding. Right now, think about what you might teach in a course on cool bikes. As you think, list the different subtopics you might talk about across your fingers. I'm going to do the same thing, although I have a feeling you know a lot more about cool bikes than I do." I was silent, gazing up at the ceiling so that I looked absolutely lost in thought over the contents of a chapter on cool bikes. As I thought, I moved my hands to progress from one finger to another.

"Whichever partner feels like you know a lot about this topic, will you tell the other partner how you might plan your chapter? And remember to say a little bit about each finger, not just one sentence."

As writers planned down one finger, I coached in, prompting them to elaborate on just the one part they were planning. For example, I overheard Anessa say to Karl, "My bike has streamers on the handlebars. And my sister has a bright purple bike."

Notice that I recruit the kids to help plan and write what then becomes a class text. This book will weave itself through the second bend of this unit. Your kids will offer different input so they'll lead you to a different book. Just watch for the characteristics of the text we develop, using our text to influence yours, as future teaching will rely on some aspect of your book being similar to ours.

I leaned in. "Anessa, can I interrupt you for a moment? You know how we talked about how we are trying to say more than just one sentence for each part? It sounded like the first part of your chapter was going to be about streamers. That *is* cool! But I was surprised when you jumped right to your sister's purple bike. Can you two work together to add some details and examples about just the streamers? Then you can go on to your second finger, where you say at least a couple things about the purple bike."

You may feel uneasy to coach a child publicly. We hope you set aside that sense of unease. Realize that if everyone is working to get better all the time, there is no shame in having more work to do.

LINK

Rally students to use the planning strategy you have transferred from earlier in the unit to plan the chapter they are most ready to write.

"Writers, of course, the real challenge is not to plan a chapter in our class book on bike riding. The real challenge is to plan a chapter in your own book. At the start of the minilesson, you starred a chapter from your table of contents that you are especially ready to write. Right now, would you use your fingers to help plan what you might write? Remember to say one finger-full of information for each part of your chapter. As soon as you have said all you can say about that one finger, go on to the next one. When you have planned with at least two fingers, zip back to your writing spot and get writing as fast as you can and get started writing a chapter. Start by copying the title from your table of contents onto the top of the chapter paper that is in a bin at the center of each table."

Be sure that the paper you leave on the tables reflects the growing expectations you have for children. By this time in first grade, you probably won't have any paper that has less than six or seven lines on a page. You definitely do not want to hold children back by not allowing them the space to grow, and you would be dumbfounded by how influential paper is in conveying expectations. Although today kids are getting their paper from bins at the center of the table and there is very little paper choice, that is not ideal, so see this as a transition. In the end, you will want kids to be able to choose from a variety of paper, but none should resemble the paper children wrote on two months ago. Kids grow very quickly, and the paper needs to anticipate that growth.

CONFERRING AND SMALL-GROUP WORK

Writing Up a Storm

THE GOAL FOR TODAY will be to help children put planning behind them and write up a storm. You absolutely will want to be sure that all of your children write several chapters today and that each chapter contains something like five or six sentences. (It is always hard to lay out expectations like that because, of course, kids are different, but the flip side to that is that if you don't expect kids to produce a lot, they won't. And if your expectations are high, the level of kids' work rises. When we suggest that you make sure all your kids are writing at least two chapters today, with essentially a paragraph of writing in each chapter, remember that many children can do more than that.)

As you work with your kids, the first thing you will want to think about is whether there might be some way for kids to get their plans for a chapter onto the page. You don't want tables of contents for each chapter, of course, but yes, the reality is that this is almost what you are asking kids to do. That is, your hope is that kids write a bunch about one thing related to the chapter heading, then a bunch about another thing related to the chapter heading. Remember that the "Bike Riding in the Park" chapter has a few sentences about grown-up bike races, another few about kid bike races, and then some about bike paths. How do you help kids reach toward the goal of writing that way? Sometimes it helps to suggest kids write some key words down the left margin of their page, almost as if they are gesturing toward using subtitles to plan. That way, in a chapter on feeding your dog, the writer might write down the left margin, "dog's food, dog's treats, dog's water." For some children, these subtopics can be sketched, not recorded in words. For example, a child working on a book about Snoopy may make a fast sketch of Woodstock, of Charlie Brown, and of Sally.

Either way, it will be important for you to sheep-dog kids along so that their plans take five minutes, not half an hour. Remember that children already spent most of yesterday planning a table of contents. So make sure you use voiceovers to remind children that by now, they need to be writing. Say things like "You guys are teachers. People are coming to you to learn tons of information. So write fast and furious; don't stop; keep your hand moving. People want to learn everything you know about the topic."

MID-WORKSHOP TEACHING
Using Voiceovers to Keep Students Writing

Instead of a traditional mid-workshop teaching time, writers today can get the most out of this independent writing time with voiceovers that encourage them to make tracks through their chapters. If some of these voiceovers don't seem right for the whole class, they can instead be channeled to individual students. But mostly these will be the voiceovers you say as children work:

- "Keep working; don't put your pencil down!"
- "Wow, some of you are using some brave and fancy words in your new books. Don't forget to check the rest of the charts for other things you could try!"
- "Stop where you are and reread your page. Make sure what you are writing makes sense!"

Writers Recall the Tips Others Have Given Us

Introduce students to the idea that they can use a new tool to help make their writing even better.

"Writers, today you are going to stay in your seats for our share. You have been working so hard, and in a moment, you'll be able to look over all the great writing you've done today and resolve to make it even better. In fact, I have a tool that can help you. It will help not just for today, but anytime you write."

Tell a story that introduces the tool—labels full of tips that students can use to remind them of the goals for information writing.

"When I am playing tennis and I hit the tennis ball like this," I punched at the air with an imaginary racket, "and the ball bounces into the net, I say to myself, 'Swing at it. Don't punch. The racket has to follow the ball and point to where I want it to go.' I know that tip, and I can coach myself that way because of all the times that other people have given me pointers about how to play tennis better.

"Well, here is the thing. You have been given *lots* of tips about how to write strong teaching books. I've put some of these tips onto a sheet of label paper that I'll pass out to you. Look over these labels full of tips and decide which tip or two would be especially important for *you* to remember, and take that tip right off the label paper and stick it in the margin of your own chapter. Then let that tip help you write better and better" (see Figures 10–1 and 10–2).

FIG. 10–1 Tip sheet printed on label paper

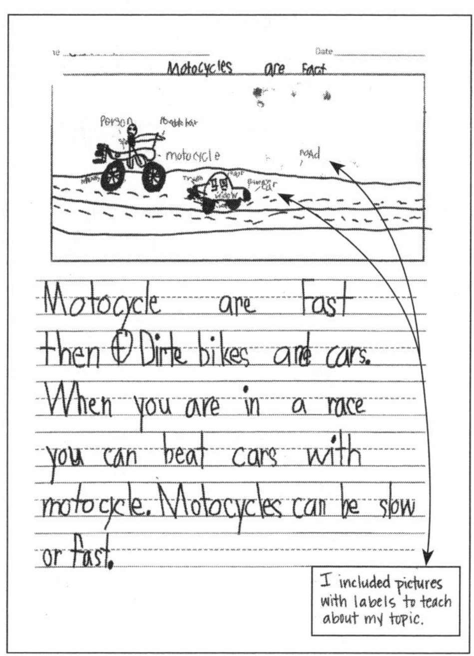

FIG. 10–2 Gabriel added labels to the pictures in his book, "Motorcycles."

Session 11

Writers Write with Details and Help Readers Picture the Details by Using Comparisons

IN THIS SESSION, you'll teach children that nonfiction writers use different strategies to say more and teach others. One strategy is using comparisons to teach.

GETTING READY

- ✔ Mentor text, *Sharks!* (see Teaching)
- ✔ Your own demonstration text that you used in Session 10 (we use bike riding)
- ✔ "How Can I Teach My Readers?" chart, to add to during the link and share

A KINDERGARTEN TEACHER with whom I work recently complained that she could never get her kids to write details. "Over and over, I tell the kids to add details, and over and over, they write in broad sweeping strokes," she said. But then one day she said to a youngster, "I keep asking you to write details. Why don't you?" The little boy looked quizzically at her, and sputtered, "But I got a lot of details." Then he turned his book to a page where the sky was filled with what looked like little balloons with strings hanging from them. "There are my *d*'s," he said, pointing to the balloon shapes, "and there are the tails: de-tails!"

This was a lesson for all the teacher-educators who work with the Teachers College Reading and Writing Project. We think we are communicating and that when kids don't do as we want, they can't or they won't. But of course, sometimes we simply aren't being clear in the first place.

Often, when we ask children to add details to their writing—or to do anything else for that matter—they do not actually know what we mean. In this session, you will not just tell your students to add details, you will show them what details look like and how and why children should be adding them to their writing. Your children added details to their narrative writing, or more specifically, they added dialogue, feelings, and internal thoughts to those pieces of writing. Today you will harken back to that work and help them add details to their teaching books. You will help them to understand that while the most common detail in a story might be dialogue or feelings, in a teaching book, writers elaborate by adding more information—more examples. But you will go a step farther and also help writers grasp that one way to make their examples and their information more detailed, more specific, and that is to use comparisons to say exactly what they want to say.

The focus of today's session, then, is on writing with more detail and, more specifically, writing with bushel loads of details! That is, this session is on the use of comparisons to make one's writing more precise.

COMMON CORE STATE STANDARDS: W.1.2, RI.1.1, SL.1.1, SL.1.4, Sl.1.6, L.1.1.g, L.1.2, L.1.5

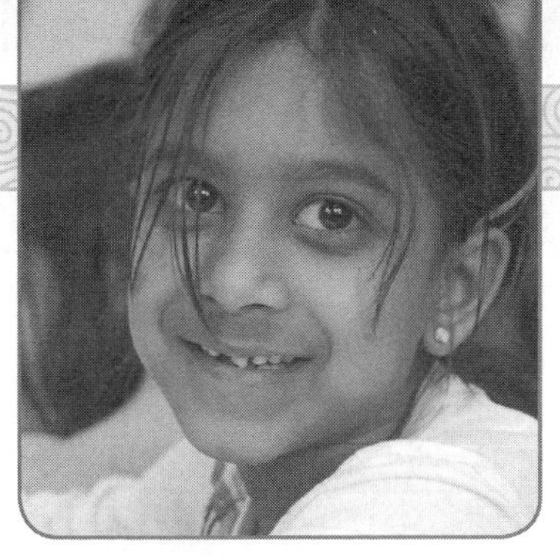

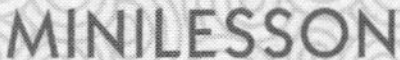

MINILESSON

Writers Write with Details and Help Readers Picture the Details by Using Comparisons

CONNECTION

Remind writers that they already know what it means to write with details. Returning to the teaching book you and the class have been working on, juxtapose what it means to write in summary versus in detail.

"Writers, I know you will all be moving on to write more chapters, and I am pretty sure that sometimes you will get to a chapter and you will think, 'Hmm, I don't have that much to say about this chapter.' For example, let's say we decided to add a chapter to our bike book called 'Getting Ready for a Bike Trip.' And let's say you didn't really have that much to say about how to get ready for a bike trip. You really just wanted to say, 'Bring some food and some water.'

"I have a tip for you that will always, forever, help you to be able to write more. It is a tip you have heard a lot of times already, but here it is. Write with details. So if you want to write a whole page and all you know is 'Bring some food and some water on your bike trip,' the secret is to tell details about the food and tell details about the water.

"'Huh?'" you ask. 'What details could I say about bringing food on a bike trip?' Well, you just think about what you would do and what you wouldn't do, and pretty soon you realize you know some stuff. Like would you pack a lunch containing an ice cream cone? No. Would you just put a jelly sandwich loose in your backpack? No."

Channel kids to quickly practice taking a sweeping generalization pertaining to the class's teaching book and rewriting it as details. Set this work up so that youngsters have quick success at it.

"So right now, pretend you had to write about ten sentences teaching readers all about packing lunch for a bike trip, and this time talk in tiny details about what to do and what not to do. With your partner, figure out what details you could write. Go!"

The class erupted into conversation. I stopped them fairly quickly.

Name the teaching point.

"So, writers, you already know how to write in details. You just sometimes forget to do it. Now today I want to teach you that you don't just tell a fact (a detail). You help readers to picture the fact (the detail) and to understand why it matters. One way you do that is by using comparisons."

◆ COACHING

Often in the connection, you will remind children of what they already know by motioning to a chart, a list. But remember that the best way to bring home what someone has already learned is to share some details about that prior knowledge, to plunge into it a bit deeper. In this connection, you essentially teach a quick review minilesson, one that sets writers up to be ready for the more advanced work in the actual minilesson. You may decide, however, to break this session into two minilessons, given over two days, with the connection as one minilesson and the rest of the minilesson as the second.

TEACHING

Tell a story that illustrates how using a comparison can help readers understand something that is unfamiliar to them.

"Writers, can I tell you a story? The other day my computer froze." I began to dramatize the moment. "I clicked on the mouse and nothing happened. I pressed on the keyboard. Still nothing." I held my head in my hands. "I have a friend who is good with computers, so I called him, and he said, 'I know what the problem is. So much information has been traveling into your computer that it is like there are too many cars on a road, so there is a traffic jam and nothing can move.'

I appreciate the fact that the example here is one that could be used to teach writers of any age. Children benefit when we let them in on more complex ideas.

"Writers, when my friend said that it was like there was a traffic jam of information inside my computer, I could picture what he was saying. And nonfiction writers do that all the time. They compare something that is hard to picture with something that is easy to picture."

Show an example of how a mentor author uses comparison to help readers picture a detail.

"Writers, let me show you how Anne Schreiber uses comparisons in *Sharks!* On page 7, she is teaching all about sharks' skin. She starts off writing a detail. Then she adds a comparison to help readers picture it."

When teaching a technique, it helps to show the same technique in several texts because this highlights the transferable, universal qualities of the technique.

> *Shark skin feels bumpy and rough. It's hard like sandpaper.*

"I have never felt a shark's skin, let me tell you! But I have felt sandpaper many times. Now I can picture the shark's skin."

ACTIVE ENGAGEMENT

Set writers up to try the strategy using a page from your demonstration text.

"Writers, can you try to use comparisons to help readers picture something in our bike riding book? Let's take those paths that bikes ride on. Could you turn and talk with your partner and see if you could compare them to something?"

Notice that I select the particular detail that I hope students think about. By doing this, I accelerate the speed of their work and make it more likely that they'll have success trying the technique I've taught.

I listened in while partners talked to each other, crouching next to a few to help them get started. Julissa said, "The bike paths are like roads. Just smaller."

"Julissa, you're really on to something there," I said. "It might be helpful for people to think about the bike paths as small roads. And that they're just for bikes, not cars."

After I moment, I reconvened the class, and Julissa shared her idea. I said, "Let's try some others, okay? Pretend you were writing a book about airplanes. What could you compare an airplane to?"

The children talked, generating the obvious connections to birds and kites.

"What about if you were writing about the *Tyrannosaurus rex*? To what might you compare its teeth?"

LINK

Remind writers of all of the strategies they know to teach readers.

"Writers, let's add this to our 'How Can I Teach My Readers?' chart." I added "Make a comparison to something they know." "Let's be on the lookout for other ways we can teach more, and we can add those to our list, too. As you go off to write today, remember that your job as writers of *chapter* books is to teach readers as much as you can about your topic. To teach well, you need to say a lot of stuff about your topic. As you go off to write, think about how you can make the new chapters you write today bigger and even more chock-full of great information than ever before."

FIG. 11–1 Comparison from Caroline's book

I know that puppies are cute as cute as bunnies. They are both fluffy. They both have wiggly noses and they both have waggily tails.

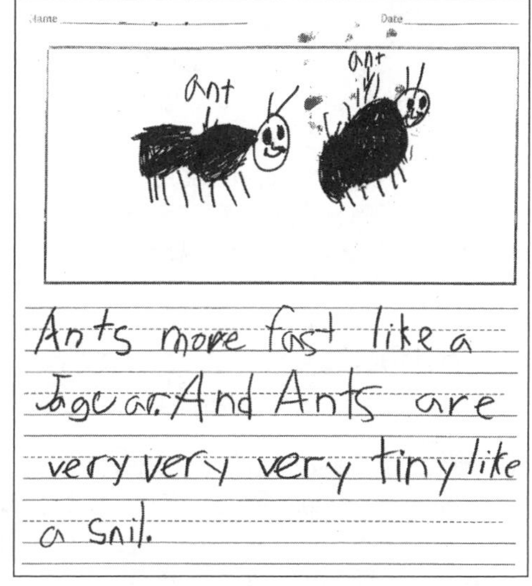

FIG. 11–2 Comparison from Joseph's book, "Ants"

Ants move fast like a jaguar. And ants are very very very tiny like a snail.

CONFERRING AND SMALL-GROUP WORK

Conferring to Ensure Students Have Grasped the Essentials of the Unit

KEEP IN MIND THE BIG PICTURE of all that you need to support today. Just because your minilesson illuminated the fact that writers of informational texts include details and sometimes use comparisons to help readers picture things does not mean you will want to pound that one point home in each conference. Your conferences and small-group work can sometimes scaffold students to try the work of the minilesson, but it is more common for you to use worktime as a chance to support all the essentials. Today's lesson was enrichment. If some kids pick this up and make great use of it, that is wonderful. But you should approach today already knowing that you can also use today to support essentials in the unit.

You'll recall that many children began their chapter books with tables of contents that were fashioned in ways that made it likely that the children would end up finding that they simply didn't have enough to say in some chapters. Remember that chapter on dog's ears? No matter how detailed the child gets in his writing, it is unlikely that a six-year-old will have a lot of success writing on a very tightly focused subtopic like that. So part of your time today might be devoted to helping students rethink their original plans for their books in light of what they are now discovering.

Then, too, you will find that the idea of dividing a big topic into related subtopics and then writing all about a subtopic on one page is not as easy as it sounds. In the midst of a chapter on one subtopic, children will skid right into other topics.

Of course, some writers will take to writing with comparisons. They're apt to have five conflicting comparisons on a single page. The bike paths are like roads that bikes fly down like planes, going as fast as race cars. All of us overuse whatever we first learn, and in time we become more moderated.

For children who take to comparisons, instead of helping them get PhDs in comparisons, you might suggest they work together to mine yet more incredible lessons from the mentor text (see Figure 11–2). Leave four kids with the book and with a pack of Post-its and charge them with finding yet more things that the mentor text does that they could try.

MID-WORKSHOP TEACHING **Writers Reread, Looking for General Statements to Expand with More Detail**

"Writers, remember that we began today by saying that sometimes you forget to write in details? Like you will write 'It is good to pack a lunch if you are going on a long bike ride,' but then you don't tell any of the details about wrapping the food up and which food works well for that sort of a lunch.

"If you finish your book, instead of starting a new one, you might want to reread and revise your book. One thing you can do is reread, looking for places in any of your chapters where you wrote a big general thing like 'Dogs like to do tricks' and forgot to add, 'for example' so you can tell the detailed tricks that dogs do.

"If you reread and you find sentences where you wrote the big general things, you can just use a flap, tape it onto the page, and write, 'For example, . . .' and then tell a lot of details.

"Listen to Sasha's chapter, for example. If you hear a place where she wrote a big general thing, give a thumbs up."

I am going to teach you all about writing workshop. In writing workshop we write a lot of different kinds of things. We work very hard.

By now, some children had already signaled. I nodded and reread so that all of them heard the general statement. "If Sasha got a half sheet of paper and taped it onto the edge of her book and wrote details, what might she say?"

Soon the children had listed all the kinds of writing they'd done so far and were rereading their own books to find similar big general statements.

SHARE

Adding Details to Writing to Help Readers Get the Point

Highlight one student who added a lot of detail to his or her writing, showing how adding comparisons, examples, or other details to one's writing helps readers to understand what the writer is trying to convey.

After convening the students on the rug, I said, "Writers, I saw so many of you writing with detail today. Some of you helped your reader picture what you were writing about by comparing your subject, your thing, to something else. Others of you took a general statement and elaborated on it by writing examples. This is great work, writers. When you write with detail, including comparisons and examples in your books, you can be sure that your reader will learn all there is to know about your topic.

"Let's take a closer look at Riley's book, 'Places in Long Island City.' She gives her reader tons of examples throughout the entire book, so that they can learn *all* about Long Island City—and not just a little bit. This part here, the chapter about the Food Cellar, shows how Riley makes sure she teaches her readers all of the information about the neighborhood grocery store. In this chapter, she writes":

> Food Cellar sells you food. You can buy bread and you can buy cereal and you can buy chips.

"Riley could have written, 'Food Cellar sells you food' and stopped there, but she didn't. Nope! Riley kept going, giving examples of some of the food you can buy. The more examples she gives, the more her readers learn. Quickly reread the book you brought with you to the rug and find a place (or two!) where you added details—a comparison or an example or something else—so that you can be sure your reader will learn all there is to know about your topic. Once you've found a place, turn and share with your partner."

As the students shared, I added "Give an example" to the "How Can I Teach My Readers?" chart.

FIG. 11–3

Session 12

Different Kinds of Writing in Teaching Books

Chapters Can Contain How-To Writing, Persuasive Writing, and Stories

IN THIS SESSION, you'll teach children that writers draw on everything they have already learned to teach their readers, including writing how-to pages, persuasive writing, and stories in their teaching books.

GETTING READY

- ✓ Paper choice options for the writing center: full-page diagram paper, how-to paper, narrative paper, list paper, teaching paper
- ✓ Sample student chapters that could be how-to pages
- ✓ How-To paper to hold up for students to see during the connection
- ✓ Chart paper and markers, to write the guiding questions of the lesson (see Connection)
- ✓ Sample child's how-to text (see Teaching)
- ✓ Sample lists from other texts, such as a glossary of terms or a list of questions and answers (see Active Engagement)
- ✓ How-To paper and list paper, to pass out at the end of the active engagement
- ✓ Information Writing Checklist, Grades 1 and 2

Common Core State Standards: W.1.1, W.1.2, W.1.3, W.1.5, RI.1.1, SL.1.1, SL.1.5, L.1.1, L.1.2

IT IS A GREAT FEELING IN LIFE to find that you can draw on what you already know to be more proficient at something you had expected would be totally new for you. For your children, this unit can provide that same rush, that same sense of "Oh wow! I'm not as new to this as I thought." Here's why.

A nonfiction chapter book is apt to contain chapters that reflect the genre that children have already studied. For example, a book on bike riding is definitely apt to contain a chapter with a title such as "How to Do Wheelies." And if your children were in a writing workshop throughout kindergarten, chances are good that they already know how to write that chapter. They know all about writing in steps, including cautionary tips, relying on labeled teaching pictures, using transition words that sequence the activity, and the like.

Teaching chapter books often contain other kinds of writing as well. For example, a book on bike riding might contain a persuasive chapter, perhaps advocating a way to solve the problem of children who live where streets aren't safe for bike riding. Again, children who have grown up in a writing workshop can be reminded that they already know how to use persuasive writing, filled with opinions and reasons, to solve problems in the world.

Then, too, informational books often contain lists. A book on soccer is apt to have a chapter about soccer teams or soccer stars or the positions in a soccer team. In any of those cases, that information could be written in the genre of a list. Perhaps a list does not qualify as a genre, but certainly it is something that kids could profit from learning to write with deliberateness.

Today's minilesson reminds children that when approaching a new piece of writing—and a new chapter qualifies as a new piece of writing—it is always helpful to think, "What kind of writing will I be doing?" and then to set oneself up to write according to the form or genre of that kind of writing. And children should realize they can notice how other authors organize their chapters, and attempt to write in a similar way. This sort of text study and experimentation can lead children to write pages that are glossaries or that are organized into a question-answer framework or a host of other options.

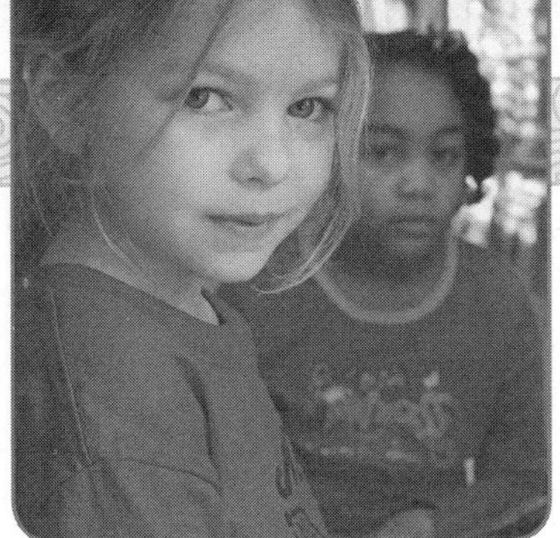

MINILESSON

Different Kinds of Writing in Teaching Books

Chapters Can Contain How-To Writing, Persuasive Writing, and Stories

CONNECTION

Provide students with an example of a different genre—a how-to page or a narrative story—within an informational text.

"Writers, bring your folders with you when you come to the meeting area." Once children had settled, I continued. "Will you quickly get out the book you are working on?"

Once all the children had their books in front of them, I continued. "Writers, Rachel just discovered the coolest thing. She was working on a book about horses and was starting to write one of her chapters, titled 'How to Canter Your Horse,' and she stopped and said. 'Wait a minute. Holy moly. This chapter is called '*How to* Canter. . . .' That means this is a how-to page, like the how-to books we wrote last year.' How many of you remember writing how-to books when you were younger?" Many hands shot up.

Have students search their chapter books for pages that could be written in a different form or genre.

"So, Partner 2, put your book between you and your partner and will the two of you look through the book and see if you, like Rachel, have a chapter that already could be a how-to chapter?"

As the children looked at their books, I helped them see that a number of them did have pages that could have been how-to pages, had they only realized it. "Listen to these chapters and give me a thumbs up if this could have been a how-to page," I said. Then I listed some that I'd just seen:

> You Can Get a Headband at a Store (from the book "Headbands around the World")
>
> Flat Surfaces (from the book "Coloring")
>
> Pizza Men Make Pizza (from the book "Community Workers")

◆ COACHING

In an instance like this, when my teaching champions what one child has done and that child is not in your classroom, you'll of course want to find your own example of a child who has done similar work. In this instance, the writer didn't need to be making a how-to text. The important part is that the writer is making a kind of text that the class has studied.

"Writers, here is a challenge. Would you and your partner think about whether, if I gave you how-to paper," and I held some up (see Figure 12–1), "you could rewrite the how-to chapter you already have or write a new how-to chapter? The new how-to chapter would need to go with your whole book. What could you teach people how to do? Turn and talk."

Name the teaching point.

"My point is not really that you have how-to pages in your books, although you do (or you could). No, the thing I want to teach you is bigger than that. I want to teach you that whenever a writer goes to write something new—even if it is a chapter, not a book—the writer pauses and thinks, 'What kind of writing am I making?' Then the writer makes sure that his or her writing follows the rules of that kind of writing."

I wrote the question "What kind of writing am I making?" on the chart paper. Then I wrote, "What are the rules of that kind of writing?"

TEACHING

Using the shared book that you and the class have been writing, solicit children to join you in thinking about the kind of text your upcoming chapters might be. Once children are engaged, demonstrate how you would go about thinking about this.

"So let's think about the kinds of writing we might do in our book about bike riding. Do you remember the other day we talked about how we might include a chapter that talked about packing a lunch for a bike trip? I suggested it would be better not to write, 'We should pack food for a bike picnic,' but that, instead, it helps to write with details. So if we were to describe how to pack a picnic lunch for a bike trip, we could just start writing. But today we learned that it helps to ask, 'What kind of writing am I making?'

"What kind of writing would a chapter be that was called 'How to Pack for a Bike Picnic'?"

The kids, of course, were primed to realize this would be a how-to text and called this out. I nodded. "Now, the next thing to do, remember, is to think, 'What are the rules of that kind of writing?' or 'How does that kind of writing usually go?'

"Let's see if we can remember how how-to writing usually goes, so we can make sure our chapter, 'How to Pack for a Bike Picnic' follows those rules. Hmm."

I displayed a child's how-to text and said, "Oh, yes, it is written in steps, right, with a drawing for each step. And lots of teaching labels."

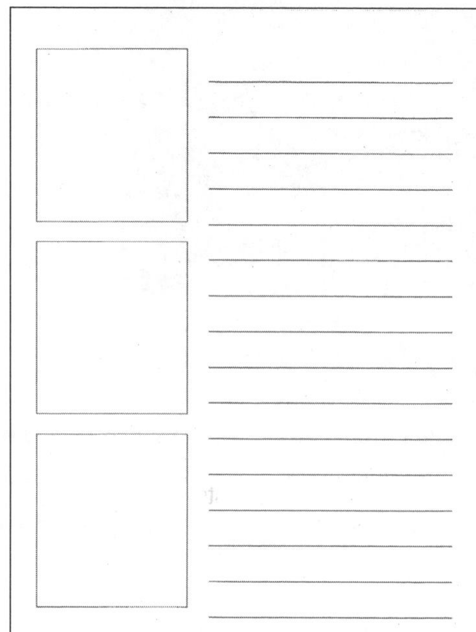

FIG. 12–1 Sample how-to paper

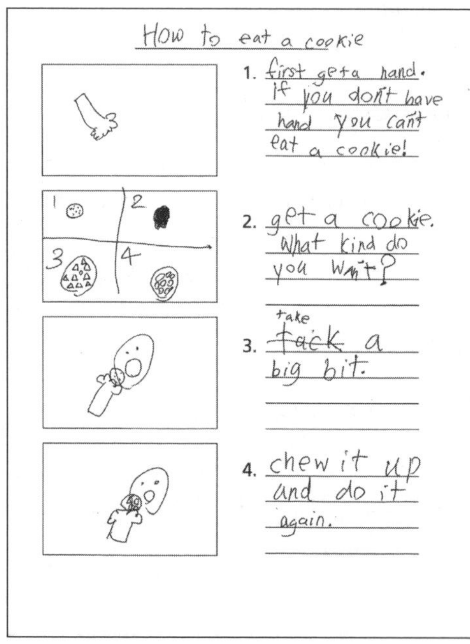

FIG. 12–2 Using numbered steps can help tell "how to."

ACTIVE ENGAGEMENT

Channel children to practice taking time to think, "What kind of text am I about to make?" Do this with especially concrete and simple kinds of writing.

"But let's say we wanted to write a chapter about the different kinds of bikes, and we wanted to tell that there are tricycles and dirt bikes and motor bikes. What kind of writing would that be, and—here is the harder question—what are the rules for that kind of writing? Let's see if we can figure that out," I said. "Turn and talk."

Julie said, "So would it be a list, like of bikes?"

I nodded, fascinated by the suggestion. "And what is the harder question that we need to ask next?" I asked and gestured to the question on the chart paper. Children read it aloud together. "What are the rules of the kind of writing?"

Marco said, "The rules of lists?" When I agreed that the job was to think about how lists tend to go, about the rules of lists, he said, "Well, you put all the things down." I gestured for him to say more. "You have a little bit of information about one thing and then the next and the next."

I showed the students a few different lists from different books: a glossary of terms and a list of questions and answers.

Debrief in ways that help writers transfer what they are learning to the books they are writing.

I passed out two kinds of paper: a page of how-to paper and a page of list paper. "Writers, right now will you and your partner work together to see if there is a how-to page or a list page that you could write for *your* book?"

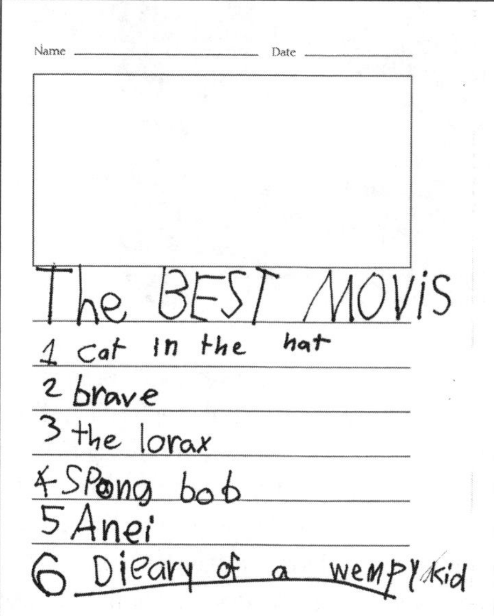

FIG. 12–3

LINK

Send children off to write more chapters, encouraging them to take the time, before they start a chapter, to ask, "What kind of writing am I making?" "What are the rules of that kind of writing?"

"I know you are dying to get to work on your own writing. Will you bring out your table of contents and think about which chapters you have already written and which you are going to write today? You can probably get two written today. Right now, point to one chapter on your table of contents that you are going to write today."

The kids did this. "So before you write, you have a lot to do. You still want to plan the chapter across your fingers, thinking about all the stuff you might say in it. But you also want to ask, 'What kind of writing am I making?' If you are writing a how-to chapter, use the paper with steps on it. If you are writing a list, use the list paper. And if you are writing some other kind of writing, surprise me. Show me the idea *you* come up with! Get started."

You always want your minilessons to be multi-level. Leaving open the possibility that children might come to the conclusion that they could write other kinds of writing—stories, persuasive letters, jokes, maps, mysteries—allows space for writers who want to think outside of the box.

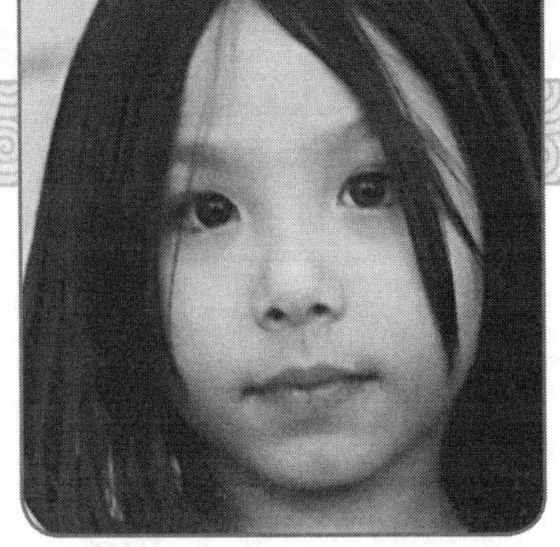

CONFERRING AND SMALL-GROUP WORK

Support Volume and Thoughtfulness

As YOU CONFER TODAY, you'll again want to light a fire under your students so that they write several chapters in a day. To promote fluency, it helps to remind children to write in sentences of thought, not in phrases. So instead of thinking, "My cat" and writing that and then thinking, "makes faces," you'll coach writers to think of a whole idea and then write it, not stopping until they have written the whole idea: "My cat makes faces." If the child seems accustomed to taking a little break at the conclusion of every sentence, point this out and encourage the child to keep writing, not stopping for that breather until reaching the end of the chapter. "Keep going. Don't stop," you can coach. Soon the child has written more.

> My cat makes faces. Some faces are happy. Some faces are sad.

If the child seems at a loss for what to say next, you can always encourage the writer to add his or her thoughts. "What do you think about that?" When the child starts to tell you what she thought, act fascinated, but don't hear the whole thought out. Instead, say, "Write it, fast and furious, before you lose the thought. Don't stop. Just write." This particular child produced this thought.

> If your cat has a mad face on, you should lean down and say, "I'm sorry."

"What an expert you are. I can't believe how much I am learning from your book," you can say. "What are you going to teach me next?"

Promoting volume, supporting elaboration, and teaching with high expectations and great respect—these all go together. Think about times in your life when you have gone to tell someone something you know, and halfway through talking to that person, you realize she is not listening. All of a sudden you feel like you have nothing to say anymore.

MID-WORKSHOP TEACHING **Writers Also Include Small Moment Stories in Their Teaching Books**

"Writers, can I interrupt you for a moment? Tamara just did something wise. She was writing her book on soccer, and she said, 'There is another kind of paper that I want to use to write my chapter on scoring my first goal.' Then she asked if it would be okay if she used story paper to write her chapter, and pretty soon she'd written a Small Moment story about scoring her first goal—putting that paper inside her soccer book."

"When Tamara said, 'There is another kind of paper I want to use,' I think she actually meant that there is another kind of writing that she wanted to include in her chapter book on soccer. And she was right. We've talked about a few kinds of writing today, but the truth is there are lots more kinds of writing than the ones we have listed, including stories.

"So, writers, let's say that in our bike riding book, we want to write a chapter titled 'The Day I Got My First Bike.' Will we write a how-to page for this chapter?"

Children called out, "Nooooo!" I acted surprised and said, "Then what type of writing should we make?" Some children whispered, "Stories," while others thought for a moment.

I continued. "Writers, lets add stories to the kinds of writing we've been doing today. Even though you are writing teaching books now, not stories, you might decide that one chapter in your teaching book should be a Small Moment story. Back to work!"

On the other hand, think about times when people have listened, spellbound, to your thoughts and insights, raptly following your points and asking questions that show a deep fascination in your knowledge. All of a sudden you feel as if you could hold court forever on that topic. You find yourself realizing you know more than you ever thought. That sort of listening is what will prime the pump in your children and help them write with gusto.

You also want to be careful to welcome what they produce. The page I quoted above is on my mind because when a first-grader produced that page, her teacher was upset that she'd used the first-person pronoun *I* in an information book. The teacher wanted her to write about cats without drawing on any of her own experience. It is understandable that sometimes you can feel pressured by the world to teach that way, but don't go there. The great best-selling nonfiction writers would never dream of not using the first-person pronoun. Even this book, frankly, is a nonfiction, information book, and there is lots of use of the first-person pronoun.

As you listen to children and encourage them to write in their own voices and to include their own ideas, you'll find that teaching responsively leads you to grow your own teaching ideas. Go for it!

SHARE

Using the Information Writing Checklist to Self-Assess

Channel students to self-assess as writers of information texts, returning to the Information Writing Checklist.

After calling students back to the meeting area, I said, "Writers, you've been working so hard today on writing chapters for your teaching books. Many of you have added how-to chapters and lists and even chapters with whole-page diagrams and stories. This is amazing work, writers. You also used our Information Writing Checklist—and similar checklists for writing narratives and how-to books—to help make sure you were including everything in your chapter that the type of writing calls for.

"Let's return to our Information Writing Checklist and take a look at what things you are getting better at as writers of teaching books, and what things you may still need to work on." (This checklist can be found on the CD-ROM.)

Information Writing Checklist

	Grade 1	NOT YET	STARTING TO	YES!	Grade 2	NOT YET	STARTING TO	YES!
	Structure				**Structure**			
Overall	I taught my readers about a topic.	☐	☐	☐	I taught readers some important points about a subject.	☐	☐	☐
Lead	I named my topic in the beginning and got my readers' attention.	☐	☐	☐	I wrote a beginning in which I named a subject and tried to interest readers.	☐	☐	☐
Transitions	I told different parts about my topic on different pages.	☐	☐	☐	I used words such as *and* and *also* to show I had more to say.	☐	☐	☐
Ending	I wrote an ending.	☐	☐	☐	I wrote some sentences or a section at the end to wrap up my piece.	☐	☐	☐
Organization	I told about my topic part by part.	☐	☐	☐	My writing had different parts. Each part told different information about the topic.	☐	☐	☐
	Development				**Development**			
Elaboration	I put facts in my writing to teach about my topic.	☐	☐	☐	I used different kinds of information in my writing such as facts, definitions, details, steps, and tips	☐	☐	☐
Craft	I used labels and words to give facts.	☐	☐	☐	I tried to include the words that showed I'm an expert on the topic.	☐	☐	☐
	Language Conventions				**Language Conventions**			
Spelling	I used all I knew about words and chunks (*at, op, it,* etc.) to help me spell.	☐	☐	☐	I used what I knew about spelling patterns (*tion, er, ly,* etc.) to spell a word.	☐	☐	☐
	I spelled the word wall words right and used the word wall to help me spell other words.	☐	☐	☐	I spelled all of the word wall words correctly and used the word wall to help me figure out how to spell other words.	☐	☐	☐

Rally students to celebrate the things they are doing well, and encourage them to think about areas in which they can continue to grow.

"Writers, I'm going to read through the list, and as I do, will you think about whether you are doing each item in the teaching book you are working on today? If you are, that's great, writers. Continue with that goal each time you start a new teaching book. If you are not doing the item in your teaching book, this is something you can do as you revise the book you worked on today or as you start new teaching books tomorrow. Also, as I read, star or mark the places that show you are doing that work. After I'm done, you'll have a chance to share with your partner the ways you are becoming an expert at writing teaching books." I pointed to each item as I read them aloud to children, and then gave them several minutes to turn and talk, showing their partner their "expert" work, as I listened in.

Introductions and Conclusions

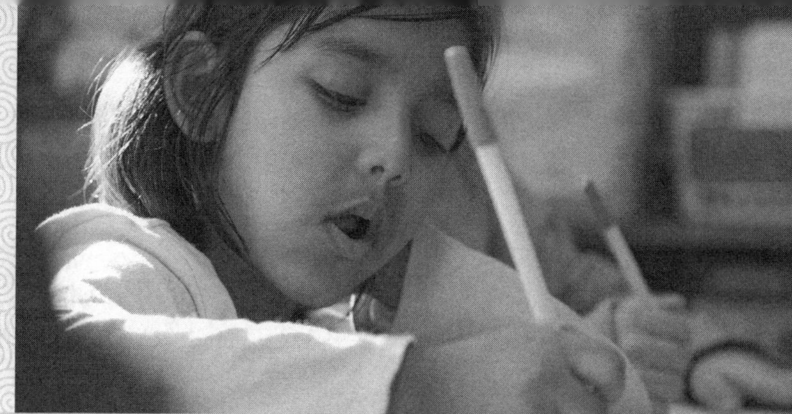

Dear Teachers,

Pascal once said, "The last thing one settles in writing a book is what one should put in first." That sounds backward—writing the beginning at the end—but the beginning of a book often helps the reader know what to expect, almost like the beginning of a tour might, and it is not until a book is finished that the writer really knows what the book will contain. We suggest, then, that this session be a time for you to teach children about writing the introductions and conclusions to information books. The topic is an important one because introductions and conclusions add structure and form to a book and also link the reader to the book.

This lesson is also important because in the land of the Common Core, writing introductions and conclusions is one of the main ways that expectations for first-grade writers of informative/explanatory texts differ from expectations for kindergarten writers of informative/explanatory texts. Kindergartners' main tasks, according to the Common Core, are to name what they are writing about and supply some information. First-graders must do this as well, and in addition must name a topic and provide a sense of closure.

Your children will have already been introduced to the concept of beginnings and endings. Although the introductions and conclusions in first-graders' books need not be more than a sentence in length, to do this work really well, a writer must think about the whole of his or her text and think also about why the information matters.

MINILESSON

One possible way to begin your minilesson might be to help children think about the fact that every school day has a beginning and an ending. Every summer has a beginning and an ending. Every book has a beginning and an ending. It would be confusing indeed if there were no beginnings and endings to a school day, a summer, or a book. You will want your teaching point to be crystal clear. You might say something like "Today I want to teach

Common Core State Standards: W.1.2, W.1.7, RI.1.1, RI.1.2, SL.1.1, L.1.1, L.1.2

you that when you write a teaching book, readers expect that your writing, like a school day, will have a beginning and an ending. And readers expect that at the start of your writing, like at the start of a school day, there will be ways you tell readers the big things that they will be learning about and usually how the learning will go—what will come first and next."

For the teaching component of the minilesson, you might want to point out that it is helpful at the start of the school day to show children the schedule for the day. An introduction at the start of a book, and the table of contents, too, act like the schedule for the day. They help people know what they will learn so people can get ready for that learning.

Then you might show children a few different ways that authors have started their books, reminding them that they are looking at this to get ideas for how to write the very start of their own books.

Sharks!, by Anne Schreiber, begins:

What is quick?

What is quiet?

What has five rows of teeth?

What glides through the water?

CHOMP!

It's a shark!

Change It!, by Adrienne Mason (2006), begins with the following lines.

Matter is all around you.

You are matter, a toy boat is matter and water is matter.

Matter is anything that takes up space.

Matter can be a solid, a liquid or a gas.

You could point out that Anne Schreiber begins her book with questions. The questions pull her readers in and get them to think, "What is quick, quiet, and has five rows of teeth?" Adrienne Mason, on the other hand, gives an overview of her topic in her introduction. The facts she provides on the first page in her book give readers the topic they will learn about right away. With this, you can show children that sometimes writers wait to introduce their topic, while others teach about their topics right off the bat, not waiting until the middle of their chapters to give some of the most important information about their topic. Of course, you may want to share other introductions with students from the class's favorite informational books.

Then, in the active engagement, you could guide writers to study other mentor texts you have chosen in a similar fashion, looking closely at the texts' introductions and thinking about what the authors did that they could try in their own books. You might also consider making a quick one-day chart to capture in writing what your students are noticing. You might start a chart with the heading: "Introductions can . . . " and bullets such as start with a question, start with an action, start with a little story that pulls the reader in, and start with a big idea about the topic.

You could decide also to channel children to go back and look at the books they wrote during the first bend in the unit and to reconsider their beginnings, thinking about alternatives. Because they wrote so many books, reconsidering them will give the readers plenty of practice. Of course, children can also talk with partners about several different possible ways they could begin their chapter books. Nudging children to generate and choose between options is a wise idea.

CONFERRING AND SMALL-GROUP WORK

As you confer with writers, you may gather a group to study how a variety of informational books begin. Taking time to linger over and name the moves writers make across a variety of texts will show a repertoire of introductions. You may want to add to the chart you started during the minilesson with students' new observations. You will find that authors typically ask questions, introduce the topic, or begin with some of the same craft moves in small moments: sound words, action words, and so on. You can do the same study around conclusions. A group can gather around some informational books and study how they conclude. You can help students name some of the big things authors tend to do in their endings: give a message or an idea, connect to the beginning, send the person off to get more information.

You could also point out that writers of teaching books often talk to the reader in the introduction and the conclusion and, in fact, all the way through the book, asking the reader questions.

MID-WORKSHOP TEACHING

Then, in your mid-workshop teaching, you will want to shift your focus to conclusions. Conclusions leave the reader with a big thought or idea. Children could do the same work with endings that they have done with beginnings—making a chart of ways to end a book, studying endings in books they know, rereading their earlier books to reconsider their endings, or composing alternate endings for their chapter book. This is a lot to do, and I am not suggesting students would be able to do it all.

SHARE

Then, because tomorrow will likely be the last day your writers will spend on their current books, you may want to encourage them to spend the next fifteen minutes or so working like the wind to get all their pages done. That is, you could skip the share, giving writers a bit more time to develop their writing and to feel as if they've gotten something developed that has yet to see the light of day.

Good luck!

Lucy, Kristi, and Barb

Session 14

Fix Up Writing by Pretending to Be a Reader

IN THIS SESSION, you'll teach children that nonfiction writers fix up their writing for readers by pretending to be a reader and also by thinking, "Does this match what I know about how to write this kind of writing well?"

GETTING READY

- ✔ Page 1 of the mentor text, *Sharks!*, enlarged (see Connection)
- ✔ A student's teaching book, containing punctuation and spelling errors (this can be a book from your class or another class or an anonymous child's writing)
- ✔ "Ways to Spell Words" chart from Session 5, to reference during teaching
- ✔ Students' teaching books, to practice rereading and editing
- ✔ Star stickers, for students to mark the chapters they want to share (see Share)
- ✔ Designated areas for two partnerships or four students to meet and celebrate their writing (see Share)
- ✔ Sample student teaching books, edited, for the share

COMMON CORE STATE STANDARDS: W.1.2, W.1.5, RI.1.10, RFS.1.4, SL.1.1, L.1.1.d,g; L.1.2.c,d,e

THIS SESSION BRINGS THE CONCEPT OF AUDIENCE into the editing work you'll ask your writers to do. All year, you have been reminding your students that they are writing for readers, just like professional writers write for real audiences. And you have asked students to consider their audience with questions like "How can you teach your reader that?" and "What questions would your reader have?" Today students will continue this work of thinking about their reader, but this time with a focus on editing rather than drafting. Today students will ask themselves, "How can I make my writing clear for my reader?" and "Will my reader be able to read what I have written?"

Today, then, you will transfer the editing work students did in Session 7 of the *Small Moments* unit to the editing work you will ask them to do in their teaching books. In the *Small Moments* unit, you taught children that writers go from being the writer to being the reader. And when writers reread their own books, they read just as if they were reading a published book. In that session, you taught children to reread their stories so that they could catch if something didn't make sense—misspellings, missing punctuation, missing words, and so on.

"Today, students will ask themselves, 'How can I make my writing clear for my reader?'"

This session continues that work but asks children to apply their growing knowledge of language and mechanics to the writing they are doing in this unit. The Common Core State Language Standards state that by the end of first grade, students will, among other expectations, use end punctuation, use commas in a list, spell high-frequency words correctly, and use inventive spelling for less common spelling patterns. Repeated work around these standards helps them become accessible, just like your tennis backhand or that recipe you have been making for fifteen years. It is essential, therefore, that you have sessions like this one that remove the multiple demands of writing to focus on just one: editing. In this session, your students' books are written and their attention shifts to rereading with a singular focus on language and mechanics.

This session also has a powerful reciprocal relationship with reading. When you ask your children to reread their own writing fluently, you are working to build their understanding of pace, prosody, and phrasing, As your children get closer and closer to levels G and H, your emphasis on fluent reading has probably grown exponentially. Level H signals the start of the transitional stage of reading development, a stage that emphasizes fluency. Therefore, you may want to leave some extra time at the end of the lesson for your end-of-workshop share so that you can set writers up to share parts of their chapter books in small groups, celebrating both the increasing clarity of their writing and the increasing fluency of their reading.

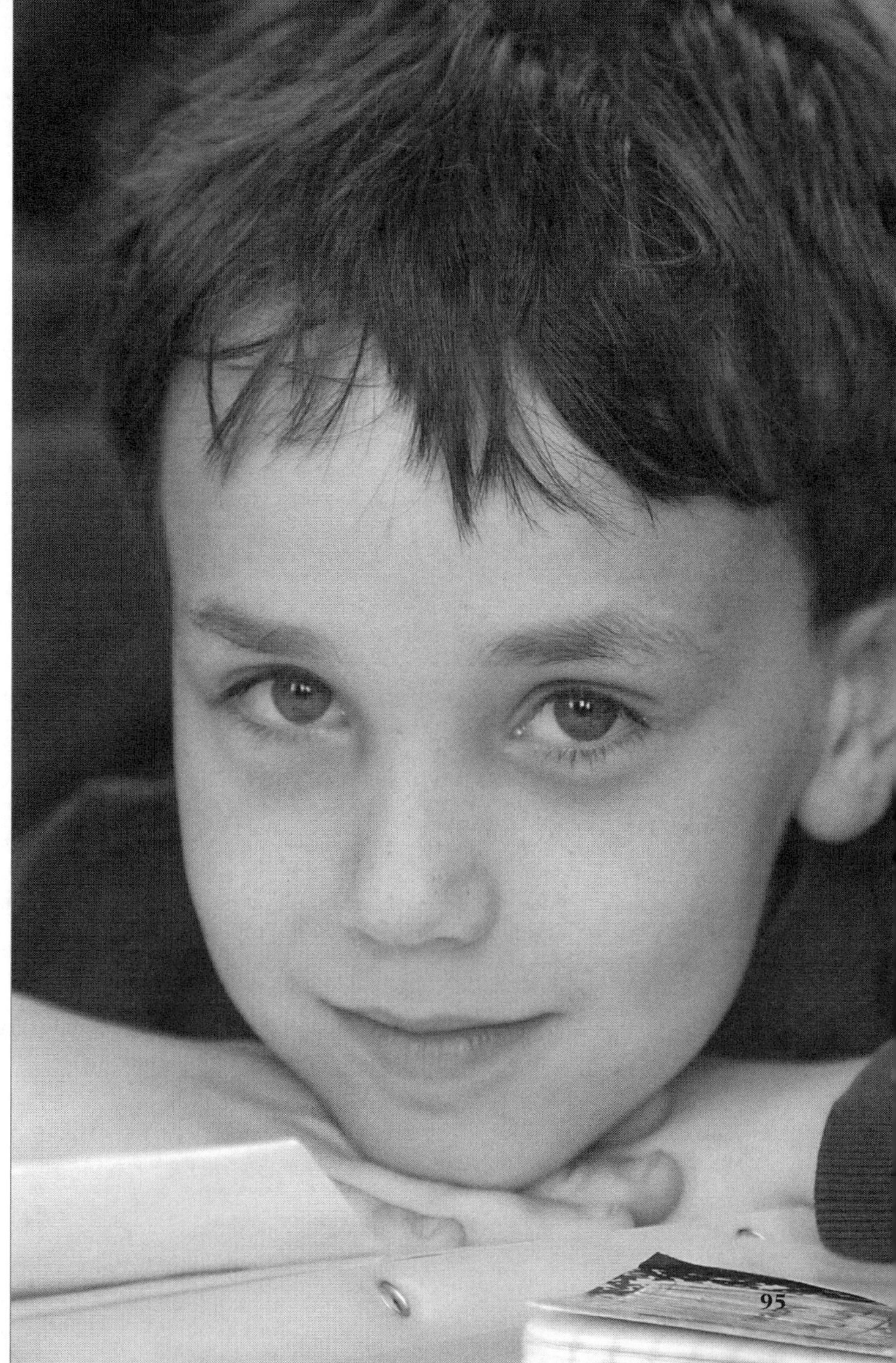

MINILESSON

Fix Up Writing by Pretending to Be a Reader

CONNECTION

Reread the introduction of *Sharks!* in a smooth voice, with dramatic emphasis on the punctuation.

"Writers, let's go back to one of our favorite pages in *Sharks!* And when we read it together, let's really focus on making our voices match the punctuation and sound smooth like talking." I displayed the first page of *Sharks!* and put my finger by the lines as we read them aloud.

> *What is quick?*
>
> *What is quiet?*
>
> *What has five rows of teeth?*
>
> *What glides through the water?*
>
> *CHOMP!*
>
> *It's a shark!*

"One of the things I love about the page is how Anne Schreiber wrote it in a way that makes it fun to read it aloud. It is so easy to read. That got me thinking that Anne probably reread her writing carefully, checking to make sure it sounded good and to make sure there weren't any mistakes or confusing parts. She probably did that so that her readers could read it as smoothly as we just did. Later today, we are going to have a mini-teaching session in which we teach each other all about the topics we've been writing about. But first, we need to get our books ready."

Rally children for the editing work ahead by connecting it to previous work they did with their Small Moment stories.

"And writers, it dawned on me that if we want to get your books ready for readers, to publish them, you'll need to reread your book, checking that you have spelled everything the best you can and that you have checked your writing for punctuation and capitals. One way you can reread your writing is to pretend you are the reader, reading it for the first time. You did this with your Small Moment stories at the beginning of the year. And now you can do it with your teaching books. Writers do this a lot. They take a step back from their writing and pretend to be the reader. They do this so they can catch things they didn't notice while writing."

◆ COACHING

Notice that I regularly return to one or two texts that youngsters come to know very well. Because children know these texts, I can focus on just a page or two where the author has done something we hope students will do as well. I can bypass most of the book to focus on one page, and yet students have the whole book in mind.

The connection actually teaches content that is more sophisticated than that which is forwarded in the minilesson. You might remind your more proficient readers that the sounds of their texts matter.

Name the teaching point.

"Today I want to teach you that when writers get ready to publish, they first reread their writing, thinking about how to get it ready for their readers. And one way they get their books ready for their readers is by pretending to be the reader, checking for any mistakes or confusing parts."

TEACHING

Demonstrate reading a page from a child's teaching book, either from your class, another class, or an anonymous child's writing, pausing at confusing parts or spelling mistakes.

"Writers, a student from another class, Philip, said it would be okay if we help him get his 'Car Racing' book ready for readers. Let's read his first chapter and look for places that are difficult or confusing to read. I have enlarged the pages of his book. I'll start reading the first page. As I do, will you remember to give me the stop sign," I motioned with my hand up in the air, "in case I forget to stop and check as I am rereading the first page?"

I sat up straight and cleared my throat, making a big show of the important work we were about to do. I started with the first sentence, reading slowly and dramatically, pointing to the words on my chart as I read them.

> Car racing is cool.

I paused and looked at the class. "That felt pretty good when I read it. I could say all of the words, so they are probably spelled right, and there was a period at the end to show me to pause. I'm going to try the next part." As I read the next part, I made a show of not pausing between parts and of getting stuck on the words *nmbrs* and *hlmts*.

> The cars have nmbrs on them drivers wear hlmts.

Revise in front of students, adding end punctuation and checking spelling.

"Writers, that part was *much* harder to read. I think there might be some things in this part we can help Phillip fix. First, I felt out of breath at the end, like I had gone for too long without taking a pause. I'm going to take another look at the punctuation. Hmm, I think this part, 'The cars have nmbrs on them,' is really one sentence, and 'drivers wear hlmts' is really another." I reread with punctuation and still made a point about not being sure how to read *nmbrs* and *hlmts*. "I think it would feel good to take a big pause between those two parts. I'm going to put a period after *them* and put a capital *D* on *Drivers*. Also, I really struggled with the words *nmbrs* and *hlmts*. I don't think they're spelled right. What could we tell Philip to do to check the spelling?" "Check the word wall!" Kevin called out. "Sound it out slowly," Takuma said.

"Great ideas. I could also have him look at our 'Ways to Spell Words' chart if he's still stuck." I pointed to the chart.

FIG. 14–1

Remember that you are role-playing Philip—a child the children don't know.

FIG. 14–2

ACTIVE ENGAGEMENT

Set writers up to try out the strategy of reading parts out loud and checking parts that are difficult or confusing to read.

"Writers, did you see how I did that? I read Philip's first chapter out loud in parts, stopping at parts that were hard to read and checking for anything that needed to be fixed. Now you guys are going to have a chance to try. Here is Philip's next chapter. Would you read the whole thing out loud? Read kind of quietly to yourself so you're not disturbing others but loud enough so that you can really get a feel for how it sounds. Take special notice of parts that feel hard to read, and start to think about how you might fix those parts."

> Car races are danshres. They come from fron bak and side.

After a minute, I reconvened the class. "Writers, I overheard many of you struggling with some parts of this. Would you turn and talk to your partner. Tell each other one part you struggled to read, and tell each other how you might fix that part to make it easier to read."

I coached in while partners shared with each other parts that were difficult to read and what they would do to fix them. "I didn't know the word *danshres*. That part was hard to read," said Kim. "I think we need to check the spelling. It's dan-ger-ous, I think," Kim said, sounding it out slowly. I chimed in, "Let's get the whole class together so we can fill them in on what we're talking about." I reconvened the class. Other students noticed the misspellings of *fron* and *bak* and worked together to sound them out, fixing the spellings.

Debrief and connect this work to editing rules you have previously taught.

"You are all doing some great work on Philip's book. As you get ready to reread your own writing, remember, writers don't just check their writing once. When writers get ready to publish, they reread their writing a couple times, maybe even more, to check their spelling, punctuation, and capitals."

LINK

Send students off to reread their books, listening for mistakes or confusing parts.

"Writers, it is always an exciting day when you get ready to share your writing with others. There are so many things you might catch when you read your writing out loud, just as a reader would. You can make sure that your sentences have punctuation marks, like commas and periods, that tell readers when to take small and big pauses. You can also check for capitals at the start of each sentence. A third thing you can check is that words are spelled correctly, especially really important ones. Writers, off you go to read your book and get it ready to share."

CONFERRING AND SMALL-GROUP WORK

Small-Group Inquiry to Support Students in Experimenting with Conventions

In his seminal work on word study and spelling development, *Words Their Way*, Donald Bear refers to the magical teaching time when children "use but confuse a concept" (2007, 9, fourth edition). He is referring to the time when you see your students using, for example, capitals, end punctuation, or commas in their writing, sometimes correctly, sometimes incorrectly, but ever present. He suggests that this is the time when children are truly ready to learn these new skills. You will want to look

MID-WORKSHOP TEACHING **Using Commas in a List and in Dates**

"Writers, pens down and heads up." I waited until I had all eyes trained on me. "Writers, there was one part of Philip's book that sounded a little confusing, but we didn't fix it when we were on the rug. Let me show you that part again." I covered everything but the last line, which was edited for spelling during the active engagement.

They come from front back and side.

"I was thinking that someone who read this might say, 'What's a front back? Is that a new thing I don't know about?'" I put on my best concerned face as children said, "No!" I looked around and lowered my voice, "Now Philip *could* go back and write *and* so it sounds like: front and back and side, but I think you are ready to hear a much more grown-up way to tell people a whole list of things without getting confused. When you write a list that has three or four or five or even one million things in it, you get to use this very cool thing called a comma." I drew one on a piece of paper. "Draw it in the air while I draw it again," I said, this time adding a swoosh sound.

"Anytime you make a list, you should use commas to let your reader know they are reading a list of different things. Watch me as I do it here in Philip's book." I read the piece aloud again, this time pausing after *front*. I added, "That is the end of one thing. Let me put a comma." I made my swoosh sound as I made the comma. Then I continued reading from the beginning. After I read the next word, *back*, I paused and said, "That is the second thing in my list. Time for another comma." I made it, saying "Swoosh." Then I read on to the end of the sentence. "So, you guys see how I made that list clear to the reader? I used commas and also the word *and* to make sure people knew this was a list of different things. Can you guys take a minute to find a place where you may have a list that you can use commas in, or add a list to your writing now?" I gave the writers a few minutes to either add commas to an existing list or make a list on a page to practice commas.

"Writers, I also noticed another place in Philip's writing where readers might get confused. It's in his next chapter on being a race car driver, which I read while you were working on your chapters today. I'll display the part and maybe you can help me figure out how to fix it."

I want to be a racecar driver. I am 16 September 18 2023.

"Writers, do you see anything missing in this sentence?" I waited several moments and then directed students' attention to the date. "Philip's reader might be confused about his birth date and his birth year because he forgot to put a comma between the day and year, just like we separate your birth day and birth year on our class birthday chart. I better add in that comma now." And I did, making the swoosh sound again.

"Writers, I am going to give you another chance to reread and see if you have whole lists of things where you can put in commas, or if you want, you can add a list and use commas there! You might also want to include a date in your writing—and if so, don't forget the comma between the day and year! Either way, you want to be close to done because we will be wrapping up our editing time in about eight minutes."

for writers who are "using but confusing" a technique today as you fashion small groups. More specifically, with your editing checklist in hand, you may want to sort children into groups based on the mechanics they "use but confuse." So you will likely have a punctuation group comprised of the children who use it after every word, at the end of every line, or once at the end of every page. You may also have a group of children who mix capitals and lowercase letters in all their words, indicating that they are now ready to learn the right time and place for capitals. Additionally, you may have a group that is experimenting with more complex sentences who will be ready to hear about the basic uses of a comma.

When meeting with a group of children who are experimenting this way, the best question to start with is, What do you think a period (capital, comma, etc.) is for? In one first-grade classroom, end punctuation begat a host of theories from "It tells you when to turn the page" to "It tells you when you can breathe." Discovering children's hidden theories allows you to address misconceptions and establish common understandings around the conventions of writing.

The next step with these groups will be to study places where the period (capital, comma, etc.) is used correctly, either in the context of a child's writing or through a sort, sentences and nonsentences, for example. Once sentences are sorted from the nonsentences, you will want to construct a rule with your group of children that holds true when tested with all the sentence examples. It could be as simple as "A sentence is a group of words with someone (or something) and what they do." Although that rule is not always true, it is a good starting point. The last step for this group will be for children to apply the rule to their own writing, asking, "Is this a group of words? Does it have someone or something doing something? If so, did I include punctuation?"

Keep in mind that these will not be groups that meet once. It will take multiple exposures, and a mini-course in end punctuation (or capitals or commas), before this becomes a habit for most writers.

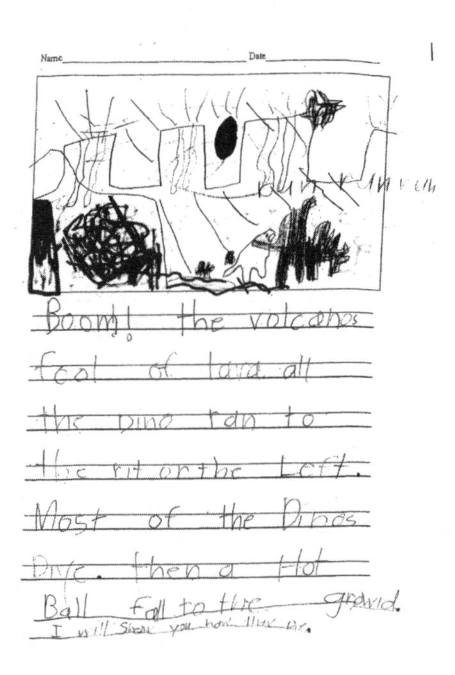

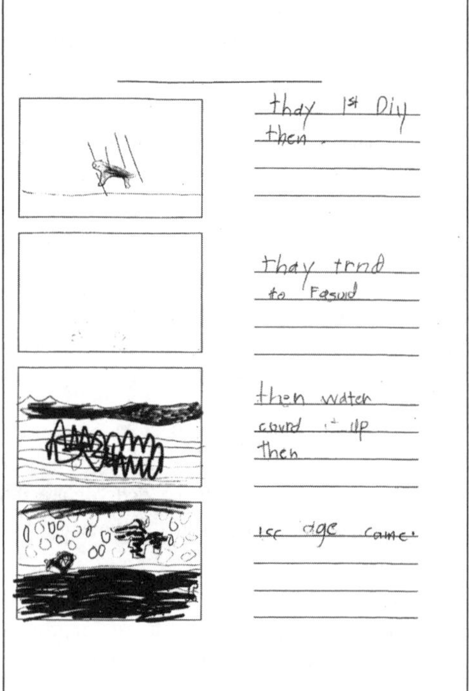

FIG. 14–3 Brian's chapter from "Dinosaurs: Danger"

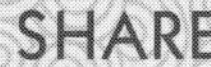

SHARE

Sharing Work as a Means of Celebration

Send writers off in groups of four to share parts of their chapter books as a way to celebrate the work they have done.

"Writers, I know you have read and reread your teaching books, and you have fixed up all of the parts that were confusing. There is so much expertise in this room that really needs to be shared. Right now, would you pick a chapter or two that you feel are your best teaching chapters? These will be the ones you will share with your small group. Marco is handing out some star stickers. Would you put a star on the chapters that you are going to share today?"

I gave the class a few moments to pick the parts they wanted to share before continuing. "Writers, can I give you a few tips that might help your presentations? Remember, when teaching, it's helpful to use not just the words on the page, but also our voice and our hands. We can slow down on important parts and make our voice go up and pause when we ask questions. And we can point to the pictures or use gestures.

"Writers, I've organized you into small teaching groups. If you look around the room, you'll see I've put the names of two partnerships, or four of you altogether, on signs in different parts of the room. I've put a letter next to each group. When I call your letter, would you head off to your teaching spot, right near your sign? And as soon as you get there, you can start teaching! Why don't you start with the person whose name starts first in the alphabet, and then have the person whose name comes second, and so on."

I named each of the groups, and the children eagerly headed off to get started. I circulated around the room, listening in and coaching writers as they presented their chapters. I walked up to a group just as Gabriel was sharing. He had the rapt attention of his group as he shared his "Motorcycles Are Very Expensive" chapter (see Figure 14–4).

> Motorcycles are very expensive. If you don't have money, you have to use your ID card. You don't need to take the motorcycle.

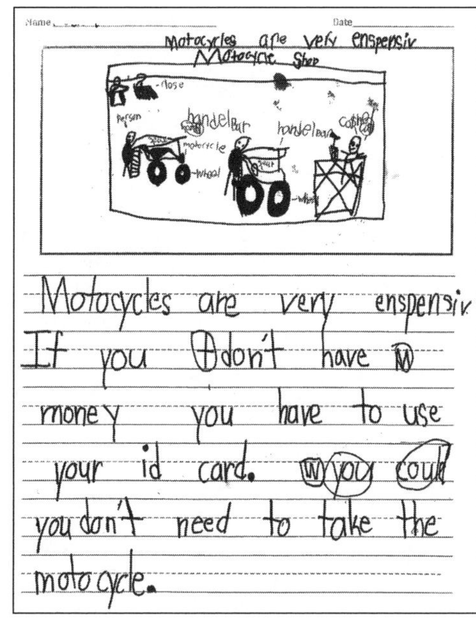

FIG. 14–4 Gabriel's chapter from "Motorcycles: Motorcycles Are Expensive"

Writing Chapter Books with Greater Independence

Session 15

Writers Use All They Know to Plan for New Chapter Books

IN THIS SESSION, you'll teach children that writers use all of the tools around them to make a plan to write their best book ever. These tools include charts, mentor texts, and other writers.

GETTING READY

- ✔ Mentor text, *Sharks!*, or another nonfiction book with special features such as headings and comparison pages (see Teaching)
- ✔ Baskets of mentor texts on each writing table (see Link)
- ✔ "How to Write a Teaching Book" chart, from Session 2 (see Link)
- ✔ "How Can I Teach My Readers?" chart, to add to during the Link
- ✔ Variety of paper choices for students in the writing center, including blank white paper (see Mid-Workshop Teaching)
- ✔ Post-it notes (see Mid-Workshop Teaching)
- ✔ Information Writing Checklist, Grades 1 and 2 (see Share)

COMMON CORE STATE STANDARDS: W.1.2, W.1.5, RI.1.1, RI.1.5, RI.1.7, SL.1.1, SL.1.4, SL.1.5, SL.1.6, L.1.1, L.1.2

IN THE PREVIOUS BEND OF THIS UNIT, children cycled through the writing process of planning, drafting, revising, and editing chapter books in a somewhat, lock-step fashion. The start of this final bend, then, marks a turning point in the unit and in your students' development as writers of information texts. It is now time to cut them loose. Your children have experienced writing one chapter book, have the vision for what it entails, and are now ready to write with increasing independence, volume, and stamina. This bend aims to move children into higher-level thinking work, asking them to transfer and synthesize all they have learned and apply their growing body of knowledge of what teaching books look like and sound like to a new book and new topic.

Whereas in the previous bend, you offered lots of scaffolds for children as they took on the challenge of writing longer and more detailed chapter books, in this bend you will not need to offer the same level of support. Rather than saying to children, "Here, try this or try that," you'll be able to say, "Use all you know about writing teaching books to help you with your new book." Your students will be the ones making the decisions in this bend, being strategic in how—and when—they use the tools you have given them. The most important lessons of this bend will come when children evaluate the options before them.

This first session of the bend reminds children that they have an array of tools from which to choose (charts, mentor texts, the author's gallery) as they revise an old chapter book or begin a new one. Today's session will be an exciting one, because you'll see the results of what you've taught in full swing: children working independently and purposefully to make plans, utilizing the classroom charts, and writing furiously, their noses pressed in close to the paper.

The sessions will build toward a final celebration. You may want to keep the date of that celebration in a clear location, announcing a countdown daily, so that you build a palpable excitement in your room. This will also keep your students mindful of the urgency in this last bend.

MINILESSON

Writers Use All They Know to Plan for New Chapter Books

CONNECTION

Celebrate the work that writers did in the previous session and set them up to begin a second chapter book, one that they will write with more independence.

"First-graders, I learned so much from each of you. The world is never going to believe that a group of first-graders can teach people *so* much! Teaching your readers tons of information has been one of your goals as writers and teachers. Go ahead and give yourselves a pat on the back right now because you've done just that!"

I clapped while the kids congratulated themselves. Then I said, "And here's the important thing. Because you've learned how to load your books with interesting information, you can be sure that not only are your readers going to be experts on headbands and the human body and Playland and sharks, but they're *also* going to care enormously about all these things!

"Writers, today marks an exciting day in your lives as authors of teaching books. Today, you are going to start a new chapter book, and *this* time you're not going to need much help from me as you write it, because you already know how to write a teaching chapter book. I'll be more like a coach, helping you along the way. And for today, what I want to remind you is that you *already know* a lot about writing information books. Draw on all that you know."

Name the teaching point.

"Today I want to teach you that as writers start new chapter books, and revise old ones, they get a new plan for their writing. To do this, they study the tools around them—things like charts, published nonfiction books, and even other writers. As writers study these tools, they think to themselves, 'How could I try that in my writing?' And then they do it."

◆ COACHING

You'll come to see that most books in this series use Bend III as a time to challenge writers to make more decisions, drawing on all they have learned. You'll rally them to do this work as if you are fully confident that they'll rise to the occasion—but the truth is that some children will need for you to teach and coach into them assuming increased responsibility.

TEACHING

Demonstrate how you use a tool, in this case a mentor text, to plan a new kind of chapter.

"Let me show you what I mean. I want to start a book about a place called Queens. I love to visit Queens because there is so much to do there. So my job now is to think of what I already know about planning a nonfiction book. I'm remembering that before we planned a table of contents page by thinking about what the parts might be and telling them across my fingers. For example, the parts might be different places in Queens, how to get to Queens, and things to do in Queens. I'm going to jot these chapter ideas down." I did this, jotting it on a small piece of paper in my lap.

"I also know another way to think about how my book might go. I could look at a mentor text, a published nonfiction book. Let's look at our mentor text, *Sharks!*, and notice what this author did to teach and explain the information. Remember, I am not writing about sharks, so I am not looking for information about sharks. Instead, I am looking for what this writer did that I could also do in my book about Queens."

Model the steps of studying a mentor text, using that text to help you plan yours.

I opened the book and began flipping through it, squinting my eyes as if studying it intently. I muttered, "Hmm, let's see. One thing I notice is that the author not only has a table of contents but she also uses headings on each page. This page shows all different kinds of teeth and that gives me an idea for my Queens book. I could tell about all the different kinds of restaurants in Queens.

"Writers, you know what the author did here? She put all of these different kinds of shark teeth on this page and taught us about them one at a time. In my book on Queens, I could write a whole chapter about different kinds of restaurants, just like Anne Schreiber did with shark teeth!"

Demonstrate how you use another tool, in this case a class chart, to plan a new kind of chapter.

"Writers, I can also use one of our class anchor charts to remind myself how I might plan my chapters. Let me see. Hmm. I'm looking at our 'How Can I Teach My Readers?' chart." I pointed to it, hanging front and center in the meeting area. "And I'm thinking that I can use the tip 'Think about questions my reader might have' to help me come up with more chapters for my Queens book. Hmm. I'm thinking that my readers will want to know who lives in Queens, what people are like there, and what they do, so I think I'll have a whole chapter on people in Queens. I think I'll get started on that right away!"

Debrief, reminding writers that they can use anything they recall and any tool, including a mentor text or a class chart, to help them plan their books.

"Writers, did you see that even though no one told me what to do to get started on a new book, I used everything I know how to do to choose a topic and to start writing a table of contents? I used a mentor text to help me, and I could have used a class chart, too. Now I know what some of my chapters will be!"

ACTIVE ENGAGEMENT

Channel students to choose one tool from the classroom—a mentor text, an anchor chart, or other writers in the room—to find one feature they can use in their teaching books.

"Writers, will you look around the room and find some thing that can help you as you plan your new teaching books today? You might look at one of our mentor texts, our classroom charts, or even other writers in the room to help you think, 'What should I do to get started on a new book today?' When you have found a tool or a resource that can help you get started, thumbs up!"

When most of the class had their thumbs raised, I asked them to take a minute to do some noticing. What can they learn about information writing? Then I asked them to share what they had noticed with a partner. I listened in, taking note of students whose responses would be particularly helpful to share. "Writers, listen to what Peter noticed. He noticed that on this page of our mentor text, there are all these little boxes that say, 'Quick Fact!' He's thinking that after he plans his table of contents page, he might try to make a list of cool features he wants to include in his book, like these little boxes."

I continued, "Peter's giving me an idea for my book! I'm thinking, for example, that I could add a box in my 'Who Lives in Queens' chapter that tells facts like over two million people live in Queens! It's the second most populated borough of New York. I could add this quick fact—and I'll think of some others too."

Debrief in a way that highlights the transferable work that students did.

"So writers, my bigger point is that when you go to write an information book, you don't need a teacher telling you, 'Do this,' 'Do that.' You can use charts and monitor texts and other writers to help you know what you can do."

LINK

Remind writers to use not only mentor texts, but all of the tools in the classroom, as they begin drafting new chapter books.

"Writers, I think you get the idea. You can use all the tools in the classroom to help you plan your writing. When you go back to your writing spots, you'll see there is also a tub of books on your table from our library that you can study.

"Don't forget there are other tools too. We have our 'How to Write a Teaching Book' chart from the very beginning of the unit. We also have our Information Writing Checklist to help you remember what to include and check for in your writing. We also have our 'How Can I Teach My Readers?' chart. I've put copies of all of these on your tables.

"And writers, one more thing: today, as you start your new chapter books and you think about what new kinds of teaching you will do, also remember what you know about *how* to start chapter books. Usually, writers of teaching chapter books start by planning a table of contents."

FIG. 15–1

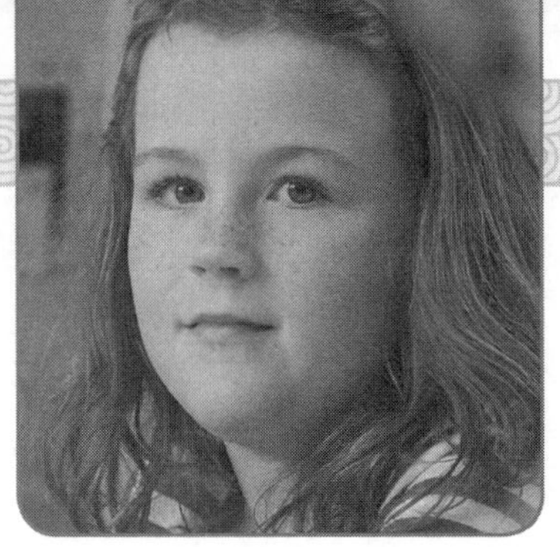

CONFERRING AND SMALL-GROUP WORK

Independence Means Thinking I Can

IN TODAY'S MINILESSON AND OTHERS, you will have encouraged students to initiate plans and to use tools to help them move forward with more independence. It is likely, though, that you will have some students who struggle with these steps and prefer the safety of a partner or a teacher to help them. It can be tempting to swoop in and help a child get started by asking lots of questions, but if you do that, the tool the child learns to rely on will be you. Some conferences then, are not about teaching a strategy to solve the writer's problem, but rather teaching the writer strategies that will help her independently solve her problems, strategies that will help her get unstuck anytime she runs into trouble.

When I pulled alongside Alyssa, I knew some things about her as a writer. Her past few teaching books had been about her deep love of food. She had tackled these with gusto, covering virtually every imaginable angle on that topic and creating pages that were chock-full of facts and examples. Today was different. Alyssa had clearly lost that motivation. She sat staring gloomily at the blank papers in front of her. I had noticed this pattern in her before; when Alyssa got stuck, she got *stuck*, and it was difficult for her to move past the point of trouble.

"Hey Alyssa! Can we talk about your writing? What is your plan for today?" I asked, smiling and making eye contact.

Alyssa had tendencies toward the Broadway stage. She collapsed with her head on her arms and moaned, "It's *sooo* hard. I don't have *anything* to write about anymore." She looked up and around her and said, "And *everyone* is writing but me. I already wrote everything I know about!"

Immediately, strategies for generating ideas came to mind, but I held myself back from suggesting these. More pressing, it seemed, was that Alyssa learn more global strategies about what to do when faced with troubles. Students will be more receptive if you begin with positives, so I began by saying, "Alyssa, one thing I have noticed about you in the drama center, is that you know how to take charge. When kids don't know what

MID-WORKSHOP TEACHING

Creating Paper for Different Kinds of Chapters

"Writers, can I interrupt you for a moment? Henry was searching in a nonfiction book for some ideas for how some of his chapters could go. He noticed that, in this book about frogs, there is a chapter that shows the steps that a frog goes through when it is turning from a tadpole into a frog. Look at all these boxes with arrows that show us the order of the steps. And Henry thought that having a chapter like that would be really cool in his book about plants, which shows how a plant grows. But then you know what? He went to choose paper to help him, and he couldn't find any that matched the kind of page he wanted to make. So he feels a little stuck, and he would love some help from you. What do you think, writers? What should he do? Turn and talk to the people at your table."

"He can just make it!" said a few of the writers at table one.

"Yeah, he can use Post-its," said another.

"Writers, this is great. When you want to try making a new kind of page, and you don't see any paper that matches it, you can just make your own. It's that simple! Watch me as I help Henry. I'm going to put Post-its on the page in place of the boxes. Henry can draw on and label each Post-it. Then, I'm going to draw some arrows to show that it is a series of steps. Finally, I'm going to make a few lines under each Post-it so Henry can write about each step. And voila! I have some paper that Henry can use to show steps of a plant's growth. You all can become page designers too. Off you go, first-graders. Keep your hands flying down the page!"

they want to act out, you give lots of suggestions, and when you need a special prop, you get the materials to make it. I even remember when you felt like the kids in blocks were making too much noise, so you asked me if you could do drama on the rug to make it quieter. You are a can-do kid! You are a problem solver!" Alyssa nodded and began to sit up a little straighter.

"I have been thinking that a can-do kid in drama is the same as a can-do kid in writing. You just need to know that you *can do*."

Alyssa nodded in agreement, saying, "I can do lots of things."

"So let's make a list of all the things that will help you be a can-do writer when you get stuck." I pulled out a piece of blank paper and quickly drew a stick person I labeled "Alyssa," and added a crown on her head for an extra dose of can-do-ness. I wrote "I CAN" at the top and waited.

Alyssa stared at me, expectant. I decided to give just a start and see what happened next, "For example, when I can't spell a word, I can go to the word wall." I wrote "word wall" underneath "I can" with a quick sketch next to it.

Alyssa began to warm up, "I can stretch words." I added "stretch words" to the page and waited. "I can actually go to the spelling chart," she said, scanning around the room until she found it and pointed. I added "spelling chart" to the list. As she glanced at the charts, I asked, "Any other charts you can use?" She rattled off the titles and I added these to the list, too. Her list now had five items. Knowing that if I added too many more the list would be useless and overwhelming to her, I quickly said, "Yup, and you can look at books, too, like we talked about during the minilesson." She agreed and then I asked, "So Alyssa, which of the tools on this 'I can' list are you going to use to help you get unstuck?" She pondered the list for a second and pointed to the "Use the 'How to Write a Teaching Book' chart."

"Great," I said, "Why don't you grab your folder and head over to that chart, and if that doesn't feel like it's working for you, try something else on the 'I can' list." I handed her the list, giving her one last thought, "Alyssa, you are a can-do kid, and can-do kids use all the tools in their toolboxes to help them out of trouble." She smiled and I headed off to the next conference.

SHARE

Reviewing the Checklist and Writing New Goals

Remind children of the first-grade goals for writing strong teaching books, on the Information Writing Checklist.

After calling students to the rug, I said, "Writers, as you get better and stronger at writing teaching books, you will notice that you do not need to go back and add so much in. You will see that you write lots of information from the start. So let's go back through and read the list of goals for first- and second-grade information writiers. I'm going to start by reading the first-grade list. As I read through the list, be thinking, 'Which of these am I a superstar at using, and which of these do I sometimes forget?'" I read through the list, editorializing on the bullets, saying things like, "Oh my gosh. This one you all do! It's almost too easy now!" or "This one I see you do sometimes, but it seems a little trickier!" (This checklist can be found on the CD-ROM.)

Information Writing Checklist

	Grade 1	NOT YET	STARTING TO	YES!	Grade 2	NOT YET	STARTING TO	YES!
	Structure				**Structure**			
Overall	I taught my readers about a topic.	☐	☐	☐	I taught readers some important points about a subject.	☐	☐	☐
Lead	I named my topic in the beginning and got my readers' attention.	☐	☐	☐	I wrote a beginning in which I named a subject and tried to interest readers.	☐	☐	☐
Transitions	I told different parts about my topic on different pages.	☐	☐	☐	I used words such as *and* and *also* to show I had more to say.	☐	☐	☐
Ending	I wrote an ending.	☐	☐	☐	I wrote some sentences or a section at the end to wrap up my piece.	☐	☐	☐
Organization	I told about my topic part by part.	☐	☐	☐	My writing had different parts. Each part told different information about the topic.	☐	☐	☐
	Development				**Development**			
Elaboration	I put facts in my writing to teach about my topic.	☐	☐	☐	I used different kinds of information in my writing such as facts, definitions, details, steps, and tips	☐	☐	☐
Craft	I used labels and words to give facts.	☐	☐	☐	I tried to include the words that showed I'm an expert on the topic.	☐	☐	☐
	Language Conventions				**Language Conventions**			
Spelling	I used all I knew about words and chunks (*at, op, it,* etc.) to help me spell.	☐	☐	☐	I used what I knew about spelling patterns (*tion, er, ly,* etc.) to spell a word.	☐	☐	☐
	I spelled the word wall words right and used the word wall to help me spell other words.	☐	☐	☐	I spelled all of the word wall words correctly and used the word wall to help me figure out how to spell other words.	☐	☐	☐

Then I said, "Writers, I think you are ready for more challenges—grown-up ones. So I'm going to read the second-grade checklist. (Whoa!) I want you to think whether you maybe—with work—could do some the items on this list."

Channel partners to choose one item and look for it across their entire book.

"Now, partners, will you share things that you only do sometimes that you think you could work on during the last few days of our unit." I'd soon channel children to write new goal sheets for themselves.

End by preparing students for tomorrow's minilesson, in which they'll need a photograph or picture that goes with their topic.

"Writers, one more thing. Tomorrow you're going to have a chance to think about how to make your books into even more powerful teaching texts by doing a little bit of research. Professional writers do a lot of research for their teaching books. So I'm giving you some homework tonight. When you're at home, look for photos about your topic. There are a few ways to do this. You could ask your parents if they have any, or you could look in a book or in a magazine or even on the Internet—with your parents' help that is. So, for instance, Annie, who's writing about superheroes, could look at home to see if she has any books with photos of superheroes. And Liam, who's writing about parties, could ask his family if anyone has any photos of actual parties that he could bring."

Session 16

Writers Do Research, Like Finding Images or Photos, to Help Them Say More

IN THIS SESSION, you'll teach children that nonfiction writers use images and photos to help them say more about their topic.

GETTING READY

- ✔ Photograph that supports your demonstration text (see Connection)
- ✔ Students' photographs they brought from home, to be brought to the meeting area (see Connection)
- ✔ "How Can I Teach My Readers?" chart (see Link and Share) 

Common Core State Standards: W.1.2, W.1.6, W.1.8, RI.1.7, RI.1.10, SL.1.1, SL.1.2, SL.1.4, SL.1.5, L.1.1, L.1.2

UP TO THIS POINT IN THE UNIT, the information in your students' books has been derived entirely from personal experience. As children make their way through the world, they interpret the things around them and make theories—some correct, some incorrect. Since the chapter books students have been writing are intended to teach, today's session invites a layer of research that lends more validity to the statements they are making.

What exactly does research mean to a six-year-old? It can be challenging for first-graders to get a book from the library, read it, take notes, and use those notes to write a more comprehensive book. Sometimes there are no books on a topic, or the child just copies directly from one source into her book, unsure what the words say or mean. When working with young children, then, we interpret research much more broadly.

Researchers look at photographs and media, conduct experiments, polls, and surveys, and read widely for more information. Even the most novice writer can use these tools to gain a deeper understanding of a topic. This session teaches the essential idea that when writing a teaching book, writers might first look inside at their own personal experiences, but then they look outside, too, to fill in details and supplement their knowledge. By consulting additional sources, they create a richer, more accurate portrait of their topic. Earlier this year, you taught students that details matter in stories. Now you'll teach them that details are also important in teaching books.

In this session, you will highlight the fact that students can use visual sources such as photographs and images for additional information in their books. Free-use photographs are available at everystockphoto.com, and the site has an easy search feature to find photos about almost any topic. You will want to assist children in using this site because it really does have *every* free stock photo on the Internet, including ones that will not be appropriate for your kids. You can also ask your students to bring in photos from home that go with their topic or to look through magazines for photos or images. While this research may seem rudimentary, it will lay the foundation for an important habit of mind: sometimes people have to look around them to find out more.

MINILESSON

Writers Do Research, Like Finding Images or Photos, to Help Them Say More

CONNECTION

Share with students a photograph that goes with your demonstration text, showing how a picture can tell a lot about a place or thing.

"First-graders, hurry to the meeting area and bring the photograph you found for homework last night. I have something really special to share with you."

When all the children were in their spots on the rug, I said, "Close your eyes. I am going to teach you something really important about Queens. Are you ready?"

Eyes closed, they nodded.

"There is a place in Queens that is really special. It has this big thing in it and lots of other things. It is peaceful and pretty." Then I paused and commented on my teaching by saying, "Isn't that interesting? Can you guys get a real clear picture about what I am describing?"

"No!" several children announced in unison.

"Now look! Everyone, open your eyes!" I revealed a photograph, showing the pond in Kissena Park in Queens. "Is this clearer?"

"Oooh!" many students exclaimed. Eyes widened and heads nodded. Tonia said, "That's much better."

I continued, "Yes, the photograph gives you lots more information, doesn't it? Writers, they say a picture is worth a thousand words. Let me explain what that means. It means, when we look at a picture, we instantly know a whole bunch of stuff about the place or the thing, because we can *see* it."

◆ COACHING

The saying that a picture is worth a thousand words illuminates the power the photographs can have for helping writers learn that outside sources can help them say more.

In these books, there's a whole progression of minilessons that teach writers to examine photographs and use them as sources of information. You might want to contrast this session with some of the others that address this same topic in more sophisticated ways. Look, for example, at the information writing unit in fifth grade as a contrast.

Name the teaching point.

"Today I want to teach you that writers research—or look for—photographs or pictures that are connected to their topics. Writers look closely at these, mining them for specific details that will teach people even more about their topics. Then they put into words what they've learned and add this to their writing."

TEACHING

Demonstrate studying a picture you've brought that relates to the text you are writing. Then show that you transfer information from the picture to your text.

"Writers, I want to show you how I use my photograph of the pond in Kissena Park to help me add more to my Queens book. Let me study this photograph. Hmm. The first thing I notice is the size of the pond. It's really huge! I think I'll add that the pond is giant to my writing." I recorded this on chart paper, for students to see.

"The next thing I notice, writers, is that there are lots and lots of animals near the pond. There are fish and squirrels. Do you notice anything else that I'm missing, writers?"

Peter called out, "I see a swan!"

"Oh, you're right. There are swans and other types of birds too. I'll add that to my writing."

Channel students to join you in studying the photograph you've brought, using it to help you elaborate.

As I write this next part, think about what other details you notice in the picture. Then turn and talk with the person next to you." I recorded what we had noticed so far on the chart paper while children talked quietly about the other details in the picture.

It may seem to you that this section of the minilesson feels like the active engagement section and you're right. When teaching this, you may decide to lop off the existing active engagement, streamlining the minilesson. We left this here because we felt that the level of work is not overly complicated. We expect that this will move quickly.

Before long, children noticed there were trees and flowers, and I added that to our description. I also added that is calm and beautiful.

> There is a giant pond in Kissena Park. It has lots and lots of animals living in and near the pond. It has fish, squirrels, swans, and other types of birds. It has trees and flowers as well. It is calm and beautiful because it has all these plants and animals.

Debrief in a way that highlights the transferable work students have been doing.

"Writers, do you see how we didn't just give any ol' details. We gave *specific* details. We named the kinds of animals and wildlife you can find in Kissena Park, and I used the word *giant* to describe the size of the pond. It really is huge! Photographs and pictures tell us a lot of information—if we look closely. Photographs and pictures can spark us to tell our readers things we would never imagine writing on our own. Like I forgot that swans were here, right in Queens. But when Peter studied the photograph, and saw swans, it reminded me to add that detail into our writing."

ACTIVE ENGAGEMENT

Recruit children to describe their pictures in great detail to their partners.

"Writers, now it's your turn to give this a try with the pictures you brought today. You should have brought those with you to the rug. Whichever partner has photographs with you—you start. Don't show your photograph to your partner just yet. Instead, describe your photograph with as many *specific* details as you can. Then, when you're finished, you can show your photograph to your partner and see if the two of you can find even more things to name."

Debrief, emphasizing strategies writers can use other days and in other books.

"Writers, I want to share some things I overhead that I think might help all of you. First, I heard Sergio describing his picture of a soccer game. He described the way the players were moving to protect the goal and help the goalie. And I thought that was so great, because he didn't just tell about the people and the things that were in the photograph, he told about the *actions*. He wrote about what people were *doing*.

"I also overhead Tonia telling Karl all about her photograph of the beach near her house. She told about the objects that were there, like shells and rocks, and she also used a few words to describe the objects so that Karl could really picture them. She said there were *pink* shells and *big* rocks. She used *color* and *size* to help describe her picture. Those kinds of details really help readers get a picture in their minds. Nice work."

LINK

Send students off to continue drafting their chapter books.

"Writers, I know you have so much you want to do today, so I'm going to send you off now. I will add this strategy—study a picture or photograph to add more information—to our 'How Can I Teach My Readers?' chart so you can use it not only today, but on other days and in other books. Remember to use all you know about making your chapters as chock-full of good information as possible. In addition to using photographs, you can do any of the things on this chart! Writers, tell each other what you'll do first today, and when you are ready to work—get started!"

FIG. 16–1 Another version of the "How Can I Teach My Readers?" chart

CONFERRING AND SMALL-GROUP WORK

Forming Research Groups around Surveys, Videos, and Reading about Your Topic

RESEARCH NEED NOT BE LIMITED TO PHOTOS AND PICTURES, and you may gather some groups around additional types of research: videos, polls and surveys, and reading about a topic. Think about the types of topics children in your class are tackling and pull a few kids whose topics will benefit from similar sources of information (or who have similar needs) into research groups that will help them gather relevant information.

You might have one group come together around polls and surveys. You will want first to let children know that this is something researchers do all the time: come up with questions and use the answers to learn something. Although understanding and using question words is a Common Core State Standard for kindergarten, you will find that you have some children who still need support with forming questions, especially English language learners. You can help this group formulate questions for surveys or polls that they can ask students in the classroom or experts at home. Pair each of the question words with an icon that will help children remember their different meanings. (For example, *who* could have a person next to the word to remind students that it is a question word that usually has to do with a person.) Children can use these words to compose questions like "What is your favorite video game?" Or "Who do you like

MID-WORKSHOP TEACHING **Teaching Readers What New Words Mean with Words and Pictures**

"Writers, can I interrupt you for a moment? As you look at pictures and find out more information, I am seeing your writing grow down the page. I am also seeing lots of interesting words pop up. When Isabella was studying her picture of a soccer player, she added some information about what soccer players wear. She wrote, 'Soccer players wear cleats. Soccer players always wear shorts.'" Isabella nodded.

"This is great information, but as Isabella and I were talking she realized I had *lots* of questions about cleats. I asked her, 'Do you wear cleats on your head? Like a hat?' Isabella rushed to say what she knew, exclaiming, 'Cleats go on your *feet*.'

"Writers, not everyone knows what you know! When you explain what certain words mean, like Isabella did for me, you are giving a definition, and that is something nonfiction writers do all the time."

I moved to the easel and rewrote Isabella's sentence: "Soccer players wear cleats."

"Writers, if you use a special word like *cleats*, you have to give a definition, which means you explain to your reader what the word means, and one way you can do that is with a word box." I drew a box at the bottom of the easel. "When you make a word box you explain what a word means, like this." I wrote the word *cleats* and then made a colon and wrote: *Cleats are shoes you buy at a special store. They are pointy on the bottom.* I said the words as I wrote them, ending with, "Do you see how I made a box at the bottom of the page and explained what cleats are?" The students nodded at me. "Isabella did one more thing that was so helpful to her readers, she also labeled the cleats in her picture!" I held up the page to show the class.

"Writers, you can really help your readers by giving definitions, which means explaining what these special words mean, by making a word box or labeling it in your picture. Can you reread for a moment and see if you have place where you can give a definition?" I walked around the room making sure everyone was rereading, making note of anyone who might need a little extra support. After a few minutes I said, "Writers, as you go on in your books think about the words you use and, if you think it will help your reader, you can give a definition using a word box or labeling it in your picture."

better: Justin Bieber or Hannah Montana?" These researchers can then head off to poll other kids in the class, and you can meet them again at the end of the workshop to help them make sense of their data.

Other children might benefit from watching short videos about their topic to learn more. These could be captured from YouTube with QuickVid or something they watched at home. The key thing to teach children who use this medium for research is to reference what they learned within the text of their book. A simple phrase like "As I saw on TV . . . " or "The show 'Planet Earth' said . . . " will anchor readers to the source. That is, you'll teach that information learned from TV and video is not necessarily something they knew already and therefore deserves a nod in their writing. Again, this is about building an important habit of mind, not teaching APA or MLA formatting.

Finally, you might have a group of children whose topics can be supported by easy-to-read texts in the classroom. In this case, you may gather your group around a basket and show them how sometimes you can read things that make you think, "Zowee! I should put that in my book!" When that happens, you put the book down and try to say what you learned in your own words, not the words of the author. This can be tricky, so a little practice will go a long way. You can teach this group the same method of referencing their source, saying, "The book *Baby Animals* said . . . " or something else along those lines.

These research techniques lay the groundwork for the increasingly sophisticated writing children will do in the future. Supporting the habit of mind that information can be gathered from inside and outside establishes behaviors that will last a lifetime.

SHARE

Planning for Tomorrow Keeps the Momentum Going

Remind students that the best way to end workshop is to make a plan for tomorrow.

After gathering the students to the meeting area, I said, "Writers, today you used photos to help you research your topic, you looked at charts and mentor texts to make plans for the second part of writing time, and you wrote like the wind. To keep this momentum going, I think it will make sense for us to make a plan for what you want to get done tomorrow." I put up the "How Can I Teach My Readers?" chart.

How Can I Teach My Readers?

- Think about questions my readers might have
- Write in twin sentences
- Include pictures
  - teaching words
  - lines and arrows
  - zooming-in
- Use shape, size, and color words
- Make a comparison to something they know
- Give an example
- Use a picture or photograph to add more information

I then handed out Post-its to all the children. "Writers, sometimes it helps to write the plan you have on a Post-it so when you open your folder the next day you have a reminder of what to do, just like a note on the calendar. Can you look at the chart and write one, two, or three things you want to make sure to tackle tomorrow?" I waited while children jotted down their ideas.

"Great. Now stick your Post-it right on the front of your paper, so when you get ready for writing workshop tomorrow, it will be waiting to remind you of your plans!"

To provide different entry points into goal-setting, you may encourage children to write the words from the chart as their goal, or draw the picture from their chart as the goal. It is helpful to coach into the choices children make by asking, "What did you do a lot? What do you think you could do more of?"

Session 17

Editing "On the Go"

Varying End Punctuation to Bring Out a Teaching Book's Meaning

AS YOU NEAR THE END OF THIS UNIT, you can—and should—expect more from children's written work. Expect that they will write with greater volume and greater detail; expect that they will try out more and more of the writing moves they've learned the past few weeks to write interesting, informative books. In the midst of all this big work, don't forget the "little" work that will make the difference between a legible book and an illegible one; expect that children will punctuate!

You can draw on the work children are doing during reading to teach them to make thoughtful choices as they punctuate their writing. By this point in the year, you probably have a large cluster of students reading at or around Fountas and Pinnell levels F and G. Your reading instruction will probably channel children to read fluently, with pace, prosody, and parsing. Prosody, the rhythm, stress, and intonation of speech, has a reciprocal relationship with punctuation in writing. Studying the ways authors use punctuation sets children up to make choices for using punctuation in their writing.

In the *Small Moments* unit, and also Sessions 8 and 14 of this book, we recommend teaching ending punctuation within editing lessons, encouraging children to fix up pieces they have already composed by checking on their punctuation. In this session, we suggest you teach punctuating on the go—that you convey to children that writers punctuate *as they compose*. This, then, becomes another way children build the habits of mind necessary for fluent writing. Notice that we first encouraged you to help youngsters look back on completed work to revise punctuation. After channeling children to practice

"Teach punctuation on the go—convey to children that writers punctuate as they compose."

IN THIS SESSION, you'll teach children that writers use their voices to help teach their readers. One way they do this is by deciding how to punctuate their sentences.

GETTING READY

- ✔ A story to demonstrate how we use inflection in our voices when we talk or teach (see Connection)
- ✔ Your own demonstration text, with one sentence prewritten, but missing end punctuation for each chapter (see Teaching)
- ✔ Post-Its (see Conferring)
- ✔ Timer (see Share)

Common Core State Standards: W.1.2, W.1.5, RFS.1.4, SL.1.1, L.1.1.j, L.1.2.b,c

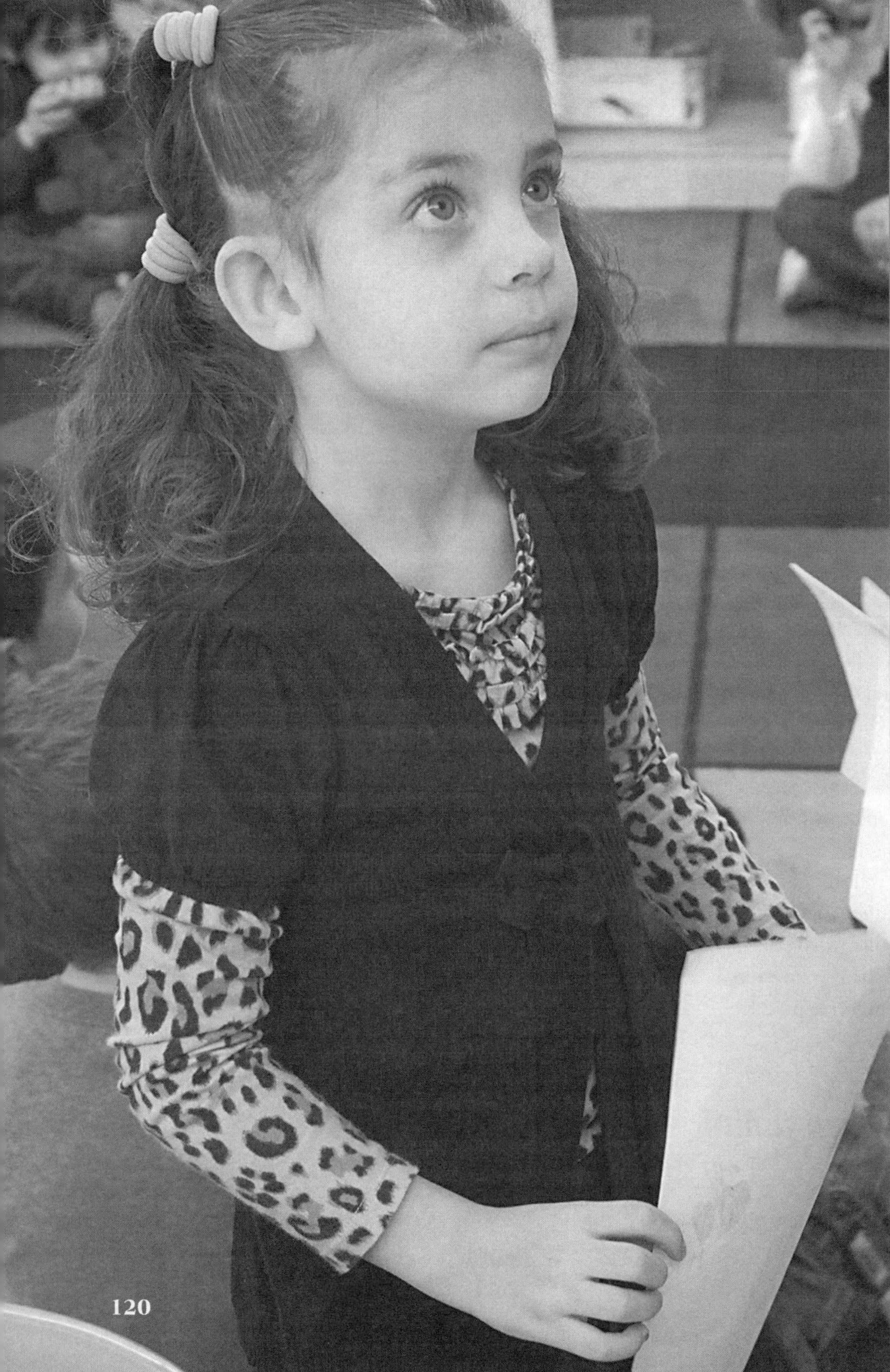

using punctuation, we suggest you up the ante and encourage children to include punctuation as one of the many things they do while composing. That's much more challenging. This progression—first teaching through revision, later through drafting—will be common throughout this series. First, you'll teach children to practice something by trying it on an already completed piece of writing, and then you'll teach them to incorporate that skill—that work—*as they write*. Punctuating while composing holds many challenges for young writers, so be prepared to welcome their attempts and give them support and reminders, as needed.

Some teachers find it helpful to teach children to say a sentence, write the sentence, mark the sentence, and then reread it. This will slow your writers down a bit, but they can then speed up once punctuating becomes a habit. You could give a small index card with these steps to each child in your class to serve as a visual cue of the strategy they are working on. Slowing down to focus on punctuation encourages children to make more deliberate choices about *how* to end their sentences, giving them more opportunities to reflect on their choices. When children stop to consider how they want their reader to read their text, they are doing work that writers the world over do when they write for real purposes and real audiences.

MINILESSON

Editing "On the Go"

Varying End Punctuation to Bring Out a Teaching Book's Meaning

CONNECTION

◆ COACHING

Use a personal story to engage children in the purpose of using our voices to help us teach.

"Writers, I was chatting with my neighbor, Jessica, the other day. I love talking to Jessica. She is a teenager, and it is almost as if she is my teacher because she teaches me about what teenagers, these days, do and think about. The thing about Jessica is this: She uses her voice in a lot of different ways to help me understand her. Do you remember that book, *Yo! Yes?* (Raschka 1993)? Remember how the characters in that book can say one word—like *yes*—with all these different moods? Yes! Yes? Yeeesssss! Well, Jessica teaches me about being a teenager and when she talks to me, she uses all these different voices to make her meaning clear. For example, when Jessica tells me something important, she practically *yells* at me. She'll say in a loud voice, 'At the movies, my friend was laughing so loud I was *embarrassed*!'

"There are other times when she knows I know practically nothing so she launches into a whole long list: listing singers or actors, or films, or video games. Then she uses her voice to shovel out one item after another on a list. One time, she said something and then quizzed me to see if I grasped her point.

"The interesting thing is that Jessica, like those characters in *Yo! Yes?* is *always* speaking with punctuation. Always?" (I made a question mark in the air.)

"Always!" (I made an exclamation point in the air.)

Clarify how the story you told relates to the nonfiction writing children have been doing.

"The thing about my conversations with Jessica is that she is so good at using her voice in different ways, that I find it really great learning from her. It is the very same thing for nonfiction writers. When nonfiction writers are writing teaching books, they can state facts, raise questions, or share exciting tidbits . . . they use their voices to help teach."

Name the teaching point.

"Today, I want to teach you that nonfiction writers choose ending punctuation that reflects how they are trying to speak. Specifically, they use periods when they want to tell facts, question marks when they want to ask questions, exclamation marks when they want to tell something exciting, commas and colons when they want to make lists."

TEACHING

Demonstrate how to think intentionally about end punctuation, pausing to reread and think about what kind of end punctuation would relay the information best to your reader.

"Watch me as I try this with our book on Queens. You might remember that one of the chapters is about places in Queens. I already wrote about Kissena Park. But there is one place that is famous in Queens. I know that this place is very important, so I am going to write in a way that lets my reader know that, too."

As students looked on, I quickly read the first sentence I had prewritten in my book—with missing end punctuation—using a straightforward voice: "'A famous site in Queens is the Botanical Garden.' That sentence is written in a voice that gives just the facts. So I think a period works best there. Periods let readers know that you are just giving them the facts." As students watched, I added a period at the end of the sentence.

"Now I want to write a sentence that conveys how great the Queens Botanical Garden is. Let me think for a minute . . . " I wrote, "Everyone should go to the Queens Botanical Garden because there are so many beautiful flowers to see!" "I really want readers to know how beautiful and special the Botanical Gardens are. I know! I'll use an exclamation point to do that!" I said this in an excited way to drive home the point. "Writers use exclamation points when they want to let their reader know that information is super duper." I added an exclamation point.

Debrief, recalling that writers think about end punctuation not only while editing, but also while drafting their teaching books.

"Did you see what I did there, writers? I didn't just write my sentences any old way. No! I thought to myself, 'How do I want to say this information? How do I want to speak to my reader?' Then I used the kind of end punctuation that would help me teach my reader the information in that specific way."

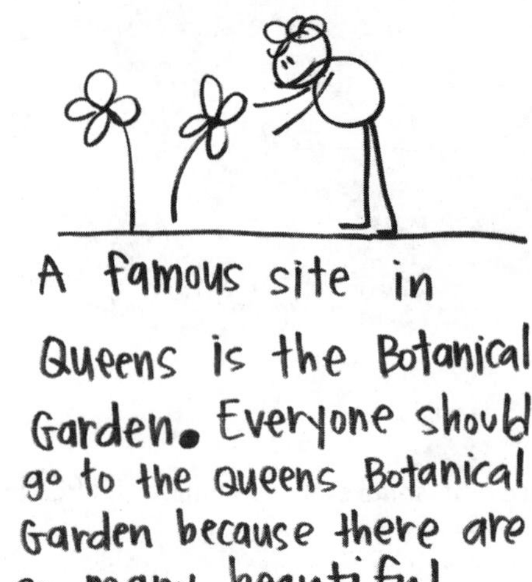

FIG. 17–1

Obviously it would be easy to continue teaching other kinds of punctuation. Using a colon, you could have listed places to go in Queens. Using the question mark, you could pose questions.

ACTIVE ENGAGEMENT

Recruit students to do the same work in the demonstration text.

"Your turn to try this out, writers. See if you can make the same kind of decisions as you help me with another chapter in our book about Queens. How about a chapter on transportation. So far all I have is, 'There are lots of ways to get around in Queens.' That leaves it wide open!

"Now, think about the next sentence we might write. As you come up with ideas of *what* to say, be sure to think about how you would want to speak the sentence to our reader and about the way you suggest punctuating the sentence. " I gave children a moment to think, then said, "Turn and talk to your partner."

As you listen in to children's conversations, you will hear how they come up with content and how they match content to the way they want to teach their reader with their voice. Some children will have difficulty orchestrating these two elements, so your coaching in these instances will be critical.

"Writers, can I have your attention? I heard Hattie telling David, 'People can take the subway train. It's high up above the cars!' I heard that and saw Hattie raise her arm way up in the air, and I was like, 'Whoa! Okay, okay. I get that riding the train is not just a little bit exciting. It's *super* exciting. When I heard how excited Hattie was, I was actually thinking to myself, 'Hmm. Riding the train *is* really great.' I bet you can figure out the punctuation.

"Then, I overhead Alaysha say to her partner, 'Have you ever ridden on the train? Did it go high above the cars?' Did you see what Alaysha did? She asked a question—a couple questions actually—so when we record what Alaysha told her partner, we'll make sure we put a question mark at the end of each of those sentences. Remember, writers use question marks when they want to get their reader thinking about the information they are teaching them."

LINK

Send students off to try this work in their teaching books, tucking in that they can do this with lots of sentences and that they can also do this as they start new teaching books.

"Writers, as you go off today, remember that if you want to let your reader know something is really important, an exclamation point will help you do that. If you want your reader to really think about what you are teaching, you might try asking your reader a question and ending it with a question mark. When you are writing the straightforward facts, a period is the way to go. If you are listing, start the list with a colon and include commas. You have choices. Even before you write a single sentence, it helps to think about not only what you'll say, but *how* you'll say it."

FIG. 17–2

CONFERRING AND SMALL-GROUP WORK

Supporting Students in Using More Complex Sentence Structures

ONE THING TO KEEP IN MIND as you plan for your conferring and small groups today is that many students will be working on other things besides end punctuation. This is something to celebrate. Since you have consistently given choices to your students about what work they will do during independent writing time, you should expect that some children will still be working on adding detail to their writing, others will be working on their beginnings, yet others will be adding comparisons or examples. Take this as a perfect opportunity to revisit the work students have been learning all year.

So, even though the minilesson today supports students' use of end punctuation as they draft their teaching books, you will want to continue to support students in writing with more sophistication. This might mean that end punctuation becomes a secondary concern for some of your writers today. This is a good thing. Your conferences should always be a reflection of the work that students are ready and eager to do next.

I sat next to Karl and opened up our conference. "Karl," I started, "Can you tell me about the writing you are doing today?" I started with this question so that I could give most of the responsibility of the conference to Karl.

"I'm good. I am working on writing more on each page."

I nodded, knowing that it is a big step for writers to talk the talk, expecting that he might not actually be also walking the walk. "Can you show me what you have been doing when you work more on a page?" Karl looked a bit stunned. Then he pointed to the chart on information writing, and said that he was using transition words.

"Oh, Karl!" I exclaimed. "That is a big step." I looked over Karl's page, and saw he'd inserted a *because*. I knew then that I wanted to support Karl's burgeoning use of connective words. I continued, "Karl, I notice you used a connecting word—*because*—to connect two parts of your sentence. You are right that *because* is what people call a *transitional word*. Transitional words are like glue. They help writers connect two simple sentences into one more complex, fancy sentence." I purposely tucked in the academic language, so that I could help Karl build his vocabulary around writing. I continued, asking him about his process of adding these transitional words in his writing.

Karl paused, with some hesitation. "Well, I don't really know how to add them in."

"Well, one thing I noticed, Karl, is that you are doing some pretty important rereading work here. Even from across the room, I could see you going page by page. I have to tell you the truth. I was wondering what it was you were doing as I saw you slowly turning your pages. Now I know that you are getting ready to add little words like *because* or *so* or *and* that can glue two parts of a long sentence together. Bravo to you!"

"What an important piece of information, Karl. Now, add that in using one of the transitional words."

MID-WORKSHOP TEACHING **Reading in Partnerships and Practicing Using a Teaching Voice**

"Writers, let's stop for a moment. So many of you are doing a lovely job adding thoughtful punctuation. Sometimes, before you get ready to share with a larger audience, it's helpful to practice with a partner. Right now, would you get together with your partner and would you take turns reading your books to each other? Make sure you read in your best teaching voice. As you read, be on the lookout for punctuation parts. If you are the listening partner, put your head together with the reading partner to see if you can find those parts so they can be read just like you are speaking to the reader."

"Keep rereading," I said. Karl reread this: "Police stop traffic. People cross the street."

"So, Karl, is there one of those little transition words you could us to glue those two sentences together?" I left a bit of silence, and then jotted a list of options. Karl selected the word *so* from the list.

"Police stop traffic," Karl started, "so crossers on a different road can go."

"That's it, Karl. See how you did that, there? You can continue to do this amazing work all on your own. "

I then quickly jotted down *but*, *because*, *so*, *as*, and *or* onto a Post-it and left the list with Karl as a reference. "If you are not sure which transitional word to use, you can use this Post-it to help you. Well done."

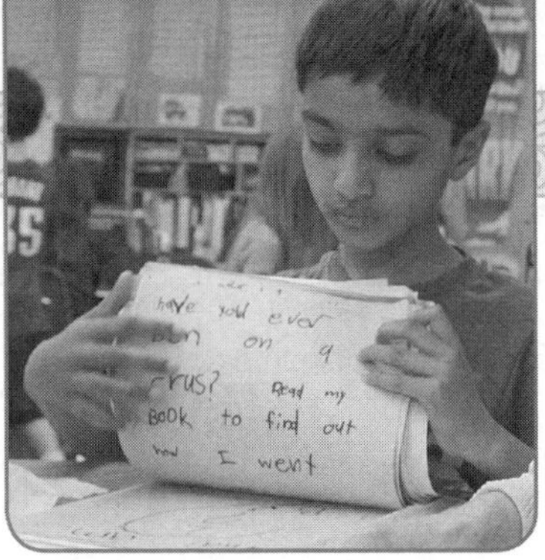

SHARE

Writers Take a "Make-Sense Minute" to Reread, Monitoring for Sense

Tell students that writers reread their writing, giving themselves a "make-sense minute" to check their writing for confusing parts.

After students had gathered in the meeting area, I said, "Writers, thanks for bringing your writing and pens over to the rug. You were so thoughtful in your use of end punctuation today. Sometimes when you work so hard, concentrating on one thing, you can forget to be thinking about all the other important jobs you have as writers to make your books easy to read.

"What if we start having a 'make-sense minute'? I will set the timer for one minute, and your job is to reread the page you are working on and make sure what you wrote still makes sense and that things aren't confusing. If things are confusing, then fix them up right away! And if you have time, you can read two pages."

I set the timer for one minute and coached some students to point under each word as they reread to make sure they read the words they *had* written, not the ones they *thought* they had written.

After one minute, I gathered their attention again. "Writers, I do not need to be the one to give you a make-sense minute. Whenever you want, you can give it to yourself. You might decide to do it at the end of every page, before you turn to the next one. Or you may decide to do it after you have finished a book. The one thing I know is that writers stop and reread to make sure their writing makes sense!"

Notice that I coached children to point under each word as they reread their writing. Without this step, children often add in or leave out words as they read. The pointing ensures focus on the print and often helps children find their mistakes before I need to ask them to look again at a certain section.

Session 18

Using Craft Moves Learned in *Small Moments*

Pop-Out Words and Speech Bubbles

TODAY MARKS AN IMPORTANT MILESTONE in the unit. Up until now, your writers have been drafting and revising furiously, starting new books and perhaps returning to old ones, all the while being encouraged that when writers are done, they've just begun. Today's session, though, will be the last chance for any new writing before the mid-workshop teaching transitions your writers into choosing one book that they want to publish, revising and polishing it for the final celebration of the unit. For that reason, you may want your mid-workshop teaching time to be a bit longer than usual, since there are quite a few steps involved: choose one book, talk to your partner, and now get going with the revising tools.

Since this session marks the transition from writing and revising to editing for publication, rather than introduce a brand new skill or strategy, I recommend instead teaching toward the important work of transferring learning from one genre to another genre. The beginning of this unit brought the writing process in from the *Small Moments* unit and taught children that they plan for their writing here too! Students also learned how to bring different types of writing—how-to pages, stories, persuasive writing—into their teaching chapter books. This session follows the same idea. In *Small Moments*, children studied George McClements' craft moves to see what he did as a writer, how he did it, and why he made those choices, and then children took on those moves in their own writing.

In this session, then, you will teach children that those delightful craft moves do not belong in narrative writing alone. Pop-out words, speech bubbles, and ellipses are sprinkled throughout nonfiction writing as a way to engage readers, highlight important information, and give little asides to readers. Anne Schreiber's *Sharks!* uses pop-out words on the first page, and ellipses make an appearance in the table of contents. Books like *Watch Me Grow: Elephants* and *Big Babies, Little Babies* (Magloff 2005) employ speech bubbles to tuck in additional information and give voice to the animals featured. Beyond the voice these craft moves give to nonfiction writing, teaching children to transfer something from narrative writing to nonnarrative writing taps into high-level thinking and sophisticated processing of strategies.

IN THIS SESSION, you'll teach children that writers rely on all the craft moves they have learned, even craft moves from other genres, to write their teaching books.

GETTING READY

- ✔ Mentor text from *Small Moments* unit, *Night of the Veggie Monster* (see Connection)
- ✔ "How Can I Teach My Readers?" chart, to reference during the connection and add to during the teaching
- ✔ Your own teacher demonstration text to show how to add pop-out words and speech bubbles (see Connection)
- ✔ Scissors, tape, Post-its, and strips of paper for revision work (see Conferring and Mid-Workshop Teaching)
- ✔ Small copies of the "How Can I Teach My Readers?" chart for the mid-workshop teaching
- ✔ Information Writing Checklist, Grades 1 and 2 (see Share)

COMMON CORE STATE STANDARDS: W.1.2, W.1.5, RFS.1.1, RFS.1.4.a, SL.1.1, SL.1.5, L.1.1, L.1.2, L.1.5

MINILESSON

Using Craft Moves Learned in *Small Moments*

Pop-Out Words and Speech Bubbles

CONNECTION

Revisit the craft moves from the *Small Moments* unit at the start of the year.

"Writers, I was moving some things around in the closet yesterday and some of the charts we used in the *Small Moments* unit fell out! When I picked them up, I reread some of the things we had learned about from George McClements." I held up one finger, about to list them off. "Pop-out words," I opened my hand and wiggled my fingers like a mini-explosion, "and speech bubbles." I touched my mouth. "It hit me then. We could use these same cool techniques in our teaching books!"

I heard a "Huh?!" and a few students had screwed up their faces at me.

"I know, I know. It sounds crazy, but it really works. We now know tons of ways to teach information: comparisons, examples, answering our readers questions." I gestured to the "How Can I Teach My Readers?" chart. "Pop-out words," I made a mini-explosion again, "and speech bubbles," I touched my mouth, "are *also* things writers do in teaching books."

Name the teaching point.

"Today I want to teach you that writers use craft moves like pop-out words and speech bubbles in teaching books to give more information or make some information stand out."

TEACHING

Demonstrate how to use pop-out words and speech bubbles in your demonstration text.

I displayed a page of the class book. The heading read, "Restaurants," and the text read, "There are good restaurants in Queens. People should eat in lots of different restaurants."

"Writers, help me see if we could use any of these techniques to emphasize key points in this text." I put a finger to my head, pausing for a moment. "I know! This chapter is all about different restaurants, so maybe I should find a way to accentuate key words. Probably the most important words in that sentence are *lots* and *different*. I can make those

◆ COACHING

If you are struggling to understand the wiggling fingers, this is meant as a description of the gesture that can accompany the term pop-out words. *Of course you can invent your own gestures—the important thing is that you go to the ends of the earth to foster engagement.*

FIG. 18–1

words important by making them *big* and *bold*, just like you did with your Small Moment stories." I made the gesture for pop-out words as I said "big and bold" so children would connect the two ideas. I quickly revised the line to read:

People should eat in LOTS of DIFFERENT restaurants.

"Whoa, that looks good! No one will miss that information. Actually, to make sure no one misses that, I am also going to draw a person and get the person to say more about the restaurant." I drew a person and a quick speech bubble and said the words as I wrote them. "Hi! Come and eat our delicious food!"

Debrief, clarifying the purpose of using certain craft moves.

"Writers, do you see that by adding pop-out words and speech bubble, I made some information seem even more important? You can use pop-out words and speech bubbles in your information writing to help your reader figure out what is important, too, or even to help you add more information. Let's add these craft moves to our 'How Can I Teach My Readers?' chart."

How Can I Teach My Readers?

- Think about questions my readers might have
- Write in twin sentences
- Include pictures
    - teaching words
    - lines and arrows
    - zooming in
- Give an example
- Use shape, size, and color words
- Make a comparison to something they know
- Use a picture or photograph to add more information
- Use big, bold pop-out words
- Use speech bubbles

ACTIVE ENGAGEMENT

Channel children to begin this work on the rug with their own writing.

"Writers, let's get started here on the rug. Can you take out the piece of writing you are working on today?" I waited as papers shuffled and students resettled with their writing on their laps. "Today is your last day to improve your writing.

One thing you might do is to see if you want to use *pop-out words* or *speech bubbles* to bring out the most important parts of your writing. In just a minute you are going to tell your partner what your plan is." I gave the students a minute to think.

Have partners share with each other and use the nonverbal gestures for pop-out words and speech bubbles to prompt children to name the parts of their writing where they'll use those craft moves.

"Okay, now Partner 1, tell Partner 2 what you will do today. If some words will be popped out or added in a speech bubble, be sure to explain why these will be the words you accentuate." I gave the partners a minute or two, and as I coached in, I saw Karl turn to the fourth page in his book, "Police." This page read:

> Police have police dogs. The dog is running so fast he can't catch up with him

He looked at his partner and made the gesture for a speech bubble, then said, "Hey! Slow down!"

After a minute, I reconvened the children. "Writers, the important thing is that you can look back on old charts and notice ways you revised your Small Moment stories—then you can try bringing some of these some techniques to your information writing. Turn and tell your partner other techniques you used *then* that you might bring to *this* unit."

LINK

Reemphasize the big picture. Writers use craft moves in their books to reach readers and to make writing interesting.

"You now know lots of ways to add last minute improvements to your writing, and I know you'll use every second today to do all you can in these final moments."

Keep writers aware of the time line and the fact they are in charge of their own writing.

"Writers, you are going to have a little less time than usual to write today because at our mid-workshop teaching time we are going to choose the one piece you want to publish, so make the most of the time you have between now and then. It will be about twenty minutes."

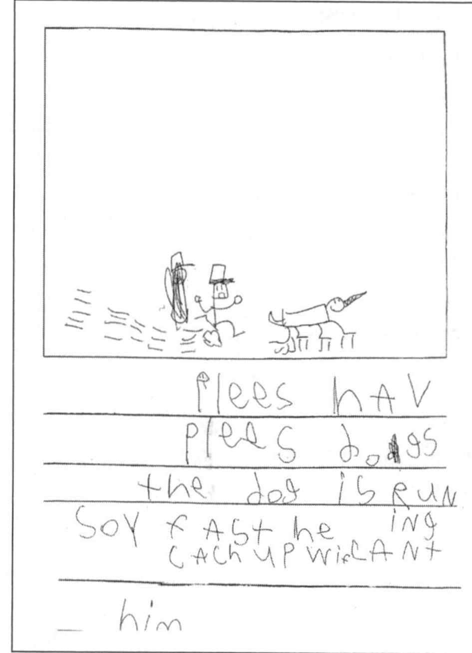

FIG. 18–2 Rereading this, Karl realized the page would be better if speech bubbles were added to the chart.

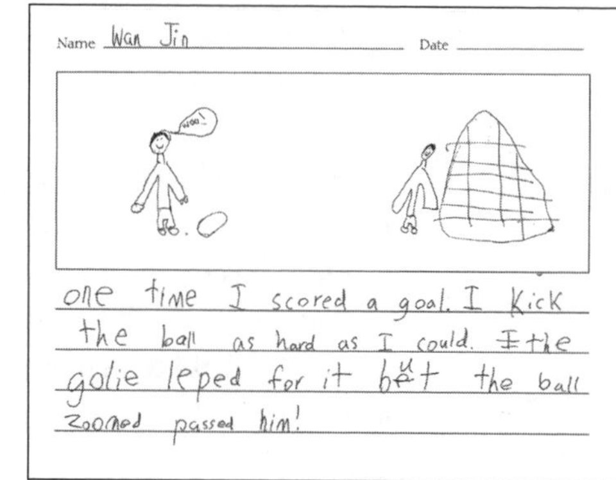

FIG. 18–3 Wan Jin used a speech bubble to make information important.

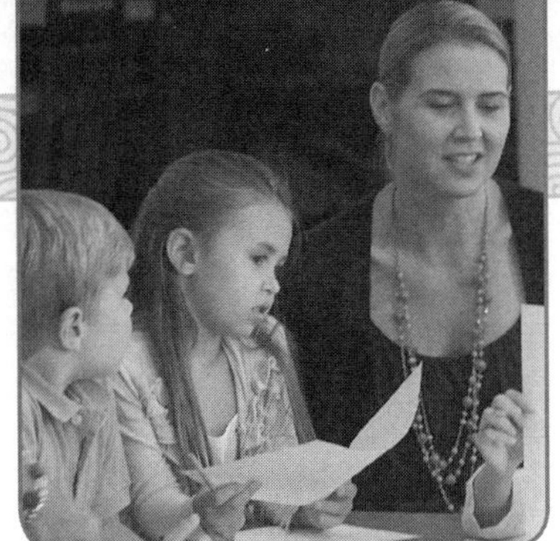

CONFERRING AND SMALL-GROUP WORK

Setting Students Up for the Final Revision of the Unit

IT WILL MAKE SENSE ON THIS DAY to use your conferring and small-group time to prepare for the work children will be doing after the mid-workshop teaching. By midway through the writing time, children need to be at a place where they can begin to revise writing for the upcoming celebration. You know that some children need extensive revision work so you might start them doing this work a bit before you channel everyone to do it.

Convene a group of children who have struggled with organization. Bring scissors, strips, and tape. If these children quickly choose the piece they want to publish, you can teach them that everything on a page should match the heading. For example, if a child has written the chapter heading "Shells," then his discussion of the games he likes to play near the ocean can't go in that chapter. This work is fun for students because of the physical act of cutting and moving and taping. It will be up to the child to decide whether to change the heading or to relocate parts of the writing.

Other children may have written a text that has missing or repeated words or sections. Reading with a partner will help these children grasp that their text is confusing. The presence of a listener can help a writer become more focused on clear communications, finding places where the writing is no longer clear. When a confusion section is located, the strips, tape, and scissors come in handy to make the writing clear. The most important goal is for children to leave this group with a book that clearly says what they want to teach.

MID-WORKSHOP TEACHING **Get Ready for Publication by Choosing and Revising One Book**

"Writers, time to stop writing!" I paused and clasped my hands expectantly. "This is *it*, this is the *big moment*! It's time to choose one book that you want to publish out of all your *finished* writing. Just like before in the *Small Moments* unit, I am going to give you a minute or two to read through your books and choose *one* that you want to share with the world."

I paused as children started shuffling through their folders. Some children went back to pieces they had written early, while others selected the one they had written last. I coached children who were having some trouble deciding, and when everyone had one book chosen I reconvened the group.

"Writers, I am so excited to see the choices you have made and the teaching you are going to share with the world. But before you can do that, you have to make sure this book is ready for its time to shine. This is where your partner can come in. I have small copies of our 'How Can I Teach My Readers?' chart for everyone to hold onto. As you listen to your partner read, look at the small chart. If you notice something the writer could add, point it out on the chart to them and help them think about where it could go." I asked the table monitors to distribute the small copies of charts as I was talking, and at this point they were in the hands of the students.

"Okay, so Partner 2 can start this time, and when you are done listening and getting a tip from your partner, you can switch roles. I am not going to tell you when to switch. You can do it when you are ready. Then, for the rest of our writing time you will be working fast and furious to revise this piece of writing. Revision toolkits are out, and I know I will see scissors and Post-its and strips aplenty! Okay, Partner 2, start reading!"

I floated from table to table indicating that children should be referencing the chart when listening and prompting them to give a tip. As partnerships finished, I sent them off to get the revision materials they needed.

SHARE

Use the Checklist for a Final Check

Channel students to use the Information Writing Checklist to make a few last revisions to their books.

I displayed the Information Writing Checklist. (This checklist can be found on the CD-ROM.) "Writers," I said, "You have revised your books with tips from your partners, classroom charts, and mentor texts. You still have one last tool you can use—our Information Writing Checklist." I gestured to the chart. "These are things your writing absolutely must have, so use this share time to check that you do each of these things in your writing, and if you don't, you can still add it in or change your writing. Your partner is next to you, so ask for help if you need it!"

I circled the rug, coaching in as needed with quick tips. After five or six minutes, I stopped the writers. "Okay, friends, tomorrow is our editing day, and then before you know it—celebration!"

Information Writing Checklist

	Grade 1	NOT YET	STARTING TO	YES!	Grade 2	NOT YET	STARTING TO	YES!
	Structure				**Structure**			
Overall	I taught my readers about a topic.	☐	☐	☐	I taught readers some important points about a subject.	☐	☐	☐
Lead	I named my topic in the beginning and got my readers' attention.	☐	☐	☐	I wrote a beginning in which I named a subject and tried to interest readers.	☐	☐	☐
Transitions	I told different parts about my topic on different pages.	☐	☐	☐	I used words such as *and* and *also* to show I had more to say.	☐	☐	☐
Ending	I wrote an ending.	☐	☐	☐	I wrote some sentences or a section at the end to wrap up my piece.	☐	☐	☐
Organization	I told about my topic part by part.	☐	☐	☐	My writing had different parts. Each part told different information about the topic.	☐	☐	☐
	Development				**Development**			
Elaboration	I put facts in my writing to teach about my topic.	☐	☐	☐	I used different kinds of information in my writing such as facts, definitions, details, steps, and tips	☐	☐	☐
Craft	I used labels and words to give facts.	☐	☐	☐	I tried to include the words that showed I'm an expert on the topic.	☐	☐	☐
	Language Conventions				**Language Conventions**			
Spelling	I used all I knew about words and chunks (*at, op, it,* etc.) to help me spell.	☐	☐	☐	I used what I knew about spelling patterns (*tion, er, ly,* etc.) to spell a word.	☐	☐	☐
	I spelled the word wall words right and used the word wall to help me spell other words.	☐	☐	☐	I spelled all of the word wall words correctly and used the word wall to help me figure out how to spell other words.	☐	☐	☐

Session 19

Editing Step by Step

EDITING CAN SOMETIMES FEEL LIKE MEDICINE FOR CHILDREN. They have already *written* the book. They now want to get to the work of coloring pictures, adding photographs, and decorating the borders. Taking a day to look at spelling, punctuation, and readability does not always come across as the most exciting thing for your students. And it might feel tedious for you, too. If so, you'll want to watch carefully how you introduce the work of editing to your students. Chances are good that if you introduce editing as a painful part of the writing process, your students will bring low energy to the task at hand, reflecting the same energy you are projecting. If you instead imbue a sense of fun and playfulness into the work of editing, you'll find that students will eagerly leave the meeting area today, rushing to their books to look for punctuation, capitals, and spelling.

In this session, you will want to add the metaphorical spoonful of sugar to editing work. We suggest taking the editing checklist from the Small Moments unit (Session 19) and turning it into a game. The checklist should be updated with the new skills students have learned during this unit. Then you might cut up the new editing checklist and put in an envelope. Partners will pull one slip out, and each will work on that item through his or her own book, and then partners can exchange books and check each other's editing before they pull out another slip from the envelope. The work they will do will be no different than the editing work they've done before, but the surprise element of drawing a piece of paper out of an envelope, working side by side with a partner, and then checking their own writing and their partner's will all add a level of play that children will embrace. The mid-workshop teaching will transition students into fancying up their writing for publication, preparing their pictures and illustrations for the celebration. You may decide to do the mid-workshop teaching toward the end of the workshop, so students have plenty of time to check their own—and their partner's—writing.

IN THIS SESSION, you'll teach children that writers edit their writing so that it is ready to be published and go out into the world.

GETTING READY

- ✔ Students need to bring the teaching book that they chose for publication to the meeting area.
- ✔ Name jar with children's names on popsicle sticks or another way to make the connection to drawing items from the editing checklist out of an envelope (see Connection)
- ✔ Updated editing checklist from *Small Moments* Session 19 to display and others cut into strips and put into envelopes for each partnership (see Connection)
- ✔ A large piece of chart paper displaying one page of a first-grade teaching book with many errors in it, either from an anonymous student or a student in another class (see Teaching)
- ✔ "Ways to Spell Words" chart, from Session 5 (see Teaching)
- ✔ Post-its, markers, construction paper, cotton balls, sandpaper, ribbons, or other odds and ends that students can use to add color and texture to their pictures (see Mid-Workshop Teaching)
- ✔ Star Post-its for students to mark the most interesting parts of their books (see Share)

COMMON CORE STATE STANDARDS: W.1.2, W.1.5, RFS.1.2, RFS.1.3, RFS.1.4, SL.1.1, SL.1.5, L.1.1, L.1.2

MINILESSON

Editing Step by Step

CONNECTION

Set the class up to play a partner game that uses editing strips drawn out of an envelope as reminders of what to edit.

I gestured to the envelopes at my side. "You and your partner are going to play a game. You pull out one strip from the envelope, read it together, and then use that reminder to fix up your writing. When you are done fixing it up, you get to check each other's work and see if your partner found all the spots to fix up. Then pull out the next strip!"

Name the teaching point.

"Today, I want to teach you that writers edit their writing before they publish it. One way they edit their writing is by using an editing checklist. They look at one thing on the list at a time and check to see they have done that one thing throughout their writing. Then they check for the next item on their list, and so on."

TEACHING

Show children that you locate one item on the editing checklist, then read carefully, checking for that one item and making changes as needed.

"Okay, I have a first-grade student's writing from another class up here," I gestured to the hanging chart, "and here is our envelope." All of you are going to play the role of the partner. I went to dump the strips all out and then stopped myself, "Wait, wait, I just have to pull *one* out. Let me do that." I pulled out one slip and read, "I used vowels in every word. Okay, let me check." I started to read the entire piece without stopping. "Woah! I need to slow down. I didn't even look for the vowels, did I?"

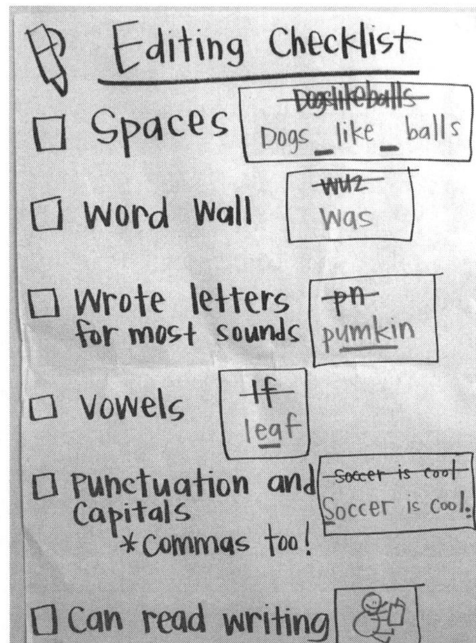

FIG. 19–1

◆ COACHING

Notice that we don't suggest writers reread their writing once, checking for everything during that one scan.

Again, notice that I make the mess-ups that I anticipate children will make, and then self-correct. This is a way to highlight pointers I believe the children will need.

Choruses of "No!" came from the students.

"Okay, let me start from the beginning. Okay, help me out. If the word has a vowel, give me a thumbs up." I went through the piece, missing some words that needed vowels so children could help. Each time a word needed a vowel, I used a spelling strategy from the "Ways to Spell Words" chart.

Clarify the role of the partner.

"Okay, writers, when you are off at your tables doing this, once you check for one thing, ask your partner to reread your writing and to see if you made the changes necessary so the piece doesn't have more of that error. Will you do that for me now? With your partner, look through this first-grader's writing and see if now there is a vowel in every word." I let children do this for a quick second and then gathered them back. "I heard lots of you saying we got them all. We are ready for the next item on the checklist. Do you see how many more mistakes we catch when we look for one thing at a time on our checklist and then use our partner as a checker?"

ACTIVE ENGAGEMENT

Start children on the editing work of the day on the rug, so you can iron out any confusions or inconsistencies.

"Writers, put the piece you are going to publish on your lap. Hattie is going to pass out the envelopes to you and your partner." After the envelopes had been distributed, I said, "Okay, Partner 1 will choose first. Okay, pull one strip out and both partners check." I circulated on the rug making sure partners were attending to the one thing they had pulled from the envelope and coached children who I saw getting bogged down in spelling if they were supposed to be looking at punctuation marks. After a minute I stopped them. "I know you aren't done, but I just wanted you to get a start."

LINK

Send students off to finish editing their writing, using the editing checklist game and their partners for support.

"Writers, we've turned editing into something that will feel a bit like a game, but I hope you remember that following the items on a checklist isn't kids' stuff. This is how pilots land planes. This is how doctors do lifesaving operations. So enjoy the game-like part of editing, but take this work seriously."

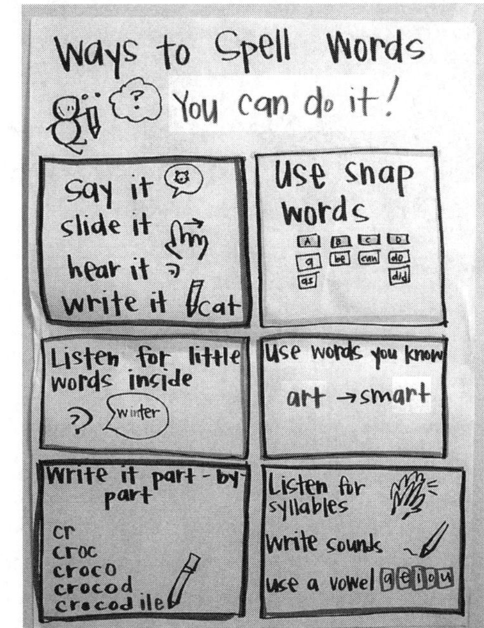

FIG. 19–2

Supporting Students' Editing Through Interactive Writing

THERE ARE SOME YOUNG CHILDREN who understand that editing can help them to reach their readers. They know that if a teaching book does not look and sound "professional," all that the author has written will be taken less seriously. If their writing is hard to read and hard to follow readers may not read it at all!

There will be other children for whom the work of editing remains elusive—even after lots of practice throughout kindergarten and the first unit of writing workshop. Interactive writing can help teach editing and small-group interactive writing can be especially helpful.

When you gather a small group of three to five children together, give them individual white boards and dry erase markers. Have a page from a writer from another class ready (with multiple editing errors in it). Begin by telling children that this student needs some extra support making his writing easy to read.

"Writers," you might begin, "if you want to be sure your readers can learn something from your writing, then you have to make sure your writing is easy to read. If not, people might not take you seriously and—believe it or not—they may stop reading your book!"

Ask children to help this mystery student edit his or her piece, using the tips they learned about editing. Start reading the piece, asking children to join in.

"Let's look at this first item on the editing checklist." If the first item suggests that writers use white space between words, call attention to the first line. If it has incorrect spacing between words, say, "This student needs some help putting spaces between words. I see that right away! Takuma, can you come up and help?"

MID-WORKSHOP TEACHING **Time to Fancy It Up: Adding Color and Texture to Illustrations**

"Writers, eyes up here." I waited until the chatter died down and all eyes were on me. "It is time to start to fancy up your work for publication!" I began to pull out Post-its, markers, and a box of odds and ends, which included construction paper, cotton balls, sandpaper, and ribbon, that students could use to show texture or color in their books. "Writers, you can add color to your pictures and use tape to make a 'lift-the-flap' feature in your book. You could use flaps to show what is happening on the inside *and* outside of anything—a building, a person, a vehicle. You might come up with your own unique way to use the lift-the-flap feature. I am also putting out some construction paper and odds and ends in case you want to add some texture into your illustrations. Make sure as you work to fancy up your book that it continues to help teach the reader and doesn't hide any of the hard work you have done so far. You have about ten minutes to do this work."

As the one child does the work, you can coach the other children to rewrite these parts, using appropriate spacing on their white boards.

As you move down the editing checklist, share the pen with other students. Children meanwhile all use their white boards to practice, and you use the white boards as a quick, on-the-spot assessment. Remember that this small-group work is meant to be quick!

SHARE

Preparing for the Celebration

Have students flag the most important parts of their books in preparation for the celebration.

"Writers, all along in this unit, when you have read nonfiction books, you have skipped around to read the parts that seem super interesting to you. I remember when we started the *Sharks!* book, everyone wanted to hear the 'People Attack?' chapter, so we read it first. For our celebration, you are not going to share your *whole* books, but the parts that seem really super cool and interesting. I have grabbed some star Post-its so you can mark those pages." I dropped piles of star-shaped Post-its among the children on the rug.

"Okay, writers, first go through and decide what part of your book you want to share. You can find two, three, or four parts you might want to share. You can ask for your partner's opinion if you aren't sure which part you want to pick." I gave the writers about three minutes and then began again.

Recruit writers to practice reading their favorite parts to their partners, using their best teaching voices.

"Now, writers, those parts that are super cool and important, you'll want to read them and read them and read them again so you can read them aloud and it'll sound like read-aloud time." I gave the partners some time to practice. "Okay, writers, you might want to think if there is anything from home you want to bring in that can teach people even more about your topic because you may want to use it in our celebration tomorrow!"

Give children ample time to practice reading fluently. You can then coach into speaking skills like: projecting your voice, holding the paper low down so it will not block your face, and using facial expressions and body language to emphasize points. You will soon feel like you have a room of National Geographic narrators!

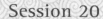

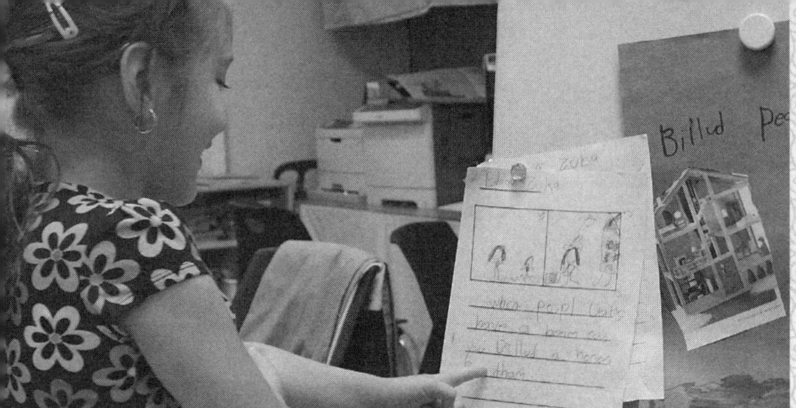

Session 20

A Final Celebration

A Letter to Teachers

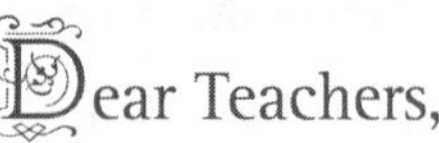ear Teachers,

Today is a day for celebration. No doubt you have watched your children grow in leaps and bounds across the course of this unit. They likely began the unit writing a line or two on a page, perhaps with some details and accompanying representational drawings. Now they are filling up books with their expertise, complete with rich elaboration, teaching pictures, and a burgeoning structure.

When planning a celebration for any unit of study remember to match the celebration to the kind of writing the students have just undertaken. Because this unit is about sharing expertise with the world, we recommend that you choose a format for your celebration that highlights expertise. For example, many first-grade classrooms end nonfiction writing with a museum celebration. You may decide to open up your classroom museum to a wider audience today, perhaps to parents and other family members.

If you decide to create a museum celebration, then before the day of the celebration, you'll want to bring your writers together and lead them to reminisce about any trip any of them have taken to a museum. Point out ways people can learn from a museum exhibit. You might say, "Museum exhibits often have displays, and these displays are where people lay out what they know about a topic. A display at a museum is like a page in a book. Displays, and pages of books, have diagrams, labels, and captions. The people setting up displays carefully choose the information they are going to include, because it's often the information that is the most important or that people really need to know. Also, museum exhibits sometimes have just a little bit of text to give viewers some extra information. Sometimes when people are looking at a display at a museum, a person comes to tell them more. These teachers at a museum are called *docents*."

Then channel writers to prepare for the celebration using these big ideas about museums. Depending on the amount of time and materials you have at your disposal, you can have your first-graders create displays, similar to the displays in a museum, with some of the most important information from their books. In some classes, writers choose a few

Common Core State Standards: W.1.2, RFS.1.4, SL.1.1, SL.1.4, L.1.1, L.1.2

special pages from their teaching books to post on poster boards. Finally, have your writers prepare for their role as "docents" by planning a very brief speech—possibly with an introduction and perhaps an important idea or two—that they can share with visitors.

After the celebration, give your writers the chance to relax and bask in the glow of a job well done. Gather them in the meeting area, perhaps offer them some refreshments, and let them debrief with their fellow docents about the experience. Then lead them in a brief discussion of the big things they learned about informational writing that they will carry with them always.

PREPARATION

You may want to set up the classroom so that it feels more like a museum. Think about your writers' topics, and consider how they could be grouped. Then push desks or tables together to create exhibit areas. You might, depending on your kids' topics, have an animal wing, a science wing, a travel wing, and a sports wing in your classroom. Make sure there is plenty of room for each student to set up his or her display. Set up a poster board or easel at each area for the pages from their books they chose to accompany their displays. Talk with your writers about the dress code. Because they are docents, presenting their expertise, they may want to dress up in their most "professional"-looking clothing.

THE CELEBRATION

As always on writing celebration days, you'll want to make sure the day has a special feel. You will likely want to gather your writers in the meeting area before the celebration and say something like "Writers, in this past unit, you not only became nonfiction writers, you became teachers! You learned how to teach others with your writing, by writing a lot of interesting details, by making your pictures into teaching pictures, by putting all of your information into chapters, and so much more. You should be very proud of yourselves. Give someone sitting near you a high five."

To set up the museum share, you might say, "Today, your expertise is on display in our class museum. Because you are the experts, you are going to be the docents. Each of you will stand by your display. You all have your docent speech ready to go. In a few moments, your family members and friends will be coming in. When a visitor walks up to your display, you can share your speech with them, and you can show them the pages from your book. Our visitors are in for a real treat. They are going to learn so much!"

Then send the children off to their spots, and if you have time, suggest that they practice their docent speeches with one another. Remind them to use their best teaching voice when they present to visitors and to point to their displays and writing while teaching. Then, open your doors and welcome your visitors to your museum. Help the visitors to circulate, inviting them to visit exhibits that aren't as crowded a others, and to get to as many exhibits as possible.

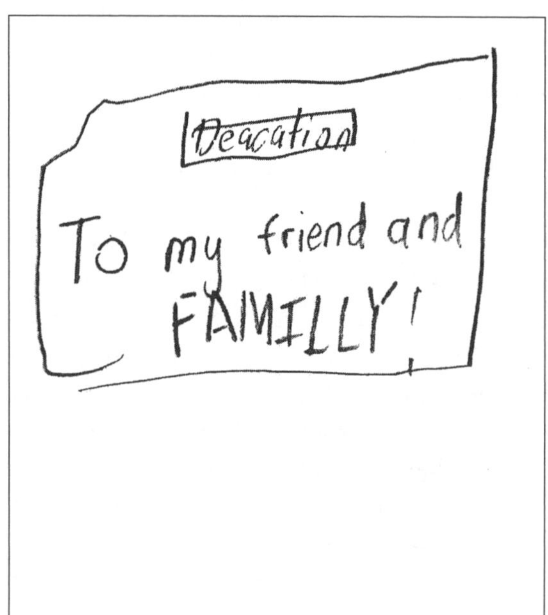

FIG. 20–1 Derek's published piece, "Plants"

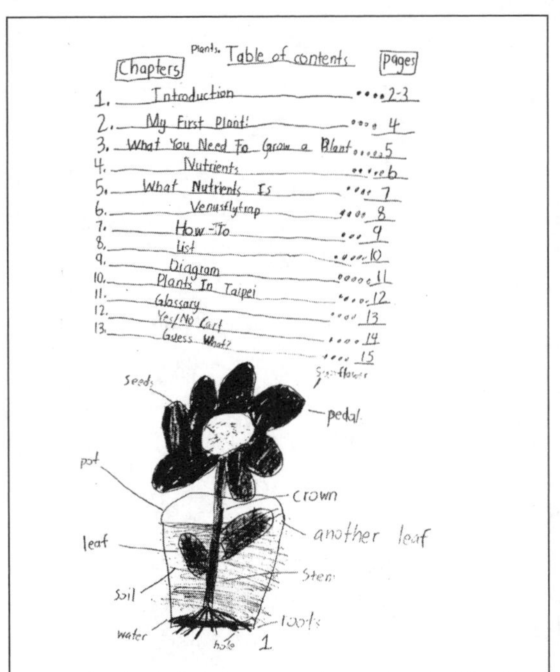

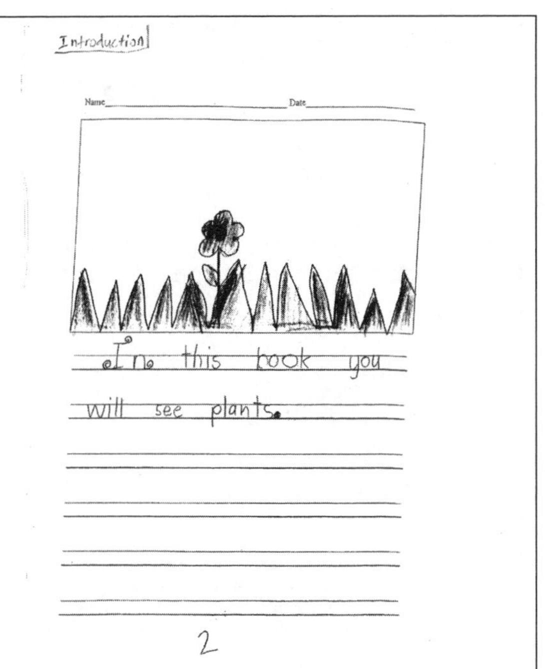

Introduction
Name
Date
In this book you
will see plants.
2

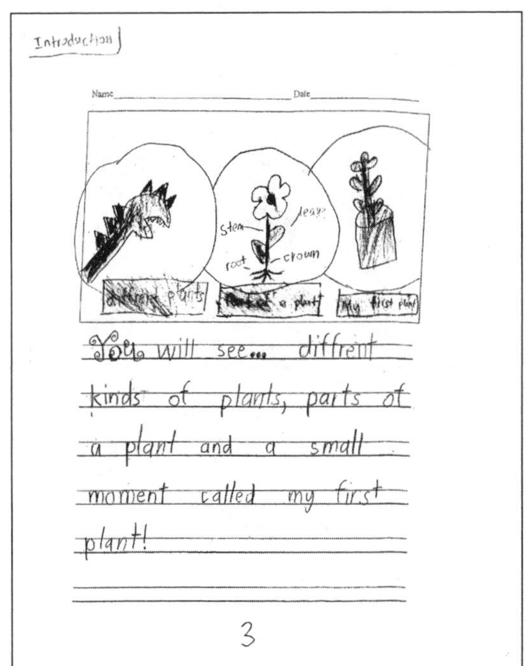

Introduction
Name
Date
stem
leave
root
crown
plants
a plant
My first plant
You will see... diffrent
kinds of plants, parts of
a plant and a small
moment called my first
plant!
3

FIG. 20–1 (Continued)

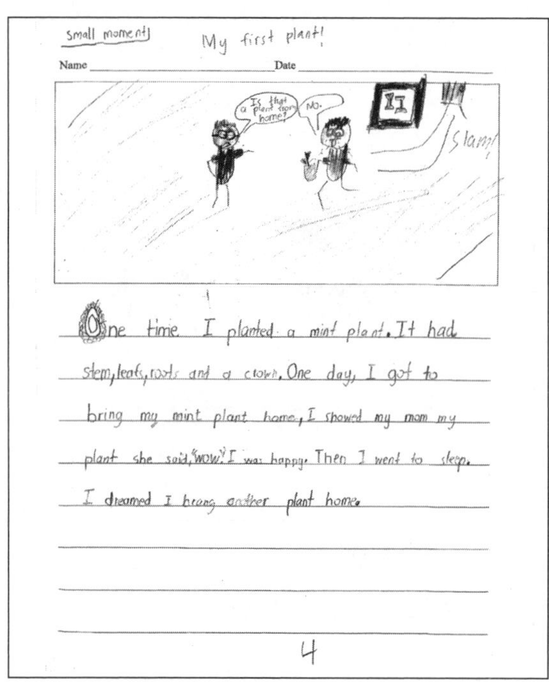

small moments

My first plant!

Name ______ Date ______

One time I planted a mint plant. It had stem, leafs, roots and a crown. One day, I got to bring my mint plant home, I showed my mom my plant she said, "WOW!" I was happy. Then I went to sleep. I dreamed I brang another plant home.

4

Plants

Name ______ Date ______

what you need to grow a plant

All about plants

1. There are many kinds of plant, but first for plants to grow you will need: water, soil, sun and nutrierts. And to grow a plant you will need a seed (to put in the soil) then water some water to the seed (attshaly every-day.)

Fancy. expert words

5

Name ______ Date ______

Nutrierts

the plant

nutrierts

2. Nutrierts are really in the soil. Nutrierts mean like medasan. so if you think you have to get a medasan add "put" it im the soil then DONT EVER DO THAT AGAIN! And you are not supposts to eat the soil too!

6

FIG. 20–1 (Continued)

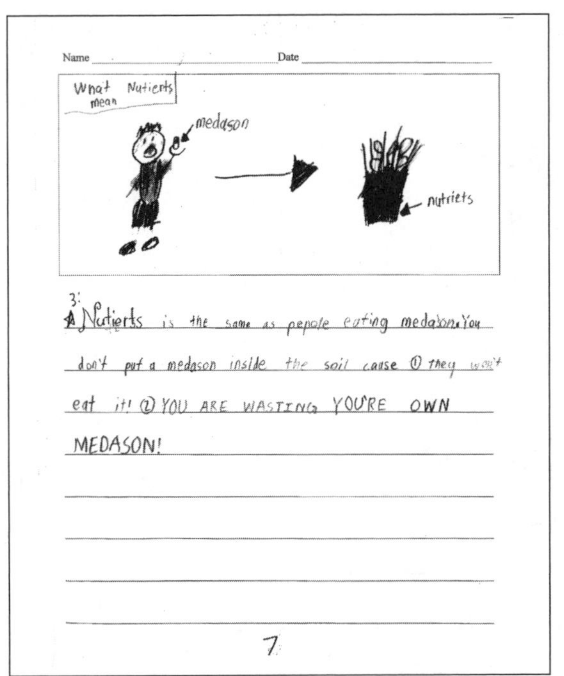
Name Date
What Nutierts mean
medason
nutriets
3: Nutierts is the same as pepole eating medason. You don't put a medason inside the soil cause ① they won't eat it! ② YOU ARE WASTING YOU'RE OWN MEDASON!
7

Name Date
venusflytraps
4: Some plants eat insests so you won't get sting or get bother. They are called venusfliptrap. It is hard to find it in the flower maket. And it is hard to find it on the groud too!
8

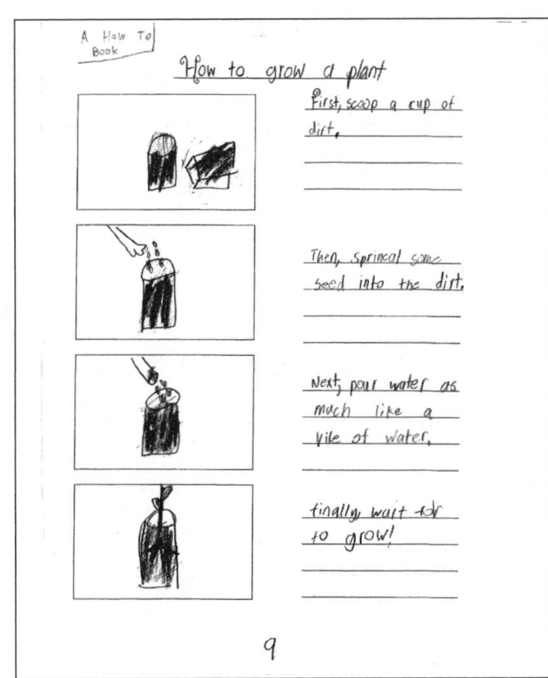
A How To Book
How to grow a plant
First, scoop a cup of dirt.
Then, sprineal some seed into the dirt.
Next, pour water as much like a vile of water.
finally, wait for to grow!
9

FIG. 20–1 (Continued)

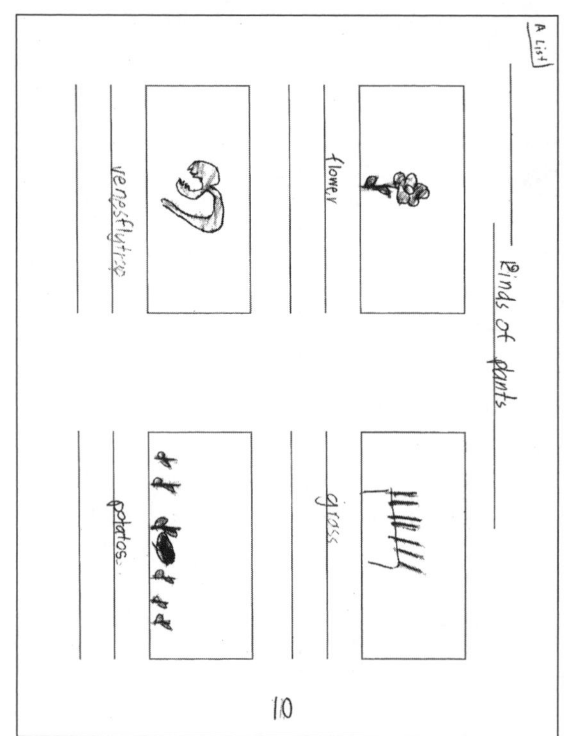

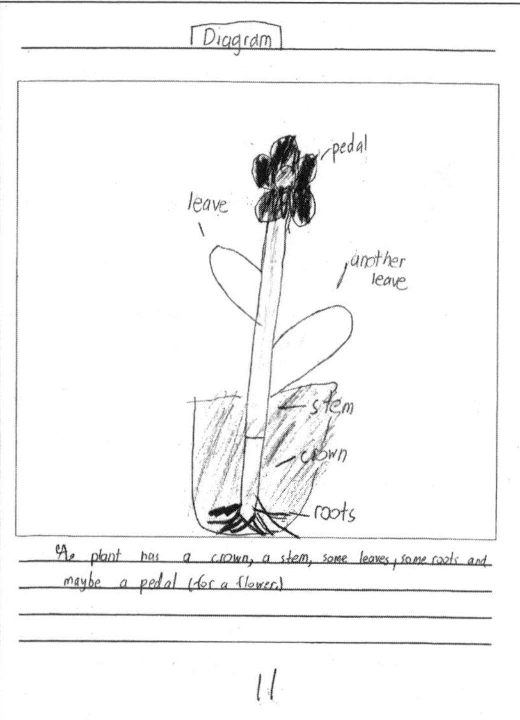

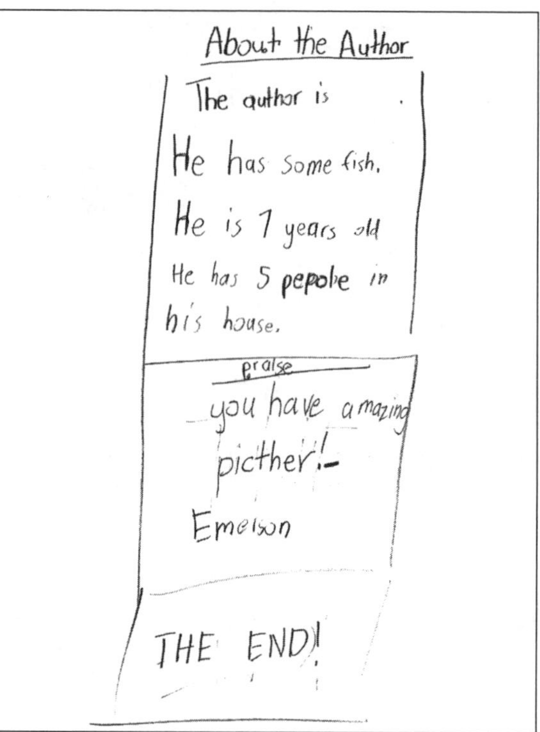

another leave

A plant has a crown, a stem, some leaves, some roots and maybe a pedal (for a flower)

About the Author
The author is .
He has some fish.
He is 7 years old
He has 5 pepole in his house.
praise
you have amazing picther!
Emelson
THE END!

brought a plant home.
What did he bring home?
let's see in this book!

FIG. 20–1 (Continued)

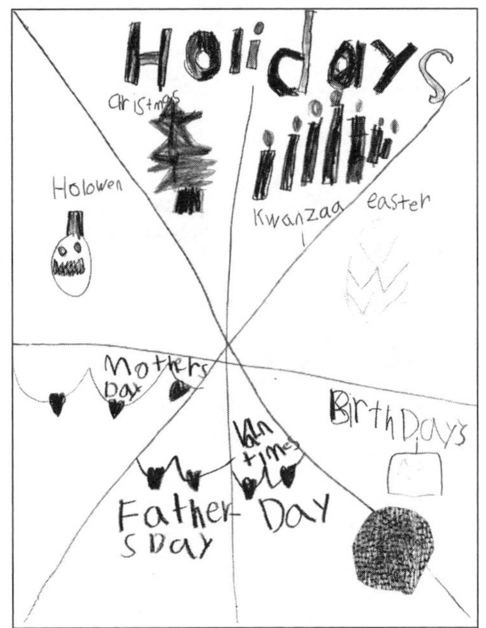

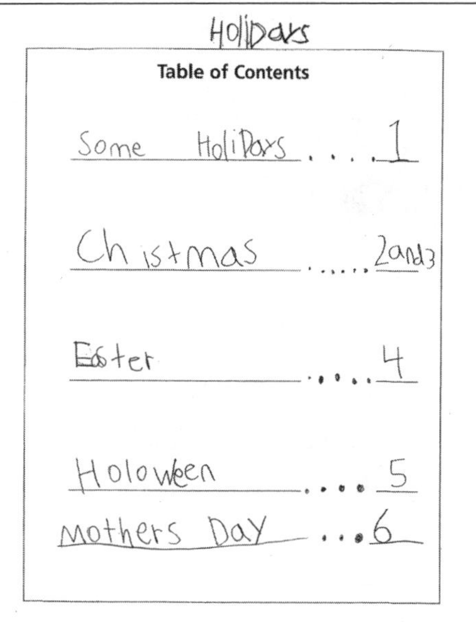

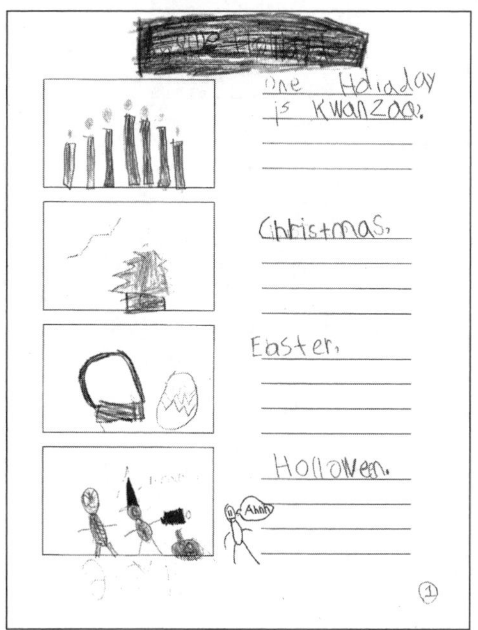

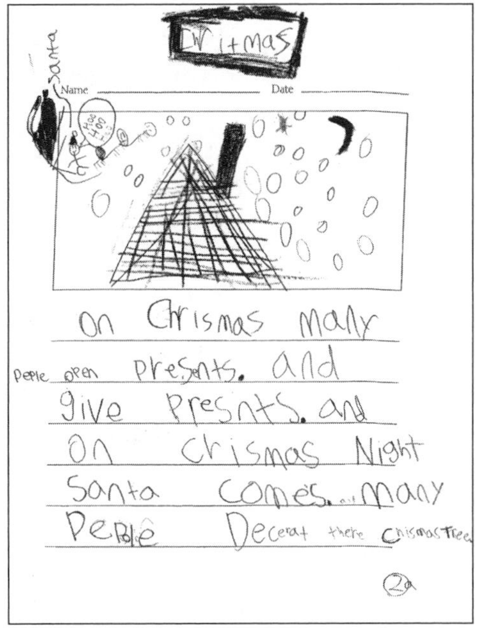

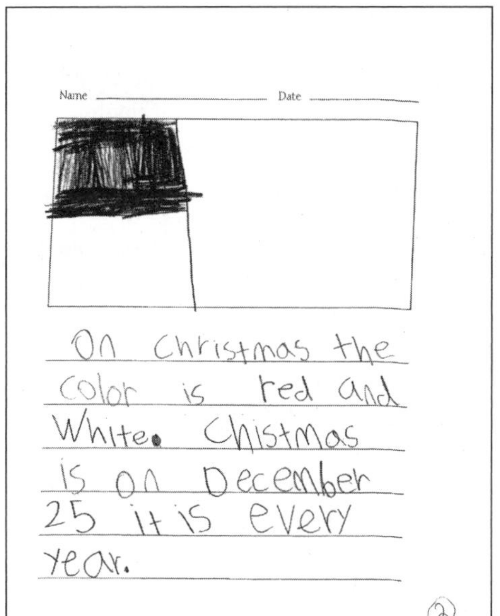

FIG. 20–2 Brendan's published piece, "Holidays"

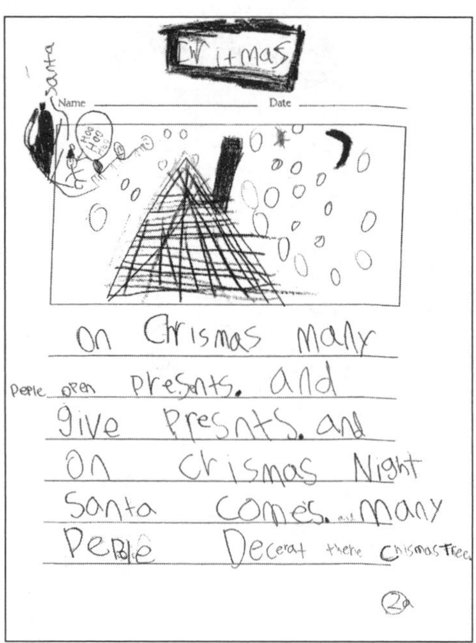
Critmas
Santa
on Chrismas many
peple open presnts. and
give presnts. and
on Crismas Night
Santa comes. many
Peple Decerat there Chrismas Tree.

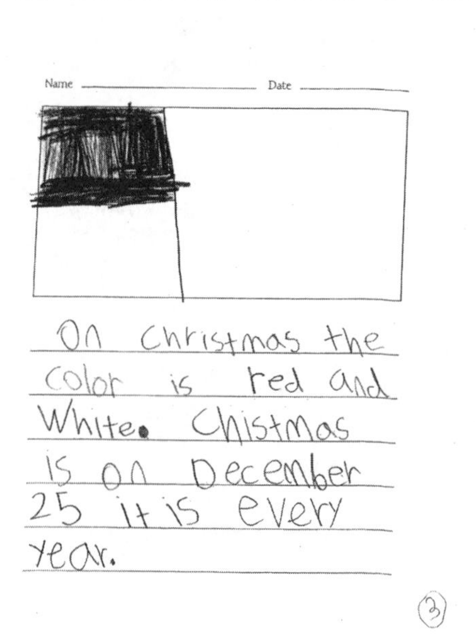
On christmas the
color is red and
White. Chistmas
is on December
25 it is every
year.

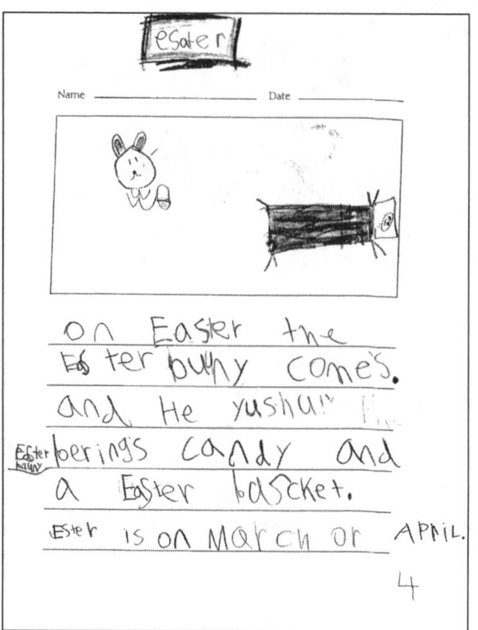
esater
on Easter the
Ester buny comes.
and He yushu
Ester buny berings candy and
a Easter basket.
Ester is on March or April.
4

FIG. 20–2 (Continued)

AFTER THE CELEBRATION

After the celebration, gather your writers in the meeting area. You might compare this day to your experiences as a teacher. You might say, "Writers, after a great day of teaching, some of the other teachers and I often gather in the staff lounge and ask each other how the day went. We share favorite moments from the day with each other. Right now, turn and talk to someone near you. Share one of your favorite teaching moments from today."

After your writers have talked for a few minutes, you could conclude with a ceremony similar to the ceremony at the end of the *Small Moments* unit in which you asked writers to place their work in the classroom library. This time, each writer could come up, say the title of his or her book, and tell the most fascinating piece of information from his or her book.

Best of luck with the celebration, and enjoy your students' budding expertise.

Lucy, Kristi, and Barb

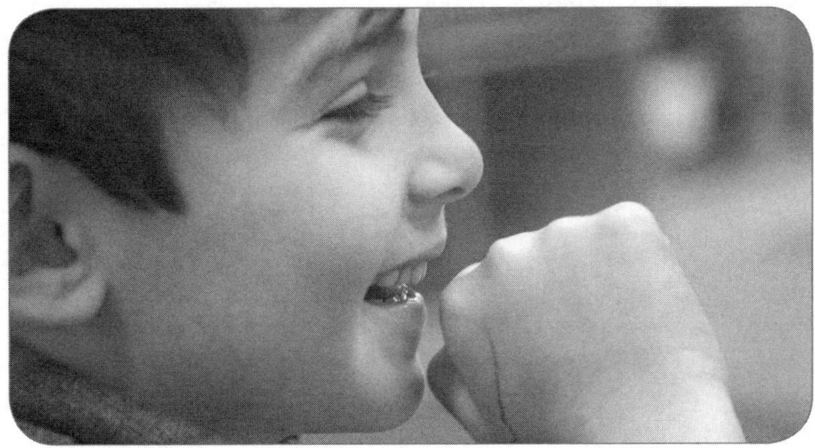